HOLLYWOOD RENEGADE

HOLLYWOOD RENEGADE

Elaine May, *Mikey and Nicky*, and the Making of a Masterpiece

Todd Berliner

University of Texas Press *Austin*

Printed in the United States of America
First edition, 2026

♾ The paper used in this book meets the minimum requirements of ANSI/NISO Z39.48–1992 (R1997) (Permanence of Paper).

Library of Congress Cataloging-in-Publication Data

Names: Berliner, Todd, 1964– author
Title: Hollywood renegade: Elaine May, Mikey and Nicky, and the making of a masterpiece / Todd Berliner.
Description: First edition. | Austin: University of Texas Press, [2026] | Includes bibliographical references and index.
Identifiers: LCCN 2026003751 (print) | LCCN 2026003752 (ebook)
ISBN 978-1-4773-3478-2 hardcover
ISBN 978-1-4773-3571-0 paperback
ISBN 978-1-4773-3479-9 pdf
ISBN 978-1-4773-3480-5 epub
Subjects: LCSH: May, Elaine, 1932—Criticism and interpretation | Motion picture industry—United States—History—20th century | Motion pictures—Production and direction—United States—History—20th century | Cult films—United States
Classification: LCC PN1998.3.M3955 B47 2026 (print) | LCC PN1998.3.M3955 (ebook)
LC record available at https://lccn.loc.gov/2026003751
LC ebook record available at https://lccn.loc.gov/2026003752

doi:10.7560/334782

The University of Texas Press gratefully acknowledges the William and Bettye Nowlin Endowment in Art, History, and Culture of the Western Hemisphere for its support of this publication.

For Sam and Jesse
who fill my heart

and in memory of Stephen Booth and David Bordwell
who blew my mind

CONTENTS

ILLUSTRATIONS

PREFACE

I have been trying to understand *Mikey and Nicky* since it first floored me sometime in the 1980s. When I saw that someone named "Elaine" had written and directed it, I was even more confused. Could Elaine be a man? I had trouble understanding how a woman could have such intimate knowledge of male friendship. Her film about a mobster setting up his friend to be killed had captured the unacknowledged rivalries, humiliations, and resentments that can plague men's long-standing relationships with other men, along with the affection, loyalty, and thrill that make those friendships deep and enduring, all of which are complicated by ambition, lust, and camaraderie. How could "Elaine"—who, it turns out, was a renowned sketch comedian and a director of Hollywood comedies—know all that? How did she render it with such compassion? How did she make it so dramatic and interesting?

My friends all knew about my love of the movie. At some point, I asked each of them, "Have you seen *Mikey and Nicky*?" "Yes, Todd, we watched it together." I grew excited if they hadn't already seen it because I could watch it with them. I rewatched it alone, too, maybe yearly. Eventually, it became the movie I had seen more than any other.

When I became a film studies professor, I screened the film occasionally in classes, mostly to share this curious Hollywood outlier. When I brought it up in conversation, even among film scholars, most people had never heard of it. I put it in my mental jewelry box of Hollywood gems that few people appreciate. It sat in there for years, along with *Thunderbolt and Lightfoot* (1974), *Tempest* (1982), *House of Games* (1987), and *Zero Effect* (1998). So when I saw that Criterion had released a Blu-ray disc of the film in 2019 and that filmmakers like Quentin Tarantino and the Safdie brothers had celebrated it, again I was confused. Was there a prestige market for this little gangster drama? I had always assumed that my affection resulted from an idiosyncratic taste for the film.

This assumption was bolstered by the fact that I did not have *reasons* for loving the movie as much as I did. I could never satisfactorily explain to anyone, or myself, what was so great about it. I barely mentioned the movie in my book on seventies cinema—even though it is my favorite film of the decade—because at that point I still did not know how to talk about it. Indeed, my primary motivation for writing this book was to understand, and to learn to explain, what makes this movie special.

I suspect that most researchers start projects like this one with curiosity and a set of questions, as I have. But I do not regard this project, which must now sound so personal, as an expression of my personal taste. Rather, it offers both a history and a practical aesthetics of the film. My goals are to persuade readers that they should also be curious about the film and, as best I can, to explain its historical and artistic significance in a way that satisfies us both.

HOLLYWOOD RENEGADE

INTRODUCTION

The only thing experience teaches you is what you can't do.
ELAINE MAY, 1975

Critics of *Mikey and Nicky* (1976) often draw a comparison that has a trace of contempt: Elaine May shot more footage than the makers of *Gone with the Wind* (1939). The first instance of this curious comparison that I can find comes from a December 1976 article by Andrew Tobias, published just days before the film's initial theatrical release. In Tobias's exposé on the film for *New West* magazine, in which he describes the eight years May spent making *Mikey and Nicky*, he writes, "It took David Selznick 475,000 feet of raw film to make *Gone with the Wind.* Elaine May shot three times that much—1.4 million feet—to make her little picture."[1] I want to focus on Tobias's phrase "little picture."

The underlying point of the comparison, I take it, is that *Gone with the Wind*—a four-hour epic that features elaborate sets, a sweeping landscape, and the burning of Atlanta—should be more difficult to shoot than May's 106-minute buddy film. Yet you could cut three *Gone with the Wind* epics with the same amount of footage that May used to make *Mikey and Nicky*, which is a study of two small-time gangsters, the opposite of an epic. The other point of the comparison, which usually appears in the context of *Mikey and Nicky*'s cost overruns, is that May is self-indulgent and undisciplined, that she doesn't know what she is doing. A few weeks after the *New West* article, Jack Kroll picked up the observation for *Newsweek*: "For this intimate, essentially two-character movie, May shot three times as much footage as 'Gone with the Wind,' brought the budget close to $5 million with delays, took more than a year to edit (she never finished that), and had the film taken away from her by Paramount after a series of legal scrimmages."[2] Kroll emphasizes how small May's movie is ("intimate," "two-character") compared to *Gone with the Wind,* yet May did such an incompetent job that studio professionals had no choice but to take it out of her hands in order to get it into theaters. Similar comments appear in the *Chicago Sun-Times, Village Voice, Sight and Sound,* and *New York* magazine, as well as in numerous other commentaries on the film.[3] The comparison gets repeated so often that we can consider it a meme. Catchy and repeatable, it is a kind of accusation: Elaine May is an amateur.

But why shouldn't May's "little picture" shoot three times the footage used to shoot *Gone with the Wind*? *Gone with the Wind* is a series of set pieces, preplanned with precision so as to get each shot with the least expenditure. That is standard practice in Hollywood; that is the business model. In the commercial filmmaking industry, a professional director realizes the vision laid out in the script on time and on budget. But Elaine May couldn't make her movie that way. I don't know for certain that she shot more footage than the makers of *Gone with the Wind*; perhaps she did. We can say for certain, however, that to make the *Mikey and Nicky* that we have, May had to shoot a lot of footage.

In order to explain why May needed so much footage, I first must explain something elementary about the production of live-action commercial films. The most expensive stage of the production process, by far, is principal photography, when cameras are used to shoot the movie. Photography requires actors, sets, and locations (which cost money for rentals, construction, traffic control, permits, security, etc.); a lot of crew to set up, operate, and break down the equipment; and crew to handle makeup, costumes, props, sound, catering, housekeeping, and a range of other activities. Every day of photography costs a lot of money—in the case of *Mikey and Nicky* reportedly $12,000 per day (the equivalent of about $90,000 per day in 2026).[4]

I once heard a film director compare principal photography to running in front of a moving train, the pressures of time and money driving forward as directors try to realize, with desperate speed, their creative plans. Photography normally entails a series of compromises as the practical realities of the shooting process collide with a director's artistic vision. So filmmakers prepare for photography for months or longer during preproduction in order to save time on set. They finalize the script, storyboard key shots, design and build sets, rehearse actors, and perform "camera rehearsals," all of which allow the film's creative participants to decide how to perform and shoot each scene. Then, during photography, the director follows plans laid out in preproduction. Notice that, in this model, almost all the creative decision-making occurs before cameras start rolling in order to make photography as efficient and cost-effective as possible.

For the moment, however, we should stop thinking about filmmaking as if we were businesspeople. Instead, we should think like artists, like Elaine May, who reconceived the traditional relationship between preproduction and principal photography. If we ignore money—and May seems to have ignored it—then why not extend the process of creative experimentation all the way through principal photography? Experimentation on set enables creative discoveries and fortunate accidents, which the time pressures of photography can stifle. Dustin Hoffman said about working with May on *Ishtar* (1987), "It was about creation for Elaine. She loved process. Those are dirty words when you're shooting."[5] With her background in improvisational theater, May understood that her vision of *Mikey and Nicky* required slowing down principal photography. She did not seem to care much about time and money or about the fact that one of her leads, Peter Falk, was going to have to leave the shoot after sixty days in order to film a season of his *Columbo* television series. She had other people, in particular her producer Michael Hausman, to worry about those details, people who put obstacles in front of the train to keep it from crashing into her movie. Instead, May focused on creating the conditions that would encourage creativity and afford the actors performance opportunities. This singular focus meant shooting scenes with multiple cameras simultaneously; moving sets, props, and actors around for different takes; reshooting scenes again and again; and letting the cameras roll. She did not want to miss something the actors did that might benefit her film.

Mikey and Nicky relishes the small moments—not the grand scenes of *Gone with the Wind*—and, to create the naturalistic work that May was aiming for, such moments required actors to tease out nuances of character and situation spontaneously on camera. May and her actors also had to figure out how they would deliver story information obliquely through subtext, facial expression, physical behavior, and vocal inflection, not the speeches and declarations of traditional Hollywood storytelling ("Frankly, my dear, I don't give a damn"). She cast John Cassavetes and Peter Falk, who were invested in doing that work and already had a close rapport, and she created an environment in which they could experiment with their characters and exploit her script's potential for complex performances. That kind of filmmaking takes more time than it took to make *Gone with the Wind* because working with actors in this way is time consuming. May might indeed be a self-indulgent director, if "self-indulgent" means that she was thinking not about the studio that financed the movie, nor about the time and money pressures that typically weigh on production, nor about whether her film would find an audience or get good reviews, but rather about getting all that she could from each moment of her "little film."

May's filmmaking process on *Mikey and Nicky* is untenable in a commercial film industry. As a production model, it cannot be replicated on a commercial scale. It is too uncontrolled, too hit-or-miss, and too reliant on the dedication of extraordinary artists willing to work for years on one small film. For a film like *Mikey and Nicky*, which would not appeal to a mass audience, her process also cost too much money, creating cost overages on the production, originally budgeted at $1.8 million but eventually growing to $4.3 million in negative costs. That amount excludes the cost of lawsuits between May and Paramount Pictures, which raised Paramount's total expenditure to almost $5 million (or about $36 million in today's dollars) at a time when the average cost of production was $2.3 million.[6] Paramount sued May because, after more than a year in post-production, she was still editing *Mikey and Nicky* and burning through money. By many accounts, she was obsessed. Within the context of Hollywood's standard practices, hers was indeed an amateur's approach to filmmaking: she did not make the film for money, careerism, or popular success; she did it out of love.

The term *amateur* generally denotes two things. In its primary meaning, an amateur is someone who has not mastered the technical skills required of a professional, skills that are largely interchangeable.[7] We expect a professional electrician to have the same set of skills that every other professional electrician has. The same is true of a professional Hollywood film director, whom the industry expects to have skills that every other Hollywood director has. An amateur does not have all those skills. But an amateur is also someone who does an activity for love, not gain. This is the original meaning of the word, which comes from the French *amateur*, meaning "someone who loves." That is probably what John

Cassavetes meant when he called himself "an amateur filmmaker and a professional actor."[8] Cassavetes acted for money; he directed for love. And it is the meaning that some filmmakers and scholars have drawn on when praising amateur filmmaking.

People tend to think of amateur cinema as inferior to professional cinema, but in film studies the term *amateur* can signify approbation, particularly within avant-garde film.[9] In his 1967 essay "In Defense of Amateur," filmmaker Stan Brakhage celebrated the amateur filmmaker who "photographs what he loves or needs in some-such sense—surely a more real, and thus more honorable, activity than work which is performed for some gain."[10] Professional filmmakers, Brakhage argued, should therefore take inspiration from amateurs, not the other way around. Filmmaker Maya Deren, in her 1959 manifesto "Amateur vs. Professional," argued that the amateur has artistic and physical freedoms that are the envy of professional filmmakers. The amateur, she said, need never "sacrifice visual drama and beauty" to the "relentless" imperatives of professional storytelling. Nor is the amateur "expected to return profit on a huge investment by holding the attention of a massive and motley audience for 90 minutes." Physical freedom, Deren argued, "includes time freedom—a freedom from budget imposed deadlines."[11] Amateurs, for Deren, may see themselves as inferior to professionals, but they should embrace their amateurism for the freedom it affords their work. Unlike the professional, the amateur can experiment ("your mistakes will not get you fired").[12]

Elaine May brought an amateur's freedom to the Hollywood film industry. Cassavetes did the same in his movies, but whereas Cassavetes mostly directed outside of the industry and on relatively small budgets, May needed Hollywood money in order to fund her unorthodox filmmaking process. Her process was too inefficient and expensive for the low-budget films that studio executives contracted her to make. Still, she refused to let Hollywood's financial, industrial, and mechanical surroundings limit her filmmaking. Deren regarded the industry as a constraint on filmmakers ("burdened as they are by their many-ton monsters, cables and crews"),[13] but on *Mikey and Nicky,* May simply ignored such limitations. This conflict between May's "amateur" sensibility and Hollywood's professional structure, deadly for any director who wants to thrive in the commercial film industry, created enormous friction and resentment between her and the studio executives who financed her movie and who expected her to bring them a marketable film on time and on budget.

Of course, the word *amateur* has taken on a pejorative connotation that I hope to complicate and undo: amateurs are incompetent. May's amateurism, I shall argue, signaled not incompetence but rather an alternative approach. Scholar Jake Wilson writes about May:

> With her move into film direction, May acquired a new image, which has clung to her ever since: that of a total incompetent. Critics of her films have seldom failed to dwell on her tendency to blow out budgets and run over schedule, and to agonize over details while digging in her heels over perverse artistic choices. Much the same could be said of some of the most revered figures of cinema history, such as Erich von Stroheim or Stanley Kubrick, but where these men have long been acknowledged as rule-breaking geniuses, the consensus on May has tended to be that she simply did not know what she was doing.[14]

Production delays and cost overruns on *Mikey and Nicky* and her other films did result in part from May's inattention to certain activities inherent to professional directing in Hollywood, activities in which she seemed uninvested. "There's a big technical side to the visual stuff, which she could never master," said Paul Sylbert, *Mikey and Nicky*'s production designer.[15] Sylbert is probably right, but there are many kinds of directors, some more technically oriented than others.

As Wilson indicates, critics have often lauded male directors who ran over budget because of a fierce commitment to their art—Jacques Tati on *Playtime* (1967), Francis Ford Coppola on *Apocalypse Now* (1979), Stanley Kubrick on *The Shining* (1980), all obsessives like May, all regarded as geniuses, not incompetents. Like May, Kubrick shot numerous takes, but film commentators call him a "maverick" and a "fierce autodidact"; they praise his "virtuosity" and valorize his technical skill and stylistic eccentricity.[16] By contrast, May's actor-focused technique led some commentators to conclude that she didn't know what she was doing, despite the fact that she had mastered some of the most challenging filmmaking skills, including script writing, performance and characterization, scene development, and direction of actors. Indeed, several filmmakers she worked with expressed astonishment at her many talents. Clive Donner, who directed her in *Luv* (1967), said, "The devastating thing about Elaine is that she's better at everything—writing, acting, directing—than almost anyone else I know."[17] In 1973, Cassavetes said, "she's the finest actor's director I've ever worked with."[18] Cassavetes had already worked with Robert Aldrich, Martin Ritt, Don Siegel, and Roman Polanski. Falk called her a "Hall of Fame" director.[19] As we shall see in a later chapter, she was also an intuitive film editor—again, intuitive not in technical skill but in the way she constructed performances and designed a scene's emotional development. Decades after working with her on *Mikey and Nicky*, editor Sheldon Kahn called her "the brightest person I ever worked with."[20]

But May never mastered several craft practices expected of Hollywood directors, such as meeting contractual deadlines, staying on schedule, working within her budget, and handling the many technical components of the filmmaking process; perhaps she never tried. She did not necessarily need to know those things in order to make the films she wanted to make, so she let other people (her producers, assistant directors, cinematographers, and editors) handle them. For a director like May, attending to such things might have interfered with her effort to maintain freedom, creativity, and spontaneity on set. "She works on impulses, intuitions," said Sylbert. "It's easy to do on a typewriter, but impossible to do when you have other people standing around."[21] Working on impulses and intuitions during photography is indeed "impossible" for directors invested in conserving studio money, adhering to deadlines, and being viewed as professional by the executives and crew "standing around" waiting for the next setup, but impulses and intuitions are key components of the creative process. There is no reason—beyond a desire to conserve time, money, and effort—to limit them during principal photography.

About directing her first film, *A New Leaf* (1971), May said, "I really didn't know anything, but when I told [the studio executives] that, they thought that was my technique."[22] By the time she directed *Mikey and Nicky*, it *was* her technique. With two films already completed, she could no longer be called an amateur in the pejorative sense, yet she continued to ignore many of the same components of Hollywood directing that she "didn't know anything" about when she started. Film scholar Maya Montañez Smukler makes this very point: "If on *A New Leaf* May's tendency towards inefficient work habits can be understood—in part—within the context of a beginner thrown into extraordinary circumstances, the way she ran the set of her third film was *her* process."[23] Despite pressures to professionalize, May maintained an amateur filmmaker's sense of freedom, which involved a deal of inefficiency with regard to scheduling and time commitments, inattention to some of filmmaking's technical components and the costs of her artistic choices, and a lot of playful experimentation or, as Brakhage said about amateur filmmaking, the "clumsiness of continual discovery."[24]

With this book, I hope to convince readers that the very qualities that made May an unprofessional Hollywood filmmaker (in the eyes of some of her filmmaking crew, studio executives, and many journalists) also made her an innovative Hollywood filmmaker. In the Hollywood film industry, professionalism gets films in the can on budget and on time, but it limits creativity. In a public interview at the New School in 1975, May, deep in the midst of editing *Mikey and Nicky*, said, "I was much smarter in my first movie than in my second. The only thing experience teaches you is what you can't do. When you start, you think you can do anything. And then you start to get a little tired."[25] Most professional filmmakers don't try to do the "impossible"; they know better. To make a "little picture" like *Mikey and Nicky*, you cannot shoot more footage than it took to make *Gone with the Wind* and still bring it in on budget; that would be impossible. And you cannot film over a period of ten months and edit for two and a half years and still make your contractual delivery date. If we want to have a film like *Mikey and Nicky*, however, then it has to be made by someone who does what a professional Hollywood director won't do. Elaine May could not make a professional Hollywood movie, so instead she made a masterpiece.

Labeling May's film, or any artwork, a masterpiece raises some thorny philosophical issues regarding artistic value, issues that extend back to Plato and Aristotle and that philosophers of art continue to debate. I do not propose to settle such issues, but I do want to suggest what we might mean when we call an artwork a masterpiece. We mean, perhaps, that the work is innovative or daring, that it breaks new ground artistically or transcends previous works in the same mode.[26] We might also mean that it satisfies certain aesthetic functions—that it succeeds, through its design features, in moving us, delighting us, or engaging our intellect in a profound or brilliant way—or that the work executes its artistic aims with excellence (superior skill, ambition, or success).[27] We might furthermore mean that the work has an enduring propensity to provide aesthetic rewards, that our experience of it grows richer upon repeated encounters, that it stands the test of time.[28] Philosophers have pointed to other indicators of artistic value, but the criteria above are some of the most common, precise, and objective. *Mikey and Nicky*, I hope to show, satisfies all of them. And I am not alone in regarding the film as a masterpiece; in the past few decades, many critics have come to the same conclusion.[29]

Nonetheless, the film did not appeal to the mass audience that Hollywood films—including more "professional" Hollywood masterpieces, like *Stagecoach* (1939), *North by Northwest* (1959), and *The Godfather* (1972)—are normally designed to satisfy. May was not cut out to make that kind of film, although she worked within the same industrial system that produced them. Instead, she made a film more suited to her artistic skills and background, a work of uncommon subtlety, complexity, and density within a commercial context that discourages these aesthetic properties. This book highlights May's artistic achievement in light of the pressures, constraints, and challenges that she faced within the Hollywood system of filmmaking.

Indeed, one of the surprising things about many of the commentators who repeat the *Gone with the Wind* observation is how much they admire May as an artist, whether they hated her "little film" or loved it. Andrew Tobias, in a postscript to his devastating 1976 exposé in *New West* magazine, goes on to call May "one of my all-time heroes."[30] Jack Kroll says, "She is one of the few artists in movies with a touch of genius."[31] Writing for the *New York Times*, Caryn James calls *Mikey and Nicky* "a small-scale drama about two gangsters, for which she shot about twice as much film as 'Gone with the Wind' needed," but she also calls the film "brutal, brilliantly acted, startlingly good."[32] In 2006, Manohla Dargis flipped the meaning of the *Gone with the Wind* comparison, writing, "May shot more than twice as much film as it took to get 'Gone with the Wind' in the can, but her struggles to get her modestly scaled wonderment into the world were worth every frame, dollar and drop of blood."[33] This is not contempt but admiration.

This book sets out to explain *Mikey and Nicky*'s artistic and historical achievements, which scholars have had difficulty pinpointing. Jeremy Carr offers the only rich aesthetic examination of the film to date in an essay that focuses on the thematic, narrative, and stylistic similarities between *Mikey and Nicky* and Cassavetes's independent films.[34] Other scholars who have tried to describe what makes the movie special end up offering indeterminate praise. "Every shot is a separate event, a movie in miniature," writes Kent Jones, "and every scene, practically every moment, is a seemingly impossible continuity built from a million discontinuities, the rhythm simultaneously broken down and improbably flowing and surging forward."[35] Ray Carney writes that May "doesn't hold our interest with gimmicks but by showing us interesting things about our emotions. She doesn't use suspense to scare and surprise us; she gives us a scary, surprising conception of who we are. . . . *Mikey and Nicky* does what great art always does: it invents a new language of feeling."[36] You can hear the authors struggling to explain their enthusiasm for the movie.[37]

I quote these scholars not to criticize them but to illustrate the difficulty commentators have had explaining May's artistic achievements. That difficulty results in part from the fact that the film's delights cannot be distilled into distinct artistic devices that we can readily identify just by watching the movie, such as *A Clockwork Orange*'s (1971) audacious use of classical music or *Nashville*'s (1975) interlocking stories. *Mikey and Nicky*'s artistic achievements are harder to pinpoint because they result from May's attention to making each moment of the film dense, subtle, and complex. To understand those achievements, we must therefore study May's working processes and artistic intentions. May designed every scene, even minor ones, as a performance event; she made every character, even peripheral ones, nuanced and memorable; and she gave every moment in the movie multiple areas of interest and some unexpected detail in the story or characterizations. She worked day after day to exploit each opportunity that her script afforded for density, subtlety, and complexity. To try to understand the artistic and historical significance of *Mikey and Nicky*, we must therefore analyze not just the film itself but the ways in which May's unorthodox approach to writing, directing, and editing dictated its artistic design.

In an effort to understand how and why Elaine May made *Mikey and Nicky* in the way that she did, this study offers a *historical poetics* of the film. This approach to film study, championed by David Bordwell, attempts to explain the ways in which films have been designed within "particular empirical circumstances."[38] A purely historical approach, while interesting in itself, does not sufficiently explain May's accomplishment. History tells us of the film's unusual production methods, cost overruns, legal disputes, and box office failure, followed by later adulation and commercial success. Although *Mikey and Nicky*'s history offers a number of unique turns, we have heard similar stories about other productions, including *Citizen Kane* (1941), *Apocalypse Now* (1979), *Blade Runner* (1982), and *Brazil* (1985)—all interesting films, but not in the same way that *Mikey and Nicky* is. History alone cannot explain what makes each of these films a unique artistic achievement. For that, we need a *poetics* of film. The term (derived from the Greek *poiêsis,* meaning "formation" or "making something new") denotes the study of an artwork's aesthetic principles and artistic design, as well as the "functions, effects, and uses" of its construction.[39]

But poetics alone would not do the job either, not with this film. A purely poetics-based approach—which involves studying the artistic properties of the finished film—would not fully explain *Mikey and Nicky*'s particular artistic achievements, which are intimately tied to its production history. That history includes May's work as a comedian, writer, and film director, her intentions and working processes as *Mikey and Nicky*'s scriptwriter and director, the work of the actors and crew, and the film's extraordinary production and reception history, all within the context of the Hollywood film industry in the 1970s and other films that the industry was making at the time.

The pages that follow set out to answer three perplexing questions that speak to this film's significance.

First, what in May's background enabled her to make *Mikey and Nicky*? Known for satiric comedy, she then came out with a domestic tragedy about middle-class gangsters. How did her background, her unorthodox directing technique, and her singular talents as an artist lead to this film?

Second, how did such an uncommercial film get the backing of a major Hollywood studio? *Mikey and Nicky* is an outlier in Hollywood history, but historical factors in the 1970s enabled the production. A strange confluence of economic-industrial conditions encouraged the major studios to court outsiders like May and other inexperienced filmmakers, who brought an unusual, sometimes radical, filmmaking aesthetic to the commercial film industry. The production of *Mikey and Nicky*—its history, the troubles May had with studio executives, and the lawsuits over it—helps illuminate the ways in which the film industry functions by relying on a particular notion of professionalism. Professionalism allows the industry to function *as* an industry, but it marginalizes or outright excludes alternative artistic practices. This book explains how industry conditions characteristic of the early and mid-1970s enabled *Mikey and Nicky*'s production and shaped its artistic design.

Finally, what is so great about *Mikey and Nicky*? Critics mostly blasted the film when it came out, and it flopped at the box office, alienating the mass audience that Hollywood movies are normally designed to please. But it has endured among a coterie that sees something special in May's film, something difficult to pinpoint without closely studying both its history and artistic design. An understanding of May's unusual filmmaking methods helps illuminate the artistic achievements of a movie that almost didn't make it into theaters. Ultimately, I hope to show that what critics and audiences initially regarded as incompetence in fact represents an intentional deviation from Hollywood norms. May made the movie she intended to make, and to appreciate her accomplishment we need to understand her artistic aims and her efforts to achieve them.

To answer these questions, we will study Elaine May as an artist, Hollywood in the 1970s, and *Mikey and Nicky*.

PART I

ELAINE MAY

1 COMEDIAN

Humor is just a way of looking at things. I mean, you look at it this way, and it's a disaster. And you look at it this way, and it's funny.

ELAINE MAY, 1975

On the face of it, the grim themes explored in *Mikey and Nicky* represent a serious departure for Elaine May. She had directed two earlier films, both comedies, and before that had achieved fame in the late 1950s and early 1960s for her work with Mike Nichols as one-half of the famed sketch comedy duo Nichols and May. Before a preview screening of *Mikey and Nicky,* May asked Julian Schlossberg, a vice president at Paramount, to remove her name from publicity because "people will think it's a comedy."[1] Even the film's publicist, Tom Miller, assumed it was a comedy until his last day on set.[2] Although she had never made a serious film before *Mikey and Nicky,* her prior work prepared her for it. So let us turn to the period 1957–1961, when she was performing sketch comedy with Mike Nichols.

Nichols and May performed in nightclubs, toured the country, made three acclaimed comedy albums, appeared regularly on radio and television, and eventually capped their live performance career with the hugely successful 1960 Broadway show *An Evening with Mike Nichols and Elaine May.* An audio recording of four sketches from the show won a Grammy in 1961 for Best Comedy Performance. Shortly after that, the duo disbanded, although they collaborated on numerous other projects over the years, including performing as George and Martha in a celebrated 1980 stage production of *Who's Afraid of Virginia Woolf?* Later, Nichols directed May's scripts of *The Birdcage* (1996) and *Primary Colors* (1998).

May met Nichols in Chicago in the early 1950s, and together they worked for America's first improvisational theater, the Compass Players (later transformed into the Second City). Both had studied acting with disciples of Konstantin Stanislavsky, Nichols with Lee Strasberg in New York and May with Maria Ouspenskaya in Los Angeles. Nichols and May together developed their improvisation talents working with Paul Sills, the legendary director and son of an even more legendary improvisation teacher and theorist, Viola Spolin. Sills led Compass and popularized his mother's work. "Paul brought my work into the world," Spolin said.[3]

To teach improvisation, Spolin had designed a series of "theater games." Her 1963 book *Improvisation for the Theater*, which explains the games and lays out Spolin's philosophy and technique, is among the most significant books for teaching actors, outselling Stanislavsky's *Building a Character* by more than two to one.[4] Her teachings contradicted Stanislavsky and proponents of "the Method." Method actors focused on developing their character's backstory and recalling "sense memories" from their own personal experience. Spolin and Sills taught actors to unleash their creativity through games that focused on the present moment.[5] May directed Compass workshops using Spolin's technique in order to keep actors in the present, but she also relied on her Stanislavsky training by encouraging sense memories.[6]

According to Spolin, her theoretical work developed not through her experiences in professional theater but from supervising the amateur performances of the Chicago WPA Recreational Project, as well as spontaneous "operas" and games of charades with her family and friends.[7] "Everyone can act," she wrote. "Everyone can improvise. Anyone who wishes to can play in the theater and learn to become 'stage worthy.'"[8] Spolin brought her amateur aesthetic to professional theater, training actors to improvise onstage. Her handbook, she says, "is equally valuable for professionals, lay actors, and children."[9] In fact, she preferred the older term *player* to *actor* because it captured the spirit of spontaneity that she regarded as central to creative experience. The approach to acting promoted by Spolin and Sills enabled Nichols and May to develop live sketches, "without," as Spolin says of her games, "benefit of an outside playwright."[10] This approach, we shall see, also influenced the production of *Mikey and Nicky*.

After they left Compass, Nichols and May teamed up and hit the road, developing their sketches and performing improvisations onstage. We find nothing in their sketches about friends setting each other up to be killed, but we can see in their comedy the seeds of the themes, character interactions, and storytelling techniques that May would develop to maturity in her gangster drama, particularly observational comedy and improv.

Observational Comedy and Observational Tragedy

Several lines in *Mikey and Nicky* express May's style of humor, witty lines such as "I came as soon as I got your towel" and biting lines such as "I'm glad you told me what you think because I've got a lot of respect for your mind." After Nicky threatens to bust down his wife's door, she says, "You really have changed, I wouldn't have recognized you." When the hit man asks Mikey if he is sure that the man walking down the street is not Nicky, Mikey replies, "You want to shoot him just in case?" And the following exchange between Nicky and Mikey could have appeared in a Nichols and May sketch (or even an Abbott and Costello sketch):

> NICKY: Can I have your watch?
> MIKEY: You want to wear my watch?
> NICKY: I'll be very careful. I want it for luck, just for luck.
> MIKEY: All right, I'll let you wear my watch. Will you let me carry your gun?
> NICKY: What for?
> MIKEY: For luck. If somebody thinks I'm you and they shoot at me, it'd be lucky if I could shoot back.

The film has pictorial jokes, too. Immediately after Mikey says to the hit man, "I didn't say he was standing in the middle of the street waiting for us," the film cuts to a shot of Nicky standing in the middle of the street. These moments don't always get laughs, although at a screening I attended at the New York Metrograph in 2024 the audience laughed uproariously at all of them.

But *Mikey and Nicky* is certainly more tragic than May's sketch comedy and her other movies. Mikey Mittner and Nicky Godolin, mid-level gangsters and old friends, spend a night together roaming Philadelphia after the bosses have put out a contract on Nicky. We realize about twenty-five minutes into the movie that Mikey is setting up his friend for the hit. We eventually learn about the history of humiliations and resentments that Mikey has built up toward Nicky over their years of friendship. The scenario is serious, a tragedy in almost a classical sense. It largely obeys Aristotle's unities (the story takes place over one night, for instance). It features suffering, hamartia, moral failure, the downfall of flawed protagonists. It is a domestic tragedy—a tragedy of ordinary people, not Aristotle's great men—of the kind that flourished on the twentieth-century stage in the plays of Lorraine Hansberry, Henrik Ibsen, Arthur Miller, and Eugene O'Neill.

It is not the kind of movie that we would expect from a sketch comedian, but it does not take too many adjustments to turn a comic situation into tragedy or a tragic situation into comedy; a change in attitude, context, or outcome will often do it. Indeed, May's dramatic gangster film addresses some of the same observations about people that she and Nichols explored in their comedy sketches, in particular the observation that, although people may appear to behave out of professionalism or duty, when you dig a little bit you find that they are really motivated by emotion and insecurity, which lead them to destructive, often self-destructive, behavior. In fact, Nichols and May devoted almost an entire comedy album to that observation, *Mike Nichols & Elaine May Examine Doctors* (1961).

The running theme of the album is that doctors may appear competent, but their fears, obsessions, and doubts compromise their work. Doctors, in the Nichols and May sketches, are just children in scrubs. In the sketch "Merry Christmas, Doctor," May plays an analyst who is hurt when her patient cancels an upcoming appointment so that he can spend the day with his family ("And you feel an hour away from the kids for your analyst will be too much time?"). In "Morning Rounds," Nichols plays a doctor who, rather than attending to his patient's ailments, fixates on whether one of the nurses has visited yet ("She's the tall, terribly attractive, dark nurse. . . . Did she mention my name?"). In "Thank You Very Much," May plays an analyst whose humblebrags about her beauty reveal her need for attention ("I think it interferes a little with the treatment"). In "Physical," May plays a "lady doctor" who becomes more interested in marrying her patient than examining him ("Come in and I'll check you again in about—an hour."). And in "A Little More Gauze," a surgeon (Nichols) obsessed with his nurse (May) badgers her with love offerings during surgery:

DOCTOR: I'm not going to finish this operation unless you say yes, Edith.
NURSE: Doctor Harris, this patient will die.
DOCTOR: I've been tortured long enough. Yes or no, which is it going to be?
NURSE: This is absolute blackmail.
DOCTOR: I don't care. I don't care what length I go to anymore. All is fair and all that.
NURSE: Doctor Harris, you're a doctor, a *doctor*. Doesn't that mean anything to you? A *surgeon*.
DOCTOR: I am a doctor, but I'm a man also, and I will not go on with this operation until you give me your answer, and it better be yes.

The sketches make the same joke again and again, but it is always funny to see the veneer of professionalism collapse, revealing the doctors' desperate need for love and attention.

Mikey and Nicky makes this same observation about the two gangsters. The more time we spend with them and the more interactions we witness, the more we realize that their relationship is plagued by insecurities and the need for love and attention. "I introduced ya, I got you the job, and now I can't get you on the phone," Mikey says to his old friend. May titled her movie *Mikey and Nicky* (not *Mike and Nick*), emphasizing the childhood names of these two adult men, who seem not to have outgrown their years of slights and minor betrayals.[11] There is a dark humor in all this—Mikey's inability to get his friend on the phone is not a serious justification for having him murdered—that is not too far from the humor of a doctor willing to let his patient die on the operating table because his nurse does not return his love. As many comedians have discovered, emotional insecurity provides endless opportunities for humor. May finds tragedy in it, too.

Nichols seems to have brought more from their sketches into his filmmaking than May did, using some of the same gags in *The Graduate* (1967), for instance, that the two of them developed in their "Teenagers in a Car" sketch, such as Mrs. Robinson blowing cigarette smoke out of the side of her mouth in the middle of kissing Benjamin. But May also seems to have drawn on aspects of that sketch as she developed *Mikey and Nicky.*

"Teenagers in a Car" became their most popular sketch. They developed it first at Compass and performed it regularly onstage and twice on television (in 1958 and 1959).[12] The sketch, which portrays a boy trying to persuade a girl to have sex with him in his parents' car, gets a dark revision in *Mikey and Nicky*, when Nicky and Mikey both try to persuade Nicky's girlfriend to have sex with them in her apartment (figures 1.1 and 1.2). However, it is not just the overall scenario that resonates but the observation that men and women approach such situations with different attitudes and communication strategies and that women in these situations must navigate a difficult set of obstacles and expectations. While the male character, in both the sketch and the film, barrels forward, the female character conveys her feelings indirectly and affects a naivete, all in an effort to fend off the man. She endeavors to evade conflict, appear unthreatening, and prevent the man from feeling injured, as she avoids alienating him or violating his expectations about her innocence and femininity. By some accounts, May does not herself behave like the female characters she invented; men often find her intimidating. After meeting May, actor Richard Burton wrote in his diary, "Elaine was too formidable . . . one of the most intelligent, beautiful, and witty women I had ever met. I hoped I would never see her again."[13] By contrast, the behavior of many of May's female characters—their indirectness, innocence, and servility—makes them vulnerable to men's manipulations.

For Nichols and May, this dance of gender roles becomes a source of humor, as their sketches reveal the ridiculous scripts and gender rules that govern sexual relationships, particularly in that era. In "Teenagers," the boy and girl first ramble about anything other than the sexual implications of sitting in a parked car by a lake ("It's just suicidally beautiful tonight," she says), then he clumsily engages her in a lengthy kiss. The boy starts to move his hand toward her breast. Still kissing him, she grabs his hand and forces it back over her shoulder and onto her back (figure 1.3). It takes all her strength, but she manages it. He continues to try to make his way to her breast, but she angles her shoulder and squeezes his body tightly enough that he cannot get his hands to the front of her blouse, as much as he tries to work his way in there. Eventually, he gives up, and

FIGURE 1.1. The kiss in "Teenagers in a Car" (1959).

FIGURE 1.2. Mikey (Peter Falk) tries to kiss Nellie (Carol Grace) in *Mikey and Nicky*.

she says blithely, "So you think you're going to go to college when you get out of high school?" as though the whole fight over her breasts never happened.

One source of humor here is that this demure girl has enough determination and strength to pull the boy's hand from her breast area all the way to her back. But the sketch's primary joke is that their athletic sexual

FIGURE 1.3. The girl pulls the boy's hand away from her breast in "Teenagers in a Car" (1959).

competition goes entirely unacknowledged. The girl can sustain the appearance of innocence because the fight happens without words and out of the couple's overt view of each other. They maintain the pretense that all that is happening, throughout the exchange, is just a kiss, even though they are in fact engaged in two interactions simultaneously, an overt kiss and a covert battle. Consequently, she can fend him off without overtly rejecting him, all while maintaining her image of shyness and femininity. Nichols and May have staged the scene so that the audience can see it all—the kiss, the battle, the pretense—and thereby register the girl's real knowingness, fortitude, and physical strength.

The "Teenagers" sketch continues the satire on sexual interactions between boys and girls in the following exchange, when the boy finally makes his desires explicit:

BOY: This is the thing, I—I only get the car once a week.
GIRL: Oh, oh, well, I think that if a girl likes a boy, she'll ride on the bus.
BOY: I—I don't think I'm getting across to you. See, Genie, the way I figure it, every human being has, uh, certain natural urges, and I got them.
GIRL: I don't know what you mean.

Instead of telling the boy outright, "Listen, buddy, don't even try it," the girl affects ignorance. She then carefully explains to him the rules of dating ("this is our *first* date") while navigating the difficult sexual politics of the situation so that he does not reject her or lose face ("when you go out, like, on your *second* date"). The girl's coy demeanor and self-deprecation convey her effort to appear unthreatening and avoid conflict, even as she rejects his advances. The sketch boldly satirizes sex negotiations in a way that people had rarely seen from comedians, or anyone else, in the 1950s.[14]

Although May continued to explore these issues in her filmmaking, many feminist film commentators have disregarded her. Molly Haskell's 1976 article "Woman Directors" barely acknowledges May's filmmaking, and Alison Butler's 2002 book *Women's Cinema* completely ignores it.[15] Others attack her for her films' depictions of women. Annette Kuhn and Susannah Radstone wrote in 1990 that May's films "feature some of the most derogatory images of women on screen."[16] Marjorie Rosen, in 1973, called May "an Uncle Tom whose feminine sensibilities are demonstrably nil."[17] Haskell's 1977 review of *Mikey and Nicky* complained of the "misogyny that binds [May] to her male characters."[18] Lynne Jackson and Karen Jaehne, in a 1987 article on contemporary women filmmakers, argued that May's financial irresponsibility made things more difficult for other female directors in Hollywood.[19] In her 1988 book *Women Directors*, Barbara Koenig Quart called May's vision of women "appalling," singling out May's character in *A New Leaf* (1971) as "stupid, passive, masochistic."[20] She called the character of Lila in *The Heartbreak Kid* (1972) "one of the most negative images of a Jewish woman on film" and the character of the WASP love interest Kelly "flat and vacuous." Quart asserted boldly, "Elaine May's work has no feminist content."[21]

May herself responded to an attack on her portrayal of women at a screening of *Mikey and Nicky* at the Gramercy Theatre in the 1980s. According to Schlossberg, May attended the screening incognito ("Elaine doesn't like to do these things"), wearing an overcoat and hat, while Peter Falk took questions from the audience. Schlossberg says that a group of women "started to attack Peter about how the women were portrayed in the movie," at which point May apparently couldn't take it. "Elaine sees what's happening to Peter, she grabs her hat, throws it on my lap, takes off her coat," and, "like Clark Kent" turning into Superman, headed onto the stage to everyone's delight and astonishment. May said to the crowd, "This *is* the way it happens with women. You may not like it, but that's the way it is."[22] Indeed, I think many feminist film scholars today would disagree with Quart's assertion that May's work has "no feminist content." Beneath their stupidity, passivity, and masochism, May's women navigate some dangerous sexual politics. We see in May's sketches and films women's effort to maintain their well-being and dignity, even as they attempt to reject men's manipulations and conform to cultural notions of femininity.

The sex scene in *Mikey and Nicky* illustrates that effort, as well as the perils that women face in such situations. Probably the most distressing scene in the movie to watch, it first depicts Nicky (John Cassavetes) manipulating his girlfriend, Nellie (Carol Grace), into having sex with him while Mikey (Falk) sits nearby. Nicky tries groping Nellie's breast while she is talking to Mikey, and she surreptitiously pulls away his hand, much in the way the girl in the car did (figures 1.3 and 1.4). Eventually, Nellie succumbs to sex on the living room floor while Mikey sits idly on a trash can in the kitchen, witnessing the whole disturbing mess.[23] Immediately afterward, Mikey tries to have sex with her himself, upon Nicky's encouragement ("I wanted to warm her up a little bit for ya"). As Mikey works on Nellie, she demurely tells him that she is not interested, taking the same indirect approach used by the girl in the "Teenagers" sketch. Ultimately, Mikey disregards Nellie's resistance and assaults her.

The scene could be played for comedy, just like "Teenagers," in which much of the humor came from an unacknowledged sexual competition. But Nicky's and Mikey's aggression makes the scene disturbing and difficult. The following exchange between Mikey and Nellie, as he tries to sweet-talk her, could have appeared in a Nichols and May sketch, if not for the overt brutality:

MIKEY: So you like the news, huh?

NELLIE: I like to know what's happening.

MIKEY: [*Puts his hand on her thigh, laughs.*] You know, that's, uh, that's unusual, because you know that, uh, most pretty girls, uh, they don't have a brain in their head. I mean, most pretty girls, they don't care about uh anything that's happening around them, except that they want to have a good time. [*Nellie laughs meekly.*] Isn't that so?

FIGURE 1.4. Nellie (Carol Grace) pulls Nicky's (John Cassavetes) hand away from her breast when he tries to grope her.

NELLIE: Yes, I guess most girls are pretty dumb.

MIKEY: [*Getting closer to her.*] It makes it nice when they're smart *and* pretty.

NELLIE: Thank you.
[*Mikey puts his arm around Nellie. She stiffens.*]
Mikey, please.

MIKEY: [*Moving his mouth closer to hers while she pulls back.*]
Ahh.

NELLIE: [*softly*] Mikey, please, don't get fresh.

MIKEY: No, I just want a little kiss.

NELLIE: Oh, Mikey please, Mikey, Mikey please, don—
[*Mikey puts his hand behind her head and forces a kiss. Nellie reacts by biting his lip. He slaps her twice.*]

This scene and "Teenagers in a Car" depict a similar type of communication between the male and female characters. Their language is just as indirect, their feelings and intentions revealed more through body language than speech. In both scenes, rather than stating their intentions explicitly, the characters speak obliquely, saying, "Do you think you want to go to college?" ("Teenagers") or "So you like the news, huh?" (*Mikey and Nicky*). In both scenes, neither member of the couple overtly acknowledges what they both know—that he wants sex from her. And in both scenes, she gently explains to him that she won't do it, without overtly rejecting him ("I don't know what you mean"; "Mikey, please"). But if the *Mikey and Nicky* scene were one of Nichols and May's comedy sketches, the characters would patter like this for a few minutes—the miscommunications and pretenses offer innumerable opportunities for humor—and it would all end with a funny resolution. At the end of "Teenagers," the girl reluctantly agrees to sex, but then the boy gets cold feet. In *Mikey and Nicky*, a scenario similar to the one that Nichols and May had satirized on stage and television becomes a dark, distressing scene of manipulation and violence.

The two scenes—the comedic sketch "Teenagers in a Car" and the tragic sex scene in *Mikey and Nicky*—not only portray similar themes and scenarios, but they also use some of the same storytelling techniques. Each scene establishes a set of social norms and limits (men and women will refrain from sex unless they both want it) in order to create a conflict (men will want sex, and women will want to avoid it), norms and limits that the scenario proceeds to violate. In the comic scenario, the girl finally gives in to the boy; however, the boy, now frightened, suddenly avoids sex with *her*. In the end of "Teenagers in a Car," the norms and limits reassert themselves in a final punch line: in an effort to divert their interaction away from the sex she has yielded to, the boy says, "Do you think you're going to go to college when you get out of high school?" In the tragic scene from *Mikey and Nicky*, the woman succumbs to sex with one man, rejects the other man, and, as a result, suffers violence and humiliation in both instances. The norms and limits in such a scenario, the *Mikey and Nicky* scene shows us, are illusory.

The emotional effects on the audience of these two scenes—in one case *mirth*, in the other *distress*—point to the similarity and the difference between May's comedy and her one cinema tragedy. Indeed, the comparison may help us understand something about the relationship between comedy and tragedy as genres. The mirth of May's comedy and the distress of her tragedy both originate in a violation of norms and limits. In both instances, our minds entertain the possibility that those norms and limits might disintegrate. In her comedy, we entertain thoughts that the real world regards as subversive (maybe boys and girls in cars will have sex, even if the girl does not want it), only to have those thoughts checked and order restored. In her tragedy, we again entertain subversive thoughts (maybe men and women will have sex, even if the woman does not want it), only to come to the distressing realization that there is no order, after all. The sex scene in *Mikey and Nicky* rewrites "Teenagers in a Car" so that the audience not only imagines but *witnesses* a world without order. It is no accident that some of our greatest comedic dramatists (William Shakespeare, Anton Chekhov, Harold Pinter, and Tom Stoppard) and filmmakers (Charles Chaplin, Jean Renoir, and Woody Allen) are also some of our greatest tragedians. Successful comedian-tragedians like May have a talent not just for breaking norms but for enabling audiences to experience the distress of a universe unbounded.

Shakespeare scholar Stephen Booth suggests that the genre of comedy violates and then restores our sense of the world's order, whereas the genre of tragedy brings us to the distressing realization that the world's order is frail and brittle. "Comedy," Booth writes, "for all its gestures of fearlessness, is not ruthless in admitting truth"; rather, it "bullies us into actively exercising a faith in limits."[24] Whether or not these principles hold for comedy and tragedy generally, they accurately describe May's work. Recall the ending of "Teenagers," in which the limits of the scenario's bold premise reassert themselves in a reassuring way: the boy and girl will not have sex after all. The scene defends the ultimate fairness of the universe when the scenario retreats from its subversive edge. The boy backs out, the universe self-corrects, and it is funny. For Booth, tragedy is more fearless than comedy because it shows us that the norms and limits that we depend on for our safety and sanity are an illusion. When norms crumble, the result is chaos, and true chaos is distressing, not funny. We witness Mikey and Nicky violate Nellie and humiliate her, and nothing in the universe is stopping them.

The scene has a dark conclusion, but May sometimes went to dark places in her earlier work, too. One of her fellow Compass players, Annette Hankin, said about May's playwriting in the 1950s, "The heroines of her plays are always very vulnerable people who are eaten alive."[25] In one of May's 1955 Compass scenarios, "Georgina's First Date," an unpopular girl is first tricked by her date to the senior prom and then raped by him. In the end, she tells her mother that she had a wonderful time. Two of her plays from the 1960s, *Not Enough Rope* and *Name of a Soup*, writes Carrie Courogen, "centered around an outcast, unattractive woman and the ways in which she's taken advantage of by society."[26] One of May's comedy sketches with Nichols shows the same tragic sensibility. In "Cocktail Piano," a sketch from their 1958 album *Improvisations to Music*, a smooth-talking, predatory boss takes his shy secretary to a bar and then coerces her to go up to his apartment, presumably to listen to music. "We'll just hop up and play the record, okay?" he says, to which she replies, with obvious reluctance, "Well, uf, alright." She giggles uncomfortably; he laughs ominously. The sketch ends there, but we know what happens next and that nothing in the universe will stop it.

Improvisation

In her careers as both a comedian and a filmmaker, Elaine May delighted in improvisation. She embodied Spolin's "players," who could "put the full range of spontaneity to work as they created scene after scene of fresh material."[27] Improvisation, Spolin argued, generates creative "explosions" as players use their imaginations to solve whatever problems the scenario has generated for them. "The energy released to solve the problem, being restricted by the rules of the game and bound by group decision, creates an explosion—or spontaneity—and as is the nature of explosions, everything is torn apart, rearranged, unblocked."[28] We see that commitment to improvisation in Nichols and May's comedy. Their Broadway show, for instance, closed each night with an improvised sketch based on audience suggestions.

The onstage explosions that delighted May, however, began to frighten Nichols after the duo obtained success. "I, more than Elaine, became more and more afraid of our improvisational material. . . . She was always brave." Nichols said that May would extend their sketches onstage and go off on tangents that would throw him off. "I couldn't invent as she could."[29] According to theater critic John Lahr, "May cared more about process, Nichols more about results."[30] David Shepherd, who founded Compass with Paul Sills, said about them, "Mike's attitude was that you want to know on top what the point [of the sketch] is. And Elaine always wanted to explore and find new points."[31] Whereas Nichols worried that the team would somehow slip in front of an audience, May delighted in the spontaneity of the improv. So what if they slipped? Slipping is just another problem they would have to solve through improvisation, and everything would be "torn apart, rearranged, unblocked."

Eventually, May broke up their comedy duo. According to Nichols, their sketches became too repetitive. "We found ourselves doing the same material over and over, especially in our show for Broadway. This took a great toll on Elaine."[32] When their routines became routine, they lost the spirit of play that had inspired them in the first place. "We stopped because Elaine got sick of it."[33] According to Nichols, their lives had become "a million deals."[34] Once Nichols and May became true professionals, with predictable shows and polished sketches, she grew tired of the work.

May brought to her filmmaking the same spirit of improvisation that she had developed with Sills, Spolin, and Nichols, but filmmaking does not encourage improv in the way that live comedy does, and her techniques proved difficult to implement in Hollywood. Her second film, *The Heartbreak Kid* (1972), came from a script written by famed playwright Neil Simon, whose contract stipulated that no words could be changed without his approval. But she incorporated improvisation nonetheless, making use of a technique she had developed while directing at the Playwrights Theatre Club in Chicago in the mid-1950s: encourage the actors to improvise, then reintroduce the words of the script.[35] The technique afforded a *feeling* of improvisation, which Simon attributed to May's direction:

> She would rehearse the words, then throw out the words, then just have them do the scene the way they wanted to, and then put back the words. It's her style of directing, and I found it wonderful. For example there's the scene where the husband tells his wife that he cannot go on with the marriage, that he's going to dump her for another girl he met two days ago. Every word that I had written was on the screen, but for a number of days during shooting Elaine threw the words out and said to the actors, "Just play those attitudes, make up your own words." They did, and so they knew what the attitudes were. Then when they put these words back in, it seemed as though they were still improvising.[36]

Contractually prohibited from changing Simon's script, May used improv to help her actors develop their characters and scenes, a technique that contributed to the film's realism and spontaneity.

May used a similar process on *Mikey and Nicky*—encourage the actors to improvise, then bring back the script. Falk told the film's publicist, "she eventually sees that you get back to her lines."[37] Cassavetes told him the same thing.[38] When asked why May encouraged improvisation, Cassavetes explained:

> Because something *better* might come out of it. A line, a quality, a mood. . . . Oh, she does get back to the script, believe me she does. I just got a note from [May's assistant] Nola [Safro] last night: "Elaine says learn the lines." I know the lines. She knows I do. I'm just not married to them. What the note means is: "Now let's get back to the script." Tonight, then, I'll say the written lines. Sequentially.[39]

Falk got the same note.[40]

May has several times insisted that none of the dialogue in *Mikey and Nicky* was improvised: "You can't improvise something that's that tight a story."[41] She did, more recently, admit to one moment of improvisation, a brief exchange between Nicky and a woman about smoking on the bus.[42] Other than that, she says, it was all scripted. Others on set disagree. But rather than try to nail down whether the actors in fact improvised any dialogue, let us instead take a broad view of improvisation so that the concept includes not just ad-libbed dialogue but any actor behavior that happens spontaneously, without making decisions ahead of time. Spolin regarded improvisation as an essentially nonverbal activity and even invented a series of games in which the actors spoke gibberish.[43]

Although May says that she did not allow actors to improvise dialogue, she encouraged every other form of improvisation. During the production, Cassavetes and Falk continually explored new interpretations of May's script, each one emerging spontaneously as the actors responded in real time to what the other actors were doing. Assistant sound editor Patrick McMahon observed wildly different performances of the same dialogue: "In one take Peter Falk would just explode, and another he'd be really calm." According to McMahon, they "improvised the performances over and over and over again," varying them with each take. "With a ten-minute take," McMahon said, "they had the time to build dynamics that were startling."[44] We might say that everything the actors did was improvised *except* for the dialogue.

Cassavetes and Falk thrived under May's direction because it accorded with their own artistic attitudes and training. Cassavetes had studied at the American Academy of Dramatic Arts under the instruction of Charles Jehlinger, who advocated listening onstage. Jehlinger would not tell actors what to do, according to Cassavetes biographer Marshall Fine, but rather offered a "string of aphorisms" that encouraged dynamism in performance. They included, "Hearing is not listening," "Human impulse is the only thing that counts, not stage directions," "Don't think of acting; think of living," and "Life is the only true school of acting."[45] Unlike Stanislavsky and his disciples, Jehlinger focused less on preparation, scene analysis, and the actor's personal connection to a role and instead encouraged actors to experience the present moment *as* the character.

Later as a film director, Cassavetes echoed some of Jehlinger's ideas about acting in his own interviews. Acting, according to Cassavetes, "is an extension of life. How you're capable of performing in your life, that's how you're capable of performing on the screen."[46] And like Jehlinger, he disdained the Actors Studio. Cassavetes had taken classes with Lee Strasberg but quit after three weeks, developing his own course of acting training that, according to Fine, he regarded as a "direct competitor" to Strasberg's.[47] In interviews, Cassavetes also echoed Spolin, probably without knowing it. His oft-expressed belief that "anyone can be an actor" came close to mimicking Spolin's "everyone can improvise. Anyone who wishes to can play in the theater and learn to become 'stage worthy.'"[48] Like Spolin, he encouraged his acting students to focus on the present moment, emphasizing spontaneous reaction and improvisation. Indeed, his audition for the Actors Studio was an improvisation,[49] and his directorial debut, *Shadows* (1958), resulted from improvisations conducted in his acting class.

Cassavetes brought to the role of Nicky the spontaneity that he and May both relished. He could tell when she didn't like his performance as soon as a take ended: "When I said cut," May explained, "John would say to Peter, 'She hated it.'" Falk couldn't understand how Cassavetes always knew which takes May was going to hate; "All she said was 'cut.'" Cassavetes seemed omniscient, but years later May figured it out: "It was because *he* hated it, and he knew that if he didn't like it I wouldn't like it."[50] Cassavetes took so well to May's approach to acting and directing because it paralleled his own.

Falk did not belong to any particular school of acting, although he studied under Jack Landau and Sanford Meisner, whose technique also focused on improvisation, spontaneity, and listening. He developed many of his performance skills in community theater, off-Broadway, and Broadway productions and, later, in film and television. But when he began working with Cassavetes on *Husbands* (1970) and *A Woman Under the Influence* (1974), he found a director and collaborator whom he admired more than anyone he had worked with. "John created a new kind of film acting," Falk wrote in his memoir. "He introduced into movies a new level of acting spontaneity."[51] Falk devoted five chapters to his work with Cassavetes, emphasizing neither his preparation for performances in Cassavetes's movies nor the results of the performances but moments of performance themselves.

On his own productions, Cassavetes would not direct actors in the way Falk expected. Like Jehlinger, he would never tell actors what to do and would instead nudge and provoke them to perform spontaneously. During the production of *Husbands*, Falk found Cassavetes's approach baffling and infuriating, but in the chapter "What Is a Cassavetes Set Like?," Falk's memoir describes how the work taught him to be "available" as an actor: "What's 'available' mean? I'm totally open to be affected by only *one* thing—by what the other actor is doing or saying. I have no preconceived ideas. . . . I'm not remembering any previous insights. Thank goodness. I'm not busy preparing a certain face or positioning my voice. I'm wide open, to the exclusion of everything else, to simply hear and see the other actor."[52] Although he never attended a Cassavetes acting class, Falk (like fellow actors Seymour Cassel, Ben Gazzara, and Gena Rowlands) attended the John Cassavetes school of acting on set, which taught him to listen to the other actors and improvise emotions in the present moment—to be "available." Between the time May cast Falk in the role of Mikey in 1967 and his performance of the role in 1973 and 1974, Falk had completed two Cassavetes films. He knew how to perform in that kind of environment.

May filmed everything the actors did on set, says Miller, because she was afraid she would "lose an inspired bit of spontaneity . . . some piece of business or an expression that could not be recaptured in the forthcoming take."[53] The delight of working with Falk and Cassavetes, who relished this type of experimentation, helps account for the lengthy production: May didn't want to stop. Cinematographer Victor Kemper says that during one take of the cemetery scene he whispered to May that there was only one minute of film left in the camera, but May let the actors continue even after the film had run out, "entranced" by the actors' improvisations. The camera was empty, the take could not possibly appear in the film, but she was enjoying the performances so much that she refused to stop the scene. Cassavetes realized after several more minutes that there couldn't be any film left and said, "We're finished."[54]

May seems to have treated the *Mikey and Nicky* shoot like one of her acting workshops at Compass. Her attitude was, *Let's see what they'll do.* She wanted her actors to surprise her. "Elaine May shoots reel after reel of film," wrote Miller. "She films in segments of sometimes 10 minutes, without calling cut. And she might call for such scenes to be done as often as 15 times."[55] In one often repeated story, May bawled out camera operator Enrique Bravo for stopping a take after Falk and Cassavetes had finished their scene. According to writer David Blum, "Falk had walked down the block to talk to a friend, and Cassavetes wandered off the set entirely." Eventually Bravo yelled "cut." Irate, May demanded to know why, and Bravo explained that the two actors had left the frame. May shot back at him, "But they might come back."[56]

This approach to shooting—relying on spontaneous decision-making, improvised emotion and behavior, and multiple takes—does not conform to professional filmmaking practices in Hollywood. It creates difficulties setting up shots and recording sound. Where do you put the camera and the boom mics? How do you keep things in focus if the actors don't hit marks? "She lets them stand wherever they want, to the dismay of her cameramen," said journalist Dan Rottenberg, who observed some of the filming.[57] The soundmen and focus cameramen, according to Miller, could not do their job properly because of "the working methods of Falk, Cassavetes and May."[58] Their methods also created headaches in postproduction. "It was like fucking opera," McMahon said of Falk's and Cassavetes's various performances of each scene: "It was musical, it was so good, but that's where it got hard to edit."[59] The on-camera experimentation generated a huge amount of footage, much of it staged in entirely different ways, causing difficulties maintaining continuity.

Some of May's contemporaries also relied on improvisation during filmmaking, most notably Robert Altman, Shirley Clarke, Sidney Lumet, Mike Leigh, Arthur Penn, and Cassavetes. But these directors mostly conformed improvisation to the requirements of professional filmmaking, ensuring that their films came in on budget and on time, or close to it. Cassavetes, in fact, used improvisation a lot less than people think.[60] Actress Gena Rowlands said about Cassavetes productions, "We start with a very complete script. . . . Then John will go and rewrite it—it's not just straight improvisation."[61] Mike Leigh uses extensive improvisation during the rehearsal period, when the actors develop their dialogue and actions and Leigh refines them, but by the time shooting starts he and the actors have settled all of that, and principal photography proceeds in a fairly traditional manner.[62] Had Elaine May employed those practices, rather than filming everything, she could have forestalled the troubles that plagued her effort to edit 1.4 million feet of exposed film down to the 10,000 feet of her final negative.

So why *film* all these "improvisations"? Falk and Cassavetes were, after all, professional film actors. They could presumably improvise in rehearsal and then, during photography, deliver the performances they had already worked out. On his own films, Cassavetes sometimes had a crew member write down what he and the actors made up in rehearsals so that they could reproduce it during the shoot.[63] Working out performances in rehearsal before photography would certainly have proved more efficient from a business standpoint, perhaps enabling May to bring *Mikey and Nicky* in on time and on budget. But by filming the actors' "improvisations," May captured a quality one does not normally get from rehearsed performances. Anyone who has enjoyed watching talented improvisers knows this quality—something is happening, right before our eyes, that feels thrilling and special. What is that thing?

To try to explain what *Mikey and Nicky* gained from unrehearsed and spontaneous on-camera performances, I want to return to May's comedy career with Mike Nichols. Although Nichols and May regularly improvised onstage, we find little improvisation in their recorded television and album sketches. The differences between the versions of their sketches seem to result from their having honed the routines onstage, rather than from May's tendency to go off script. Later versions of the same sketch seem tighter, the timing more polished, the punch lines more carefully placed and emphasized.[64]

The last track on *Mike Nichols & Elaine May Examine Doctors*, however, offers a different sort of pleasure from the other tracks. An outlier on the album, the track, "Nichols and May at Work," is an unrehearsed bit in which the two performers are figuring out a sketch involving a boy who wants to become a nurse. The track allows us to hear two talented improvisers "at work." We listen to them rethink the sketch ("Oh, no, you have to be my mother"). They suggest revisions ("Let me come to you with it, and you'll be Jewish"), drawing on each other's ideas and delighting in the collaboration. They are in perfect harmony, their creative energy buoyant and playful. At times, they cannot get out their lines because they are cracking themselves and each other up ("Stop. Stop. For God's sake," Nichols says to May). The track is messy and doesn't go anywhere. They haven't workshopped or polished it. It sounds more like a skit at a family party than the work of professional comedians. But, of all the tracks on the album, it might be the most delightful because we are witnessing the "explosions" that Spolin encouraged in her players. We are observing the act of creativity in real time.

Mikey and Nicky also captures the act of creativity. In scene after scene, we sense that something unrehearsed and unpolished is happening in front us and that the actors are working things out together in real time as they spontaneously adjust their attitudes and behavior in response to each other, the two actors in harmony and always "available." May says that she never rehearsed her actors because she did not want them to "make decisions" ahead of time, preferring instead that they react improvisationally in the moment.[65] The actors' improvised emotions and behavior led many commentators to wrongly assume that they also improvised their dialogue. But the dialogue sounds improvised because the actors' emotional energy is so spontaneous and creative, offering us the same sort of thrill that comes from watching improv comedy.

May had a massive amount of footage to choose from in editing, and she often selected takes that included some visibly spontaneous bit of action. We will examine this idea in the chapter on performance, but for now consider how often—three times total—May includes a take in which an actor slips and falls (figures 1.5, 1.6, and 1.7). Why include those particular takes? A slip is interesting because, to look real, it cannot be rehearsed. We have numerous pratfalls in silent film comedy, but they never look like real slips; they look staged. To capture a realistic slip on screen, it has to happen to the actor, impromptu, while filming. May captured countless moments with that level of spontaneity, vulnerability, and reality. The actors had to commit to the scene in such a way that they might slip, fall, and recover, and the director had to create the conditions in which the actors felt invested enough to take that risk. And to capture it all on film, even the slightest spontaneous action or expres-

FIGURE 1.5. Mikey slips in the hotel hallway when running back to Nicky's room.

FIGURE 1.6. Nicky slips on a metal sidewalk hatch when he is dragging Mikey to visit Nellie.

FIGURE 1.7. Nicky slips on the wet street in the fight scene.

Mikey and Nicky includes three shots of the actors slipping during the shoot.

sion, she had to keep the cameras rolling. Is it worth fifteen takes of each scene so that May had that many choices in the editing room? From a business standpoint, of course not. But then we wouldn't have this *Mikey and Nicky*.

It is difficult to identify the observable results of improvisation. Improvisation is a creative process, not an aesthetic object in itself. But we can see the traces of improvisation, and historical research on May's working methods helps us understand how and why May created situations in which her players had to solve problems spontaneously. These were the kinds of situations that terrified Mike Nichols when the two performed comedy. May wanted to see what her players would do when they slipped.

2 FILMMAKER

I'm not a pro as a director. I'm a pro at thinking about movies.

ELAINE MAY, 1975

Elaine May directed two Hollywood movies before *Mikey and Nicky* (1976), both dark comedies. *A New Leaf* (1971) tells the story of a man who marries a wealthy, ditzy academic, played by May, so that he can murder her for her fortune. Cost overruns and a lawsuit between May and Paramount Pictures caused trouble for May in the industry. However, the film did well enough at the box office that Twentieth Century–Fox hired her to direct *The Heartbreak Kid* (1972), which depicted a man who leaves his wife for a beautiful woman he meets on his honeymoon. *The Heartbreak Kid* sustained her in the industry and earned her a deal with Paramount to make *Mikey and Nicky*. Her only noncomedy, *Mikey and Nicky* had such a troubled production and poor reception that it damaged May's career as a director in Hollywood for several years. She did not direct another film until the ill-fated *Ishtar* (1987), which cost so much (reportedly $51 million) and flopped so spectacularly (earning only $14 million in box office revenues) that it shattered her Hollywood directing career for a second time and permanently. She continued to work as a writer and performed in film and stage productions, but aside from a documentary short about Mike Nichols for *American Masters* in 2016, she has never directed another film.

May fell into directing almost by accident. She had written the script for *A New Leaf* to sell, but her new agent, Hillard Elkins, made a deal with Paramount for her to direct the film, too. "I said, 'I don't want to direct.' And I think he said something like, 'They can't afford it if you don't.'"[1] According to May (who does not always tell the truth in interviews), Paramount was going to give her $200,000 just for the script, but the studio ended up giving her only $50,000 to write, direct, and star in the film because she had never directed anything before.[2] She also received 35 percent of the film's earnings, after Walter Matthau received his share of the film's gross.[3]

When May began directing *A New Leaf*, she couldn't even correctly point out the film camera. "I thought it was one of the lights."[4] She had little concept of editing or coverage, which involves shooting scenes from multiple angles. During her first weeks on set, she thought she was ahead of schedule because she shot each scene in one long take. Later, when she wanted to trim scenes, the editor told her they had nothing to cut to. "I knew absolutely nothing," she later said. "I had written screenplays and I could write great-looking scenes, but I didn't know there was such a thing as coverage."[5] So she had to reshoot those previously completed scenes.[6]

We should entertain the possibility that some of the air of ineptitude that May gave off could have been an act or an effort to stave off criticism—or perhaps an effort to get others to do things she did not feel equipped to do. Indeed, throughout May's career, she surrounded herself with people who protected her from the practical dangers of working in the entertainment industry. When she and Mike Nichols teamed up, Nichols handled their business decisions, as well as all the other practicalities of their professional lives, making deals, arranging appearances on radio and television, and scheduling business lunches and other networking activities. He took the lead in interviews and ensured they had proper publicity.[7]

The tendency for other people, mostly men, to help May with the day-to-day practicalities of professional life continued when she got to Hollywood. When you read about May, you find accounts of people intercepting notes, hiding things from her, even lying to her in order to protect her and her movies. "Elaine had this whole network of people that would check in on her, that wanted to make sure she was taken care of," said Stephen Rotter, her editor on *Ishtar*.[8] Producer Michael Hausman packed her suitcase for her when the production of *The Heartbreak Kid* moved from Florida to Minnesota ("She needed that sort of handling to move on," said one of the associate producers),[9] and later he helped her get just about everything she wanted on set for *Mikey and Nicky* (more shooting days, last-minute set changes, etc.), no matter how disruptive to production.

May had a team of people protecting her while she made *Mikey and Nicky*. "She's the kind of person you do everything you can to help her," said Paul Sylbert, the production designer. "She's vulnerable, and it's exposed. Look at her comedy—it's all about weird kinds of vulnerability."[10] Hausman ran interference on set between May and the film's publicist, Tom Miller, because he knew Miller's presence would upset her. To Miller's dismay, Hausman wouldn't even let May know the film had a publicist, and Miller had to pretend at various points to be a crew member or reporter so that May wouldn't ask who he was. Hausman refused to let Miller interview May, so John Cassavetes stepped in. During that interview, and in many afterward with both Cassavetes and Peter Falk, the actors made sure that May received proper credit as *Mikey and Nicky*'s writer-director, when interviewers seemed to think that Cassavetes had in fact directed the film and that the two actors had mostly improvised the movie themselves. When May had exhausted her budget on *Mikey and Nicky*, Warren Beatty called Barry Diller, head of Paramount, on her behalf, even though Beatty had nothing to do with the project.[11] He was stepping in for a friend, using his credit as a star to protect May and her movie. "Those who care for her just adore her," Julian Schlossberg said.[12] After *Mikey and Nicky* flopped in theaters in 1976, Schlossberg distributed the film himself, and he has overseen almost every other aspect of her professional life ever since. "She's great as a creator," Schlossberg said. "Life itself is not easy for her." Referring to May's ditzy botanist from *A New Leaf*, he added, "She's part Henrietta."[13]

The First Women in the DGA: Dorothy Arzner, Ida Lupino, and Elaine May

If you wanted to convince Hollywood executives to hire more female directors, Elaine May's career would not help your case. You would be better off using directors without so much baggage. "I really do believe that she set back the cause of women directors in Hollywood by ten years," said Todd McCarthy, a reporter for *Variety* who worked as May's assistant in 1974 and 1975. "Every negative notion that any male executive might want to have about how difficult it might be to work with a woman director was confirmed by her."[14] It was not just the cost overruns, the missed delivery dates, the box office flops, and her lack of technical knowledge. She was litigious. She sued Paramount on both *A New Leaf* and *Mikey and Nicky*, and those suits both went to trial. And she refused to comply with Hollywood's standard practices or with anything that interfered with her artistic process. When asked about the difficulties of being a female director, she said that women want to show, "I'm no one to be feared. I'm not one of those women who are not nice women. And in the end, when it comes down to it, you're just as rotten as any guy. You'll fight just as hard to get your way."[15] Those of us who care about film as an art form, more than just a business enterprise, regard May's defiance as heroism, but unlike her female predecessors in Hollywood, she did not help pave the way for other women in the industry.

May was only the third woman admitted to the Directors Guild of America (DGA). Dorothy Arzner had joined the guild as a studio director in 1938, two years after the guild's formation, and remained the only woman to have entered in the guild until Ida Lupino joined as a director of independent films in 1950, just as the studio system was collapsing and independent productions were beginning to blossom.[16] May entered Hollywood during a period of even greater instability, as we shall see in the next chapter.

Whereas Lupino and May fell into film directing circumstantially, Arzner sought out the job. During the studio era (roughly the 1920s through the 1950s), men dominated Hollywood even more than they do today, and female directors were nearly unheard of. Studios normally assigned women to positions considered suitable for their gender, largely clerical jobs, such as typist, secretary, telephone operator, and stenographer. But women also performed specific crew jobs, including librarian, film cutter, film retoucher, laboratory worker, publicity writer, and "script girl" (who prompted the actors and recorded information about the photography of each scene). Women also held a variety of creative jobs considered gender appropriate, such as actor, screenwriter, musician, hairdresser, costume designer, set designer, set dresser, casting director, and editor. Hollywood had employed a handful of female film directors before Arzner—including Alice Guy-Blaché, Lois Weber, and Dorothy Davenport—but Arzner was the only woman regularly directing Hollywood films during the height of the studio system. In the twenties, she had thrived as a typist, script girl, and editor at Famous Players–Lasky (later Paramount Pictures) and a scriptwriter at the small Columbia Pictures studio. In 1927, she planned to leave Famous Players for a directing job at Columbia, but B. P. Schulberg, a Famous Players producer and executive, urged her to stay. So she gave him an ultimatum: "Not unless I can be on a set in two weeks [directing] an A picture."[17] Schulberg offered her a job writing and directing an adaptation of a French play, which became *Fashions for Women* (1927).

Arzner directed sixteen features between 1927 and 1943 and codirected two more without receiving onscreen credit. Paramount generally gave her control over her films, allowing her to select her cast and crew. "No one gave me trouble because I was a woman," she said in a 1974 interview. "Men were more helpful than women."[18] Starting in 1932, she worked as a freelance director for RKO, United Artists, Columbia, and Metro-Goldwyn-Mayer. She focused on woman's films, which catered to female filmgoers, Hollywood's primary audience in the 1930s. With scripts written by both men and women, woman's films of the period were all directed by men, except for Arzner's. But Arzner's gender offered studios a means of distinguishing her films, and studios marketed her status as a female director and an expert on the affairs of women. Paramount's publicity for *Honor Among Lovers* (1931) called her "A Woman who knows women," and Columbia's press book for *Craig's Wife* (1936) promoted Arzner as "Hollywood's sole woman director."[19] She left Hollywood in 1943 and directed training films for the Women's Army Corps during World War II and Pepsi commercials in the 1950s.

Ida Lupino began in Hollywood as an actress, but she always had the attitude of an independent filmmaker, changing the lines of her scripts and refusing poorly written roles, a violation of her contract for which Warner Bros. frequently suspended her.[20] In the 1950s, the Hollywood studio system disintegrated, largely because of the 1948 Supreme Court antitrust case *United States v. Paramount Pictures*, which found that the major motion picture studios operated as a monopoly. Changes in the industry opened the door to independent production companies, which addressed product shortages left by the breakup of the studios. The independents also offered filmmakers more autonomy and the potential for profit participation. In this environment, Lupino and her husband, Collier Young, began an independent film company called the Filmakers, focusing on low-budget films dealing with social issues. When the director assigned to *Not Wanted* (1949) had a heart attack, Lupino stepped in to the position. Unlike Arzner, Lupino worked in several genres, directing a crime film (*The Hitch-Hiker*, 1953) and a variety of social-problem films addressing highly controversial subjects like unwed mothers (*Not Wanted*, 1949), rape (*Outrage*, 1950), or bigamy (*The Bigamist*, 1953). To help finance her films and control budgets, she reused sets, shot in public places, planned her films with extensive preproduction, wrote and selected scripts that could be filmed cheaply, and arranged for product placements.[21]

As film directors, Arzner and Lupino were both professionally successful and savvy, Elaine May less so. Arzner paved a path as a director through the Hollywood studio system, employed by several studios because of her professionalism and proven success. Lupino created film directing opportunities for herself by running her own independent production company, which later led to a prolific career as a television director in the fifties and sixties. May, by contrast, focused on her art. I cannot imagine Elaine May arranging product placements. Studio executives did not know what to do with a director like May. They had never encountered one like her before, and they assumed she would ultimately conform to their notion of professionalism. Frank Yablans, head of Paramount when the studio contracted to make *Mikey and Nicky*, thought he could control her because their contract allowed the studio to take over the project the moment May ran over budget or missed her delivery date.[22] In the end, as you will read in chapter 4, May was willing to sacrifice her salary, her contract, and her career in Hollywood in order to make the *Mikey and Nicky* that she wanted to make.

But before all that, May made two dark comedies. Neither film has the subtlety, density, and complexity of *Mikey and Nicky*, but together her first three films demonstrate the growing range of May's comedic and dramatic filmmaking talents.

A New Leaf (1971)

A New Leaf, the film released in theaters and available now on video, is not the film Elaine May made. Paramount executives took the film out of her hands, cut out a third of the footage, and altered the ending. May's original cut, over three hours long, never screened publicly and is now lost.

Conflicts with the studio emerged the day shooting started. In what would become a habitual practice, May shot take after take of each scene. "Do it again," she would say, according Howard Koch, one of the producers. Koch assumed that May would eventually shoot more efficiently, "but it went on and on and on."[23] In August 1969, *Variety* wrote, "The film is reported to be three weeks behind schedule and the budget has soared from an estimated $1,500,000 to $2,800,000. Difficulties seem to revolve about the directorial chores with two first assistant directors already listed among the casualties."[24] Koch wanted out of the production, so Paramount replaced him with Stanley Jaffe. "She has finished the first thirty of her thirty-four-day schedule," Jaffe said to Peter Bart, Paramount's vice president in charge of production. "But she is incredibly thirty days behind schedule. She's managed to get nothing done."[25] The shoot lasted eighty-two days total. Postproduction at the time averaged about ten weeks, and the studio had afforded May a generous sixteen weeks to edit the film, but editing on *A New Leaf* ended up taking almost ten months. The film's budget ultimately ballooned to $4 million.[26]

Paramount's contract stipulated that if the film went over budget, "Paramount shall have the right to take over production of the picture and make any and all changes and substitutions with respect thereto."[27] Had May delivered a shorter film on time and on budget, the studio would likely have allowed her to cut the film her way, but her failure to satisfy her contract enabled Paramount to take over. Early in production, a studio executive wrote to Charles Bluhdorn, head of Paramount, "We certainly have the right to step in and take over the completion of the picture; but as we all know, this is a highly volatile procedure and does not work."[28] But they did it. They cut out several scenes and redid the ending to make it more sweet. May refused to dub the final scene, and another actor impersonates May's distinctive voice in the movie's closing moments.[29] You can hear the difference.

May's cut of *A New Leaf* would have been darker and less sentimental. In May's version, Henry Graham (played by Walter Matthau), in preparation for killing his new wife, Henrietta Lowell (Elaine May), murders two blackmailers: Henrietta's lawyer, Andy McPherson (Jack Weston), and an accomplice (William Hickey). In the released film, the murder/blackmail plot is missing, with Hickey's character cut out entirely. Consequently, we never believe that Henry will in fact murder Henrietta. He merely aspires to be a killer so that he doesn't have to stay married. In the end, when it seems that he has fallen for his wife, or perhaps just grown resigned to a life with her, his failure to murder her is sweet, but it is not a relief. And it seems fair that Henry and Henrietta should live together contentedly: it is not as though he got away with murder.

Some commentators, such as Elizabeth Alsop, have suggested that Paramount chief Robert Evans took control of the project because he objected to "the prospect of a comic lead who commits multiple homicides."[30] But that very story had been the subject of commercial film comedies dating to the 1940s—*Arsenic and Old Lace* (1944), *Monsieur Verdoux* (1947), and *Kind Hearts and Coronets* (1949)—and appears in several films of the 1970s, including *The Honeymoon Killers* (1970), *The Ruling Class* (1972), and *Murder by Death* (1976). Carrie Courogen has similarly suggested that Paramount executives found the film too edgy for a comedy.[31] However, this is the period that gave us *M*A*S*H* (1970), *Catch-22* (1970), *Little Big Man* (1970), *Watermelon Man* (1970), *Carnal Knowledge* (1971), *Harold and Maude* (1971), and *The Hospital* (1971), some approved by the same Paramount executives that cut up *A New Leaf*. Edgy comedies were in. But May's cut was too long, and the executives at Paramount believed it was distracted by too many subplots. In 1969, Bart wrote to Evans: "the key objective, I think, is to continue to focus on our two central characters and their odd-ball love story and not let the story run off in too many homicidal directions."[32] So they edited the film their way.

May grew furious when they cut out the murders, which she regarded as the most inventive part of the story. "Right to the throat," May said about the executives who reedited *A New Leaf*. "I mean, they do not cut out the peripheral stuff. They cut out exactly what you wrote the thing for. They know, somehow."[33] She sued Paramount to prevent the movie's release or, barring that, to remove her name from the credits. The new version, she argued, "butchered" the film, turning it into a "cliché ridden, banal story."[34] Paramount responded that May had violated her contract and had "failed to perform her duties as a director in a timely . . . and professional manner, resulting in substantially increased costs," all of which was true.[35] The judge, who found the studio version hilarious, ruled in Paramount's favor.[36] And that is why we don't have Elaine May's cut of *A New Leaf*.

So the film we have is an artistic hybrid, part Elaine May's creation and part Paramount's, and we should evaluate its strengths and weaknesses on its own terms.

The plot affords many scenes of suspense, humor, and character development. The narrative really launches when Henry resolves to marry a rich woman within six weeks, a traditional deadline device that gives the first half of the movie its narrative drive. After he marries Henrietta, the plot shifts to Henry's efforts to kill her, but a new set of goals creeps in sideways as Henry tries to establish order within Henrietta's chaotic household. He comes into his own as he inspects her accounts, restructures her finances, and fires the lazy, thieving servants taking advantage of her. We can see that the man who we thought had no redeeming qualities has precisely the skills that his new wife needs. He teaches Henrietta to manage her servants, dresses her, and cuts the tags and brushes the crumbs off of her clothing. The side plot (sorting out Henrietta's life) eventually replaces the murder plot. During the film's climax at the river, instead of drowning Henrietta, Henry decides to save her and live with her in some resigned form of marital happiness.

The plot, simple and farcical, allows May to create funny moments, such as a wedding scene in which McPherson tries to convince her not to go through with the marriage, *as* he is walking her down the aisle, or the honeymoon-night scene as Henry patiently helps her rearrange her nightgown ("We have to get your head out of the arm hole. Where is your head hole?"). The script has offbeat throwaway lines, such as, "He was an industrialist. Or a composer. Something like that," and Henry's deadpan response after his introduction to "Dr. and Mrs. Darryl Hitler" at a party: "Excuse me, you're not by chance related to the Boston Hitlers?" Moments like these sustain the film's air of silliness, which in May's cut of the film might have contrasted with Henry's ruthless murders in the ironic way characteristic of black comedy.

Strangely, given May's talent for rich characterization, her characters come across as largely one-dimensional. She didn't even write a deep part for herself. Henrietta is a sweet, fragile, trusting, soft-spoken, clumsy botanist, and that is about all there is to her. May did not work very hard to make the peripheral characters interesting either; none of them have the nuance of even the most minor characters in *Mikey and Nicky* (such as Mel in the bar or the candy store salesman, each of whom has only one brief scene). Actor James Coco gives Harry, Henry's sadistic uncle, a maniacal exuberance, but the character has two scenes and that is plenty. McPherson was more interesting when we thought he was in love with Henrietta, but when it turns out that he is milking her for her money he becomes a caricature of a greedy lawyer. The distinguishing traits of Henry's butler (George Rose) are that he is old-fashioned and has an English accent. None of these characters are individualized or realistic; they are types. And May's script has afforded the actors few opportunities to add complexity or interest to their roles.

The most nuanced character is our protagonist, but Walter Matthau is miscast as the rich, supercilious Henry Graham. May said she wanted Cary Grant for the role.[37] A child of New York's Lower East Side, Matthau has trouble playing a rich sophisticate and overacts the part. He exaggerates Henry's arrogance and always seems to be judging the character. When Henry complains to his butler about his penury ("I don't understand, Harold, why did it happen to me, why?"), Matthau mugs and delivers the line with overstated plaintiveness, like a sketch comedian. Matthau understood how to play nuanced characters—and would exhibit that skill in *The Taking of Pelham One Two Three* (1974) and *The Bad News Bears* (1976)—but here he signals Henry's emotions in the most obvious ways. In the actor's hands, the part of Henry is mostly a lampoon of haughty wealth. According to May, Matthau said to her on the first day of shooting, "You're not going to direct me, are you?"[38] Perhaps that was the problem.

Still, there are moments of originality in the character and Matthau's performance. For one thing, Henry is interestingly asexual. In fact, he seems averse to sex. When a woman he is wooing starts to take off her swimsuit top, he screams, "No, don't let them out!" and runs away. Henry appears overly particular about his sleeping arrangements with Henrietta, and, as he observes her primping for a romantic encounter, he looks annoyed and anxious at what is for him an unpleasant nuptial duty.

Henry, furthermore, never transforms into the romantic lead that the endings of romantic comedies have taught us to expect. In a more traditional ending, Henry would desperately save Henrietta from drowning in the river when he realizes that he has fallen in love with her. In *A New Leaf*, he grows irritated by the whole rescue job ("Damn it to hell"). He saves her not exactly out of love, although he has grown to appreciate Henrietta, but rather because he has given up on the idea of murdering her, having reconciled to their domestic life. In the end, we probably think to ourselves not "Henry has finally become a real romantic hero" but rather "Those two should be fine." That is an oddly low-key version of the genre's traditional happy ending.

Matthau's two best scenes occur when Henry seems touched by Henrietta, scenes that allow the actor to show some complex emotion.

In the first, Henrietta tells him that she has discovered a new species of fern. His words are just as patronizing as in other scenes ("Well, that's very nice, very nice"), but he looks genuinely proud of her. A smile creeps onto his face, and he looks up at her admiringly (figure 2.1a). When she beams back at him, he sports a full-on grin (figure 2.1b). When she explains that she named the fern after him, he looks at first shocked and then genuinely moved. Again, his words are understated ("Yes, it's very thoughtful of you, Henrietta. I believe I am pleased"), but we can see that he is starting to like her, despite himself, and he even looks ashamed as he stares down at the frond sample she has given him to wear (figure 2.1c). In this scene, Matthau delivers his lines with an understatement that we have not yet witnessed in the actor's previously overblown performance.

The movie's final scene at the river also enables Matthau to express a range of emotion. Rather than allowing Henrietta to drown as planned, Henry rescues her. As she shivers in his arms, he cares for her and comforts her, but he also looks angry (with her and himself) for not going through with the murder. When she asks whether he will change his mind about teaching history at the college, he looks away from her and says testily, "I don't know. I have no mind as far as I can tell" (figure 2.2a), but he quickly softens his voice, "Are you still cold?" (figure 2.2b), and gently brushes the hair from her eyes. Matthau performs best during scenes in which his character shows multiple emotions, especially when Henry has been taken off guard, the character softly returning to a place of composure. Such moments add nuance to a character who had otherwise seemed a comfortable stereotype of indifferent affluence.

The judge was not alone in finding the studio's cut of *A New Leaf* hilarious. Reviewers praised the film, although some remarked that they might have preferred May's cut, had they seen it. Roger Ebert wrote, "Whatever the merits of Miss May's case, however, the movie in its present form is hilarious, and cockeyed, and warm."[39] Vincent Canby came to a similar conclusion: "Not having seen Miss May's version, I can only say that the film I saw should be a credit to almost any director."[40] The Golden Globes, awarded by the press, nominated it for Best Picture and May for Best Actress, and the Writers Guild nominated May for a screenplay award. The film earned a respectable $5 million at the box office. Critical, box office, and industry successes earned May the clout to direct another film.

FIGURE 2.1A–C. A scene in *A New Leaf* (1971) allows Walter Matthau to show a variety of emotions, including admiration, delight, and shame.

FIGURE 2.2A–B. In the final scene of *A New Leaf* (1971), Matthau displays both anger and tenderness.

The Heartbreak Kid (1972)

The Heartbreak Kid tells the story of Lenny Cantrow (Charles Grodin), a sporting goods salesman, who quickly courts and weds Lila Kolodny (Jeannie Berlin), a fellow Jew. During their honeymoon at a resort in Miami Beach, Lenny meets Kelly Corcoran (Cybill Shepherd), a WASPy, flirty college student and daughter of a wealthy businessman (Eddie Albert), also staying at the resort. Still on his honeymoon, Lenny dumps Lila and follows Kelly to her home in Minnesota in hopes of marrying her, against the objections of Kelly's father. Lenny wins her over but seems just as lost and uncertain in his new marriage as he was in his marriage to Lila.

The Heartbreak Kid remains Elaine May's only feature film to come in on time and on budget. Her producer, Edgar Scherick, kept things in check and ensured that the production adhered to a strict shooting schedule. Consequently, May had none of the problems directing *The Heartbreak Kid* that she had on *A New Leaf.* Perhaps she cared about the project less because she didn't write the script. Neil Simon, the popular playwright and screenwriter of *Barefoot in the Park* (1963 play/1967 film), *The Odd Couple* (1965 play/1968 film), and many other hits, wrote the screenplay, which he based on a short story by Bruce Jay Friedman.

Strangely, given Simon's proclivity for light comedy and farce, the film is edgier and deeper than *A New Leaf* and more similar to *Mikey and Nicky* in its tone, character nuances, and psychological insights. The film generates such unrelenting discomfort that it barely counts as a comedy, with scenes so awkward and excruciatingly long that I suspect viewers' dominant emotion during the film is stress. Like *Mikey and Nicky, The Heartbreak Kid* has characters whose appalling behavior seems plausible and justified, given their goals and insecurities. At the end of the film, Lenny, like the leads in *Mikey and Nicky,* seems to have learned nothing after the traumas and upheavals he has gone through and inflicted on those around him. Ultimately, both films express a bleak vision of people's inability to understand themselves.

May and Simon did not get along. Simon's contract compelled her to shoot his script precisely as written, but she also shot alternate versions of scenes and cut out Simon's here-we-go-again epilogue, which offered a more traditional conclusion to the film. At the end of Simon's script, Lenny grows frustrated with his new wife on their honeymoon, a replay of his experience with Lila. Simon said about his ending, "They filmed it and never showed it to anybody. I begged the producer to at least screen it in front of twenty people. He said, 'No, I won't even do that.' I was really furious at that."[41] May's ending is darker and more psychological: it shows Lenny appearing lost and awkward after the wedding to Kelly that he has desperately fought for. At the end, the film centers on character traits that have bothered us since Lenny's introduction to the film—his phoniness, self-absorption, and self-delusion. May's ending is unsettling and abrupt, unlike the satisfying conclusions of Simon's other comedies.

We could describe the entire movie as an exploration of character.

Each of the main characters—Lenny, Lila, and Kelly—displays psychological nuance, and the film maintains a curiously ambiguous attitude toward each of them. May moreover drew performances from her actors that enriched each characterization.

The most complex character is Lenny, who poses challenges for Hollywood viewers invested in endearing, likable protagonists with admirable goals. Not only is Lenny's primary goal in the movie—to leave his wife on their honeymoon and marry Kelly—impetuous and morally dodgy, but his means of achieving it are reprehensible and embarrassing. After a rendezvous with Kelly, he yells at Lila when she questions his ridiculous excuse for missing their dinner date. "My God!" Lenny shouts indignantly, "You think I'm making it up?! Talk to the patrolman who pulled me out of the car!" Lenny is mean and manipulative, and his tendency to take offense betrays deep-seated self-doubt. He fixates on shaming or charming the people around him in order to satisfy his own dubious goals.

Still, the success of the film hinges on our engagement with the character. Lenny remains engaging not because we like him (we don't) but because his behavior comes across as both shocking and plausible, an exaggeration of behavior that we can at least imagine in real people. We can also deduce the motivations behind all his desperate behavior and may even, at times, root for him. When he tries to convince Kelly's parents of his sincerity, for instance, we see through his facade, although we hope, perhaps, that he might charm them. Our understanding of Lenny's dysfunctional behavior helps make him sympathetic—or at least pathetic.

Actor Charles Grodin, in his first leading role, has the weight of the film resting on him. "If I hadn't run into Elaine May," said Grodin, "I don't know if I would have been in the movies."[42] Grodin has several difficult tasks to accomplish in combination: he has to be funny and sympathetic but also true to a character who is not only a buffoon but also obnoxious. Lenny has only a few moments of charm and likability, such as a scene in which he poses as a narcotics agent for Kelly's friends and a scene in which he grows excited about Kelly's naked challenge. Above all, he has to be engaging enough to warrant our interest; the character, after all, appears in almost every scene. We have probably never met anyone quite like Lenny, but in scene after scene he comes off like a real person.

Grodin gives Lenny an abrasive energy that emphasizes the character's unattractive features. As an actor, he has an ominous quality that

Peter Falk regarded as overly menacing when May considered casting Grodin as Nicky.[43] Lenny's aggression bursts forth in the form of forced laughter, inappropriate enthusiasm, and a tendency to shout, even when he is whispering. In otherwise light scenes, Grodin seethes with annoyance. In both an early scene, in which he grows indignant when Lila tries to show him her breasts as he is driving, and the later sunburn scene, in which he berates her for ruining their honeymoon, Grodin suddenly tenses his body, flails his arms, stretches out his fingers, and blurts his lines in a high-pitched screech, as though anger and frustration are pent up and waiting to burst out. But he can be subtle, too. As Lenny tells Lila, "Hon, don't make little circles on my chest, okay?" his smiles, kisses, and sweet voice come across as a pretense of a loving husband, his facial expression changing depending on whether Lila is looking at him. When she leaves for the bathroom, he lets out a sigh that expresses both exasperation with his new wife and the relief of not having to keep up the appearance of affection a moment longer.

May directed her daughter, Jeannie Berlin, as Lila. Lila grows shocked and confused by Lenny's anger—Berlin pauses and stares at Grodin when Lenny says something that sounds off—but she wants so much to have a good honeymoon that she couches her criticisms in an air of affection. Lila's lines sometimes challenge Lenny ("You were never quiet before we were married"), but Berlin normally delivers them affectionately in what seems like an effort to flirt with her husband and charm him. Berlin's performance earned her an Academy Award nomination for Best Supporting Actress. It is the kind of performance that the Academy considers *brave* because Berlin manages to be both funny and endearing, even as she exhibits the ugly behaviors that her new husband finds so annoying.

In Simon's script, Kelly Corcoran is drawn fairly broadly, but May helped actor Cybill Shepherd find nuances in the character. "May liked to use improvisation as an acting exercise during rehearsals," Shepherd wrote in her memoir, "although she didn't call it that. She spoke about the exploration of subtext, the meaning beneath the lines."[44] The film hints at those subtexts in a five-minute-long take in which Lenny tells Mr. Corcoran of his desire to marry Kelly. Lenny and Mr. Corcoran face each other at a restaurant table, while Mrs. Corcoran (Audra Lindley) and Kelly sit in the background of the shot, facing the camera (figure 2.3a–f). The staging allows the audience to attend at will to the behavior of each of the four characters. Each actor plays the scene in a different way (the performances seem uncoordinated), and the scene remains interesting in part because it takes on different meanings depending on which character we attend to at each moment.

Kelly's behavior is the most interesting. Shepherd's face and body language go through a number of subtle and unpredictable shifts, as she nibbles on crackers and plays with her drink. At one moment, she looks surprised by Lenny's pronouncements (figure 2.3a), but moments later she appears bored (figure 2.3b). She smiles at her father when he turns to her (figure 2.3c) and studies his reaction when Lenny tells him, "I happen to be a newlywed" (figure 2.3d). At another moment she adopts a concerned expression, as though empathizing with Lenny's effort to display sincerity. When Lenny reveals his plan to follow the family to Minnesota, Kelly leans her head forward and widens her eyes, showing real concern that maybe this whole flirtation has gone too far (figure 2.3e). But when her father grows angry with Lenny ("Five days, he's been married! Five Days!"), Kelly's face reveals her mischievous delight in the drama she is causing (figure 2.3f). Shepherd's behavior and facial expressions reflect Kelly's thought processes and emotional inner life, which, like her character in general, seem slightly detached from the thoughts and emotions of the other characters.

A relative novice as an actor—she had made only one movie prior to *The Heartbreak Kid* and had never studied acting—Shepherd was open to May's directing style. "Having Elaine as my first improv coach was such a blessing," Shepherd said.[45] May coached Shepherd toward a performance that is subtle and ambiguous. Kelly is never the focus of the restaurant scene—she has no lines and no causal role to play in the scene other than her presence—but you can spend the entire length of the scene just watching her behavior.

The film's side characters also show May's growing naturalism and nuance, a prelude to the rich side characters in *Mikey and Nicky*. Mr. Corcoran exhibits a seething impatience with Lenny ("Kelly said something about your laying your cards on the table. Were those your cards?"), and actor Eddie Albert imbues Corcoran with the cool self-confidence that comes with money. Mrs. Corcoran shows innate solicitousness and politeness, even when Lenny shocks her. Her reaction to Mr. Corcoran's anger at Lenny at the restaurant conveys a sense of routine behavior; she knows how to calm her husband because she has addressed the situation

FIGURE 2.3A–F. The staging of this scene in *The Heartbreak Kid* (1972), filmed in one long take, allows the audience to attend to the reactions of all four characters at will. Cybill Shepherd's face and body language display a number of subtle and

unpredictable shifts in reaction to Lenny, expressing surprise, distraction, concern, mischievousness, and other emotions.

before. Every character with lines, no matter how briefly they appear, has something interesting about them: Lenny's lawyer, expressing annoyance that Lenny is disadvantaging himself by divorcing Lila too quickly; a man at the wedding party steering the conversation to Thomas Jefferson because, we learn, he has recently visited Monticello; the kids at the party listening compliantly to Lenny's droning, their responses awkward and unsure, eager to leave the conversation. Such subtleties do nothing to advance the causal progress of the narrative, but they add detail and peripheral interest to the scenes in which they appear.

The critics and the film industry responded enthusiastically to *The Heartbreak Kid.* Canby praised May's direction of her actors, as well as her ability to elevate Simon's script beyond mere jokes.[46] Berlin, Albert, Grodin, and Shepherd earned nominations for various awards given by the press. Albert and Berlin, moreover, both won acting awards from the National Society of Film Critics, and Berlin also won the New York Film Critics Circle Award for Best Supporting Actress. The film earned Academy Award nominations for Best Supporting Actress (Berlin) and Best Supporting Actor (Albert), and the Writers Guild of America nominated Simon for his screenplay. Most important for May's directing career, the film did well at the box office. It stayed within its $2.6 million budget and returned $5.6 million to Twentieth Century–Fox in domestic rentals, good enough to earn May a deal directing the passion project she had been developing for two decades already.[47] But before we get back to *Mikey and Nicky* in the next chapter, let us look at the remainder of May's filmmaking career.

Elaine May in Hollywood: After *Mikey and Nicky*

After the financial and legal fiascos of *Mikey and Nicky*, it is surprising that any studio allowed Elaine May to direct another Hollywood film. For many years, they didn't, but from the 1970s through the 1990s she worked as a scriptwriter and script doctor, frequently restructuring, rewriting, and sharpening the scripts of other writers.[48]

In addition to writing the scripts for three of the four films that she directed—*A New Leaf, Mikey and Nicky*, and *Ishtar*—May is the credited screenwriter for three other films. Warren Beatty brought in May to cowrite the script for *Heaven Can Wait* (1978), his directorial debut. "I wanted to be on guard about the sentimentality," he said, "and I thought she would take care of my reservations."[49] The script earned them an Oscar nomination. Mike Nichols enlisted her to write the scripts for *The Birdcage* (1996), based on the French film *La Cage aux Folles* (1978), and *Primary Colors* (1998), based on a novel by Joe Klein. Nichols also employed her as a script doctor on *Heartburn* (1986), *Working Girl* (1988), and *Wolf* (1994). In an interview, he said, "I never once made a movie without first showing Elaine the script and listening to her ideas or bringing her in to talk to the writers."[50] May also worked as a script doctor on *Reds* (1981), *Tootsie* (1982), and *Dangerous Minds* (1995), but she took no credit.[51] Dustin Hoffman said about her rewrite of *Tootsie*, "Elaine is the one who made the movie work."[52] Although May refused writing credit on the film, director Sydney Pollack sent May a congratulatory telegram after it won the New York Film Critics Circle Award for Best Screenplay: "You really earned it."[53] There are reports that she helped also on *Labyrinth* (1986), *Ghostbusters II* (1989), *What About Bob?* (1991), and a few other film projects of that period.[54]

But Hollywood offered her only one more chance to direct a film, and it was a disaster.

Ishtar (1987)

So much has been written about the production of *Ishtar* that it would be superfluous to rehash the story of its monstrous commercial failure. However, it is worth examining May's directing techniques on the film since they caused, on a much larger scale, some of the same production problems that she encountered on *Mikey and Nicky*. More pertinent to the purposes of this book, the commercial and artistic failures of *Ishtar* help us understand better the artistic successes of *Mikey and Nicky*. May's directing methods, which worked so well eliciting career-defining performances from Peter Falk and John Cassavetes (and from Charles Grodin on *The Heartbreak Kid*), did not work with *Ishtar*'s lead actors, Warren Beatty and Dustin Hoffman. In the remainder of this chapter, I shall try to explain why I think her methods succeeded on *Mikey and Nicky* and not on *Ishtar*, because understanding *Ishtar*'s commercial and artistic failure helps us better understand some limitations of May's approach to directing.

Lately, commentators have attempted to recuperate *Ishtar*'s reputation, arguing that critics and the public underrated the film.[55] Certainly it was underrated, but at the time of its release some critics placed it among the worst Hollywood films ever made. It does not take much recuperation to improve from there. In retrospect, I think we can say that the film is not bad, but "not bad" is a low bar for an artist whom many describe as a creative genius. I think we can also say that it is May's least interesting movie. Any number of Hollywood directors could have made *Ishtar* just as well. Had it enjoyed the middling commercial success it deserved, it would have been forgotten in film history like most Hollywood movies.

The chief problem with *Ishtar*, from an artistic standpoint, is that the lead actors were miscast. I am not referring to the fact that Dustin Hoffman and Warren Beatty were cast against type, with Hoffman playing the more suave lead and Beatty playing the more insecure sidekick; despite complaints from critics, the actors were not necessarily wrong for those roles.[56] Rather, Hoffman and Beatty were miscast in an Elaine May film. They had the wrong training and the wrong skills. Both actors had worked closely with May as a screenwriter—Beatty on *Heaven Can Wait* and *Reds* and Hoffman on *Tootsie*—but she had never directed either of them before. May stocked the production with some supporting actors who knew her methods—Charles Grodin, Jack Weston, and Rose Arrick—but her leads did not have that experience. For a while, Beatty and Hoffman tried to comply with May's process, but eventually their patience ran out. They came from the wrong schools of acting.

It can be difficult to identify acting schools by observing performances (although acting teachers can sometimes do it), but the processes of preparation and performance differ depending on the actor's training. Beatty and Hoffman had studied with the two most prominent disciples of Russian actor-director Konstantin Stanislavsky. Beatty had studied with Stella Adler at the Stella Adler Studio, and Hoffman had learned the Method from Lee Strasberg at the Actors Studio. Although Adler and Strasberg differed in their approaches, both teachers encouraged actors to create "truthful" performances by relying either on the actor's own emotional memories from previous experiences (emphasized by Strasberg) or on their imaginations (emphasized by Adler). Strasberg's and Adler's teachings were similar enough that people often misidentify Adler's students (such as Marlon Brando and Robert De Niro) as method actors. In both schools, a truthful performance requires intensive emotional preparation, character study, and script analysis, through which the actor learns to embody the character; a lot of this work is performed apart from the other actors. Hence, the actors make many performance decisions before filming begins.

May had studied with Maria Ouspenskaya, another Stanislavsky disciple, so she understood the technique and used it to direct actors onstage in Chicago and later on her films. However, she was also a product of Viola Spolin's "theater games," which taught actors to unleash their creativity during performance. Spolin encouraged actors to respond improvisationally to their fellow players, even when they were speaking the lines of a script. Beatty and Hoffman were not experienced improvisers. They developed their roles through study, analysis, and emotional preparation. They did not understand that on an Elaine May film all that work is just a first stage in a longer process. On May's films, actors make their most important creative decisions in front of cameras.

To direct Hoffman and Beatty in *Ishtar*, May used the same methods she had used to such success with Grodin on *The Heartbreak Kid* and with Cassavetes and Falk on *Mikey and Nicky*. Again, she treated principal photography like a Compass theater game, relying on the actors' ability to experiment and vary their performances and refusing to block scenes or tell actors what to do. Again, she shot take after take with multiple cameras, hoping for some spontaneous bit of brilliance that she could put in her film. "Elaine May is a woman of many words," one source told David Blum for his *New York* magazine exposé on *Ishtar*. "However, the word 'cut' does not happen to be among them."[57] Grodin, Cassavetes, and Falk had thrived in that environment and revered May as a director. Falk considered her one of the industry's only "genuinely original voices," and Grodin called her "the best director that I've ever worked with."[58] The small scale of production on *Mikey and Nicky*, which had only a few sets and a limited cast, also enabled May to experiment extensively during principal photography—and even at that scale her methods led to huge cost overruns and production delays. *Ishtar* had an initial $40 million budget, a huge crew, a foreign setting, and scenes with dozens of characters, extras, and animals. A film that big does not afford the same artistic opportunities that May had exploited so successfully on *Mikey and Nicky*, whose small scale and small budget had enabled May and her actors to develop complex characterizations, dense psychological interplay, and scenes in which the nuances of performance alone could generate audience engagement. The scale of *Ishtar* did not serve May's on-set experimentation, and Beatty and Hoffman did not jibe with May's directing style.

Hoffman and Beatty could not invent on the spot in the way that Cassavetes and Falk could. They were preparers, not improvisers, and they tired of May's endless takes and lack of direction. Blum quotes a production staffer on the film:

> Dustin and Warren would do a take, and Elaine would watch them or look at the video monitor and say, "Fine, let's do it again." . . . Once or twice they didn't mind. Five times. Ten times. But by the time they got back from lunch . . . they were tired. But Elaine didn't want to stop. "Let's do it one more time," she'd say, and do it ten times. She never gave them any directions, never said to do it again this way or that way. It was always "Let's do it again."[59]

Beatty and Hoffman eventually grew frustrated with May's tedious pace, and one afternoon, after two days filming the nightclub scene in New York, the actors grew "visibly angry." Following numerous takes of the same shot, May said, "Let's do it again. We didn't quite get it," to which Beatty replied, "Elaine, we got it before lunch."[60] It is hard to imagine Cassavetes saying something like that to May (or to any other director). For Cassavetes, a scene was never really done, and, like May, he was always up for more creative exploration. Each time he and Falk performed a take, they would change it up so that the interpretation was entirely different.[61] But Beatty and Hoffman did not work like that. At one point, Hoffman teased May, "The head office just called—they loved it. And they want ten more takes, just like the last."[62]

Beatty seems to have had more trouble with May's direction than Hoffman did. "Wait, wait," Beatty said to Hoffman before one take, "What are we going to say?" Hoffman replied, "No, we're going to improvise." Beatty wanted to know, "Just tell me the first sentence."[63] He wanted direction and preparation time, neither of which May would allow. When he was having trouble with the blocking in the nightclub scene, Beatty asked May, "Look: Just tell me my moves, OK?"[64] But May would never tell actors what to do.

Her direction could be enigmatic. Jack Weston, who had previously worked with May on *A New Leaf*, talked about May's cryptic direction on *Ishtar*: "Elaine walks up, and if I didn't know her, I'd clutch. She says, 'In order to do this scene . . . I don't know . . . it depends on how you feel . . . there's a way of doing things. . . .' I think: Aha, I'm doing it too slow—she wants me to pick it up, without losing what I've already got. It's hard to explain. I know this sounds like gibberish, but it's true."[65] Falk also expressed his appreciation for May's oblique style of communication, which could be scant ("The thing about Elaine is that if she can't find the phrase, she won't say anything. For that, I love her") or almost mystical ("Now Elaine starts talking to me. She starts talking about death").[66] In an interview after *Ishtar*, Grodin said something similar: "Elaine doesn't talk much about how scenes should be played. She says virtually nothing, a sentence or two, a word. It's more like nudging." And he might have been speaking about Beatty and Hoffman when he added, "There's danger in improvisation if you don't have the right people, but if you do, it works. Casting is crucial."[67] May's communication style didn't get much from Beatty and Hoffman, and no one, not even commentators who have recently championed the film, would argue that either actor gives a career-defining performance in *Ishtar*.

The lesson we should take from *Ishtar* is not that Elaine May would have been one of the great Hollywood filmmakers if only the industry had supported her. May is not the Orson Welles of the New Hollywood. The lesson of *Ishtar*, as far as I can tell, is that May's success as a film director depended on the material and on the particular background and skills of the actors under her direction. *Ishtar* had the wrong material and the wrong actors for an Elaine May film. Not every talented actor has the instinct for spontaneous invention, an instinct that May herself developed at Compass when she was in her early twenties and honed during her years onstage with Mike Nichols. So we should not expect that May's directing methods on *Mikey and Nicky* could be replicated with success in other areas of the Hollywood film industry; they could not even be replicated successfully on every Elaine May film.

We now have some understanding of May's history as a comedian and filmmaker and the ways in which her previous work prepared her to make her gangster tragedy. But we do not yet know the extraordinary history of the film itself: how May conceived of it as a teenager, why it took almost four years to shoot and edit, and how critics and fans came to appreciate a film that was regarded, almost universally, as an artistic failure at the time of its release. Nor do we understand how she managed to secure funding for a project so uncommercial. The truth is that the Hollywood film industry would not have made a film like *Mikey and Nicky* at any other time than the early 1970s. In order to understand *Mikey and Nicky*'s history, we must understand the industry at that time and the types of films it was making.

PART II

MIKEY AND NICKY'S PRODUCTION HISTORY

3 SEVENTIES MISFITS

Directing represents a complex skill set, and it's dangerous to entrust neophytes to the process.

PETER BART, PARAMOUNT VICE PRESIDENT, ON WORKING WITH ELAINE MAY, 2011

I owe it to my ignorance.

ORSON WELLES, WHEN ASKED HOW HE ARRIVED AT *CITIZEN KANE*'S CINEMATIC INNOVATIONS, 1966

During *Mikey and Nicky*'s lengthy production history, the American film industry transformed. Between Elaine May's initial deal to make the film in August 1969 and its release in theaters at the end of 1976,[1] the industry changed its financial model, its conception of its audience, and the types of films it was putting in theaters. May received a green light for *Mikey and Nicky* when studios were still approving low-budget films, geared toward niche audiences, directed by talented but relatively inexperienced filmmakers. By the time of its release, however, *Mikey and Nicky* was in some ways already outdated.

In the 1960s, American film executives observed a curious trend: art house movie theater attendance had been rising steadily since the 1950s. Art houses played "art films," mostly from Europe and Japan, for largely college-age audiences. According to Tino Balio, the number of US art houses rose from about one hundred to seven hundred between the 1950s and 1960s, a rise that Douglas Gomery describes as "a rare trend upward in movie attendance."[2] So-called mini-majors—smaller American companies distributing independent films—responded to the trend before the major studios did. In the 1960s, mini-majors began distributing "youth cult or counterculture films" (as David A. Cook terms them) that appealed to college-age audiences.[3] Avco Embassy Pictures distributed foreign art films, such as *Divorce Italian Style* (1961) and *Marriage Italian Style* (1964), as well as American counterculture films like *The Graduate* (1967) and *Carnal Knowledge* (1971). Roger Corman at American International Pictures distributed exploitation films, such as *The Terror* (1963) and *Foxy Brown* (1974), as well as counterculture films like *The Wild Angels* (1966), *The Trip* (1967), and *Easy Rider* (1969). Allied Artists Pictures and New World Pictures also tapped into the youth market.[4]

The men who ran the major Hollywood studios in the late sixties and early seventies were still trying to understand the kinds of movies that appealed to the new core audience—college-educated baby boomers—who sought out more unconventional movies than the ones Hollywood was accustomed to making. By the time the major studios had caught on to the new trends, the American film industry was already in crisis. The industry had endured a twenty-five-year decline in film attendance, from a high of 90 million Americans attending movies weekly in 1946 to an all-time low of 15.8 million weekly attendees in 1971.[5] The studios lost $600 million between 1969 and 1971. The 1948 *Paramount* Supreme Court decision had broken up the studio system, eliminating the major studios' monopoly on production and exposing the studios to significant independent competition. Crisis conditions led to industry panic in the late sixties and early seventies as studios scrambled to sell off holdings, produce films people would pay to see, and somehow turn a profit.

By the end of the sixties and the beginning of the seventies, the studios wanted some of that lucrative counterculture film action, of all things, so they began green-lighting films designed to appeal to the college-age audience. Robert Altman's *M*A*S*H* (1970) earned Twentieth Century–Fox an extraordinary $36.7 million in domestic rentals on a $3 million investment, persuading studio executives that films geared toward the counterculture could make money. By 1970 almost all the major studios had low-budget "youth films" in development in an effort to hedge against the risks of making big-budget films exclusively.[6] The films were cheap to make, the thinking went, and maybe one of them would hit like *M*A*S*H*. So Columbia Pictures teamed with the independent production company BBS, the maker of *Easy Rider* (1969), on a deal that led to *Five Easy Pieces* (1970), *The Last Picture Show* (1971), *The King of Marvin Gardens* (1972), and other films. Metro-Goldwyn-Mayer financed *Zabriskie Point* (1970), directed by famed Italian art film director Michelangelo Antonioni. Universal Pictures gambled $5 million on five young directors: Peter Fonda made *The Hired Hand* (1971), Miloš Forman made *Taking Off* (1971), Dennis Hopper made *The Last Movie* (1971), Douglas Trumbull made *Silent Running* (1972), and George Lucas made *American Graffiti* (1973). With a budget of $777,000, *American Graffiti* earned $55.3 million in domestic rentals.[7] So that one hit returned to Universal eleven times its investment in all five films.

But studio investment in offbeat low-budget films did not last. The average cost of production rose sharply as the decade progressed (from $1.97 million in 1972 to $5.61 million in 1977, a 185 percent increase in five years), and low-budget films became increasingly difficult to rationalize financially.[8] Given the growing costs, according to James Monaco, it became "harder to make a profitable small picture than a profitable large one."[9] The studio practice of teaming up with independent production companies on films geared toward niche audiences continued into the middle of the decade—with movies like *The Conversation* (1974, Paramount Pictures and American Zoetrope) and *Taxi Driver* (1976, Columbia Pictures and Michael and Julia Phillips)—but such films were dying out, supplanted by studio blockbusters like *The Towering Inferno* (1974) and *King Kong* (1976). The target audience changed, too. By 1977, according to David Cook, "57 percent of all movie tickets were purchased by those under twenty-five, a group whose tastes were inherently more conservative than those of the late 1960s counterculture."[10] The trend toward juvenile audiences continued as the decade progressed. By 1979, half of America's movie tickets went to filmgoers between the ages of twelve and twenty.[11]

Rising production costs and the predominance of juvenile audiences led to changes in the types of films produced. By the middle of the decade, the blockbuster syndrome had fully gripped Hollywood, and studio executives were looking for movies designed not for niche audiences but for huge ones—event films, bolstered by expensive marketing campaigns, that would draw teenagers and their families. *Jaws* (1975), *Rocky* (1976), and *Star Wars* (1977) had shown executives that movies could make more money than anyone had ever imagined. "Increasingly," Monaco wrote in 1979, "we are all going to see the same ten movies."[12] Films geared toward juveniles also created a lucrative ancillary market for product tie-ins like games, toys, clothing, backpacks, and food. No one was going to buy

Mikey and Nicky action figures. Movies like *Mikey and Nicky*, low-budget films designed to turn a modest profit with a college-age niche audience, were squeezed out of an industry fixated on blockbusters. Movies with small budgets, it turned out, posed too much risk.

Storytelling in Seventies Cinema

The brief period in the first part of the decade, when the major studios still invested in low-budget niche films, offered creative opportunities for filmmakers like Elaine May. May worked as the sole woman in a cohort of directors who were refashioning Hollywood cinema during a period of unusual artistic experimentation.[13] Much of this book describes *Mikey and Nicky*'s unconventional design properties, but here I want to explain the ways in which the film fits some narrative and stylistic trends characteristic of the decade—particularly the period 1970–1977, before Hollywood, in the wake of *Star Wars*, began to focus so intently on the teenage market. As many commentators have observed, seventies films look and feel different from Hollywood films from other periods. I want to describe how.

In his essay "The Decade When Movies Mattered," film critic David Thomson writes about seventies cinema in general, but the following passage could just as well describe *Mikey and Nicky* alone:

> Many of them had unfamiliar shapes, new narrative structures or strategies. They began late. They switched course. They didn't say this guy is reliably good and that one write-off bad. They didn't stick to the rules. And they did not end well, or happily, or comfortably. Sometimes they broke off in your hands or your mind. People you had come to like took it in the head, or turned traitor. The world of the films was as complex and as frightening as anything you'd come into the theatre to escape from. And you were left there when the lights came up, having to work it all out.[14]

Seventies films could be unpredictable, at times perverse, and they embraced storytelling strategies that other Hollywood filmmakers worked hard to avoid, including ambiguous characters, tonal inconsistencies, storytelling gaps, illogical events, and inconclusive endings.[15]

Seventies films seemed intent on discomforting audiences rather than pleasing them. They resisted establishing a coherent moral order and enlisted viewer sympathy for contemptible figures. We see this trend in *Mikey and Nicky* (the original poster for the film read, "don't expect to like 'em") and numerous other films of the period, including *Patton* (1970), *The French Connection* (1971), *A Clockwork Orange* (1971), *Straw Dogs* (1971), *The Getaway* (1972), *Badlands* (1973), *Death Wish* (1974), *Shampoo* (1975), *Carrie* (1976), *Network* (1976), *The Missouri Breaks* (1976), *Taxi Driver* (1976), and *Cross of Iron* (1977). Such films expressed ambiguous attitudes toward their protagonists, who might have been villains in movies of another era. These films represent the moral equivalent of *The Man Who Shot Liberty Valance* (1962)—if Liberty Valance (Lee Marvin), not Ransom Stoddard (James Stewart), were the hero.

The films could also be confusing and convoluted. *THX 1138* (1971), *The King of Marvin Gardens* (1972), *The Conversation* (1974), and *Chinatown* (1974) presented obscure or incomplete story information, and *The Godfather Part II* (1974) and *Nashville* (1975) overwhelmed audiences with an overabundance of information, some of it inconsistent. And, after all that, the films might end unresolved. *Five Easy Pieces* (1970), *Loving* (1970), *McCabe and Mrs. Miller* (1971), *The Candidate* (1972), *Nashville*, and *Carrie* (1976) demanded that spectators resolve their endings mentally since their plots resisted complete closure.

Thematically, the films could be nihilistic. Audiences had witnessed nihilism in some film noirs of the forties and fifties, including *Detour* (1945), *Nightmare Alley* (1947), *Ace in the Hole* (1951), and *Kiss Me Deadly* (1955), but seventies filmmakers took it further. Films like *The Panic in Needle Park* (1971), *A Clockwork Orange* (1971), *Born to Win* (1971), *Deliverance* (1972), *The Friends of Eddie Coyle* (1973), *Chinatown* (1974), *The Parallax View* (1974), *Hustle* (1975), and *Taxi Driver* (1976) expressed the bleakest skepticism you are liable to find in Hollywood cinema, rejecting justice and even undermining one of Hollywood's most central thematic premises: that individual human action matters. This tendency to demote action accorded with Hollywood's investment in character study films. *Five Easy Pieces* (1970), *Klute* (1971), *Scarecrow* (1973), *The Last Detail* (1973), *Lenny* (1974), and *California Split* (1974), like *Mikey and Nicky*, seem more concerned with the personalities and emotional lives of their lead characters than with their goals, actions, and efforts to overcome obstacles.

Mikey and Nicky also *looks* like a seventies film. You can usually tell any movie from the period just by the visual style. The distinctive look of seventies cinema resulted in large part from heavy lens diffusion, fast lenses and film stocks, and the practice of "pushing" (overdeveloping) exposed film in the lab. Such practices allowed cinematographers to shoot in very low light. The practices also reduced image sharpness, creating the graininess we observe in *Mikey and Nicky* and many other films of that era.[16] Handheld camerawork, too, contributed to the bedraggled look we sometimes observe in the period's cinematography. *The French Connection* (1971), *The Last Movie* (1971), *The Long Goodbye* (1973), and *Dog Day Afternoon* (1975), like *Mikey and Nicky*, used handheld cameras, which sometimes followed *behind* the action rather than anticipating it, as is typical in Hollywood cinema. The camera, furthermore, may be unstable (*The Long Goodbye*), shots might be out of focus (*Mikey and Nicky*), images may lack definition (*McCabe and Mrs. Miller*, 1971), and the cinematographer may include lens flares (*Dirty Harry*, 1971). Seventies films could look "uncommercial" as cinematographers rebelled against the crisp professionalism and self-effacing style that Hollywood had perfected in prior decades.

Many seventies filmmakers loaded their films with stylistic ornamentation that drew the audience's attention away from the plot and toward the director's style. *Taxi Driver* (1976) mixed an amplified expressionism with documentary realism. "The overall idea," said director Martin Scorsese, "was to make it like a cross between a gothic horror and the New York *Daily News*."[17] In *A Clockwork Orange* (1971) and *Barry Lyndon* (1975), Stanley Kubrick used long tracking shots and slow zooms, extreme lens lengths that distorted the image, highly formal mise-en-scène, slowly delivered dialogue, and extended segments without any dialogue. Robert Altman's films of the period—including *M*A*S*H* (1970), *The Long Goodbye* (1973), *California Split* (1974), and *Nashville* (1975)—featured loosely structured plots, abrupt scene transitions, overlapping dialogue, mumbled lines, and slowly drifting, roving, and zooming cameras. During this period, Woody Allen grew almost as fond of long takes and uninhabited frames as Antonioni was, a tendency Allen developed in *Annie Hall* (1977) and *Manhattan* (1979).

I argue in *Hollywood Incoherent* that Hollywood films of the seventies charted a middle way between European art cinema and the classical cinema of the Hollywood studio era.[18] Films of the 1970s, on the one hand, remained anchored to classical cinema's structure and purpose. They relied on the stabilizing properties of the classical model, including goal-oriented protagonists, interdependent plotlines, obstacles, deadlines, tight causal connections between events, and a visual style that served the films' storytelling needs. Some seventies filmmakers, on the other hand, also managed to inject into their films some of art cinema's looser artistic strategies, including psychological complexity, delayed exposition, narrative digressions, obscure plotting, unresolved endings, moral ambiguity, stylistic eccentricity, and artistic self-consciousness. This "middle way" tied seventies filmmakers to a time-tested classical filmmaking tradition, yet it still allowed them to draw inspiration and new storytelling strategies from nonclassical filmmaking practices. *Mikey and Nicky* did not lead Hollywood's artistic renaissance in the 1970s; the film came too late for that. But it was a small, pugnacious effort to make something Hollywood had not made before.

Amateurs in Hollywood

To support its efforts to appeal to the counterculture, the so-called New Hollywood offered several routes for young new directors to enter the industry. In the late sixties and early seventies, entry into Hollywood as a new film director was probably easier than it has been at any time since Hollywood's inauguration in the early twentieth century.

Becoming a professional Hollywood director requires training. Film scholar Patricia Rodden Zimmermann argues that professionalism normally involves "codes of expertise," "standardization," "interchangeability of skills," and "the smooth coordination of technical rules and procedures."[19] For a Hollywood director, such training includes mastery of commercial technique and the standard practices of staging, coverage, and continuity. Aspiring Hollywood directors have to learn to work with the heads of the various departments (casting, cinematography, art direction, sound, editorial, etc.) and production staff (producers, assistant directors, etc.). They learn to oversee the production process and work within fixed budgets and strict schedules.

In the seventies, filmmakers had a variety of ways to learn these skills and enter the industry. Many New Hollywood directors of the 1970s acquired professional filmmaking skills the old-fashioned way: they worked their way up through the system. Robert Aldrich worked as an assistant director in the 1940s before directing over two dozen Hollywood features, including some prototypical seventies films like *Ulzana's Raid* (1972), *The Longest Yard* (1974), and *Hustle* (1975). Hal Ashby had a career as an editor, Alan Pakula as a producer, Paul Schrader as a screenwriter, Haskell Wexler as a cinematographer, and Clint Eastwood as an actor before they became film directors. Like many studio-era directors, Bob Fosse, Sidney Lumet, Mike Nichols, and Harold Prince had already established themselves as important directors on Broadway before moving laterally to Hollywood. And, as in the studio era, many new directors in Hollywood—including Michelangelo Antonioni, Miloš Forman, Sergio Leone, Ivan Passer, Roman Polanski, and John Schlesinger—had already achieved acclaim in their home countries in Europe. All these pathways, which had opened in the studio era, remained open in the New Hollywood, offering time-tested training grounds for professionalization.

In the sixties and seventies, however, two new training grounds opened up as well. Film schools became a new source of trained talent. Francis Ford Coppola graduated from the University of California, Los Angeles; George Lucas and John Milius from the University of Southern California; and Martin Scorsese from New York University. Other new directing talent trained in television. In the 1950s, Robert Altman directed television dramas and Sam Peckinpah directed television westerns before moving to Hollywood feature filmmaking in the 1960s. William Friedkin, Arthur Hiller, Arthur Penn, Bob Rafelson, Ridley Scott, and Steven Spielberg also began directing in television.

Still, there was one more route into the New Hollywood, not as common as those outlined above but available to a handful of new talent for a brief time in the first half of the decade: Hollywood studios put amateurs in charge of some low-budget productions. I call these young directors "amateurs" because, as outsiders, they had not learned to make a Hollywood movie through established systems of professionalization and training—apprenticeship, Broadway, international film industries, film school, or television. Rather, they learned to direct a Hollywood film by directing a Hollywood film. In addition to Elaine May, the studios offered directing jobs to Brian De Palma, Dennis Hopper, Terrence Malick, Gordon Parks, and Melvin Van Peebles, none of whom had the traditional experience that would have prepared them to direct a Hollywood feature film. But they had all shown talent and an ability to attract new audiences. And, except for May, they had made their own independent films. Together, they brought an unorthodox artistic sensibility that, for a brief time, Hollywood studios sought out. We will call it an *amateur aesthetic.*

Hollywood traditionally follows what Richard Maltby calls a "commercial aesthetic," which is "essentially opportunist in its economic motivation." According to Maltby, Hollywood's artistic properties are designed to serve commercial purposes, a whatever-works approach that offers "the maximum pleasure for the maximum number for the maximum profit."[20] And what gives mass audiences pleasure, according to Maltby? Stories with romance, thrills, intense emotion, ideological reassurance, spectacle, and happy endings.[21] "Audiences go to the movies to consume their own emotions," Maltby summarizes. "Moviemakers have to organize movies so that spectators will produce their emotions in a sequence and pattern that they find satisfying. Hollywood's commercial aesthetic is grounded in this objective."[22] According to this line of thinking, Hollywood defines aesthetic success not normatively but transactionally: give the people what they want, and they will buy movie tickets.

In the early part of the seventies, however, large numbers of the public wanted something different from movies, and studios were looking for new ways to give it to them. Several expensive flops of the late sixties—*Doctor Dolittle* (1967), *Star!* (1968), *Battle of Britain* (1969), *Paint Your Wagon* (1969), and many other formulaic films—convinced the studios that traditional aesthetic approaches were no longer profitable. Consequently, studio executives invested in new talent, including amateur filmmakers who were making movies for love, not a paycheck. These amateurs were experimenting with filmmaking practices that Hollywood, with its emphasis on commercial aesthetics, had neglected. They brought an untrained, sometimes bizarre, set of artistic devices to the commercial film industry. They were willing to work on low budgets by Hollywood standards, but the studios still gave them substantial funding, sometimes over a million dollars, which allowed them to do things that filmmakers outside of commercial cinema could not do and to reach otherwise inaccessible mainstream audiences.

The most inexperienced film director of the lot, Elaine May was hardly exaggerating when she said that she "knew absolutely nothing" when she directed *A New Leaf* (1971).[23] Paramount vice president Peter Bart was surprised that Charles Bluhdorn (CEO and chairman), Robert Evans (head of production), and Frank Yablans (president) "were willing to go with Elaine May as a director without even testing her."[24] But Paramount offered her the job because she had written the script and had been a popular cultural figure in the fifties and sixties.[25] Moreover, she was a woman, which was a selling point. Bluhdorn said to her, "I can make you another Ida Lupino."[26] The studio boasted to the press "with self-congratulatory glee at its good fortune that a woman has assumed such a triple-threat role" for the first time as writer, director, and star of a Hollywood production.[27] The publicity alone might have been worth the financial risk.

Studios hired some of these untrained directors, in part, to reach new markets and exploit previously untapped sources of revenue. So it is no accident that in addition to May, Hollywood's sole female director at the time, studio executives also invited two Black directors, Gordon Parks and Melvin Van Peebles, who helped the studios reach Black audiences. Women and people of color seeking to direct in Hollywood were less likely to have the resources, networks, and professional training to join the industry in traditional ways. However, as outsiders—*misfits*, we can call them, because they never fit comfortably within the industry—they could open up new markets. They also enjoyed less power and clout than established directors and were paid less, too. Paramount offered May only $50,000 and a percentage for all three roles in her "triple threat" on *A New Leaf*. At a time when Hollywood studios were seeking out new filmmaking approaches and new revenue sources, "amateur" directors offered studios inexpensive talent that could expand markets.

But when the industry opened the door to people like May, these inexperienced filmmakers challenged how a commercial production should look and behave. Van Peebles's brief career in seventies Hollywood offers an illustrative example. Van Peebles had been a novelist, playwright, and director of film shorts and an independent feature when Columbia hired him to direct a script called *Watermelon Man* (1970) about a white bigot who wakes up to find that he has suddenly turned Black. Scriptwriter Herman Raucher was white, and Columbia wanted a Black director to add authenticity to the production. Columbia's executives got more than they anticipated. "Columbia was afraid to make it without a black director, of whom there were not many," Raucher said in an interview. "So Melvin was given the job of directing and it became, under his aegis, more of a black power film than I'd wanted."[28] Van Peebles ultimately transformed Raucher's liberal script into a story of a Black man's growing militancy.[29]

Watermelon Man did not behave like a Hollywood movie, even by seventies standards. It was almost like an underground film, which rejects mainstream storytelling norms in favor of transgressive forms and subject matter, as in the films of Kenneth Anger, Shirley Clarke, Andy Warhol, and John Waters. With a story inspired by Franz Kafka's novella *The Metamorphosis*, *Watermelon Man* had an idiosyncratic design that made the film impossible to categorize (What genre is it?), unpredictable (Where is the story heading?), nonconformist (Why does it behave that way?), and provocative (What is it saying?). Combining an absurdist storyline, incongruous stylistic devices, a bizarre musical score, radical politics, and social satire, the film brought an underground sensibility to a Hollywood studio production. It did not cohere in the way that we expect from mainstream cinema: its perspective shifted between white and Black, its politics shifted between liberal and radical, and it adopted the form of both a sitcom and a social problem film. The result is one of the most strange and elusive Hollywood films of the seventies, an underground film in the form of a Hollywood comedy.

The studios' desire to make disruptive films like *Watermelon Man* did not last long, and most of the Hollywood misfits left commercial filmmaking after just a few movies, either by choice or, like May, by force. Although Columbia offered him a three-picture deal after *Watermelon Man*, Van Peebles abandoned Hollywood after only one film in order to make the independent hit *Sweet Sweetback's Baadasssss Song* (1971), in which he explored a more truly subversive form of filmmaking that the mainstream film industry would never support. Rambling and messy, Dennis Hopper's *The Last Movie* (1971) presents not so much a story (a chain of events in a causal relationship) as a series of moments in the lives of its characters—unpredictable, sporadically engaging, technically imperfect. *The Last Movie* failed commercially, and like May after *Mikey and Nicky*, Hopper did not direct another film until the eighties. Gordon Parks wrote, produced, and directed *The Learning Tree* (1969), his first feature and the first Hollywood film directed by a Black filmmaker. It is a coming-of-age story told from the perspective of a Black boy, another first in Hollywood. Parks went on to direct *Shaft* (1971) and its sequel, but his Hollywood filmmaking career petered out when the Blaxploitation craze did. Terrence Malick made two idiosyncratic movies in the seventies—*Badlands* (1973) and *Days of Heaven* (1978)—and, after some aborted attempts to direct more movies, abandoned filmmaking for two decades. Each eccentric in its own way, these films formed a brief trend in the seventies that ran against the limits of Hollywood's commercial aesthetic.

Brian De Palma entered the film industry at the same time as May, Van Peebles, Hopper, Parks, and Malick, but his career in Hollywood offers an illustrative counterexample because he thrived for decades in the industry. De Palma brought to Hollywood the same childlike exuberance that characterized his early low-budget independent films, *Greetings* (1968), *The Wedding Party* (1969), and *Hi, Mom!* (1970). De Palma's carnivalesque *Phantom of the Paradise* (1974), picked up by Twentieth Century–Fox, shows an outrageousness rarely seen in a film distributed by a major Hollywood studio. The filmmakers, it seems, wanted to try everything they could think of, just for the kick of it, whether or not the ideas served any overall aesthetic purpose: split screen, visual homages to other movies, long takes, arcing cameras, fast motion, irises, animation, a prologue delivered by Rod Serling, and freakish costumes, makeup, and sets. We can describe De Palma's attitude toward the production as *more is more.* Like De Palma's earlier independent films, *Phantom* has the hyperactive spirit of a creative teenager playing with his parents' new movie camera.

Unlike May, Hopper, Van Peebles, and Malick, De Palma went on to direct mainstream commercial hits such as *Carrie* (1976), *Dressed to Kill* (1980), *Scarface* (1983), *The Untouchables* (1987), and *Mission: Impossible* (1996). As the decades progressed, he abandoned some of the unorthodox design features of his early films, tempering their quirky digressions and overall absurdity. Although he remained one of Hollywood's most distinctive directors, Hollywood squeezed some of the exuberance out of his filmmaking, and we can witness his growing sophistication as a filmmaker—and the loss of some of his weird sense of humor—as he mastered the art of making professional Hollywood movies.[30]

Amateur Aesthetics

This chapter set out to situate Elaine May's filmmaking within the context of seventies cinema and, in particular, the studios' efforts at the time to hire outsiders and amateurs to direct feature films, a rare practice before the late sixties. They were not amateurs within their own professional domains—May was a professional actor and writer, Van Peebles a professional playwright and novelist, Parks a professional photographer, Hopper a professional actor, De Palma a professional documentarian—but they did not have the traditional training of a Hollywood director. They brought a new artistic sensibility to the commercial film industry that, for a brief time, Hollywood supported, as long as the films were made cheaply.

Although amateur filmmakers have idiosyncratic styles, their films share some general artistic tendencies that we can try to identify. Films by creative amateurs often display visible energy and playfulness in their presentation. They show a cavalier disregard for technical imperfections or inconsistencies in plotting, tone, or viewpoint. They delight in the individual moment (a shot, a dialogue, a scene, a visual quirk, a narrative device, an unusual performance), whether or not the moment suits the film's overall goals or obeys standard practices with regard to narrative, style, or continuity. Whereas commercial productions exhibit a cool control of film form and viewer response, amateur productions come across, to some degree, as out of control, which makes them unpredictable. They delight in experimentation. They might feature accidents in the filming process—a stray dog, an out-of-focus shot, a slip of the tongue, a slip on the pavement. Their plots appear ambiguous and spontaneous, less unified and directed than commercial productions, and contain narrative digressions and scenes of disproportionate length and emphasis. Overall, we never get the impression that a journeyman sits behind the camera. Amateurs are enthusiastic. One can tell that these films are made with devotion.

In the seventies, Hollywood courted film directors that the mainstream film industry had normally excluded. Most of them never fit Hollywood's narrow notion of a professional director, and at times they behaved as though they were making underground movies. But Hollywood does not make underground movies, and even these eccentric films had a structure and purpose that suited Hollywood's commercial aims. Unlike underground films, they also had budgets large enough to polish anything too ragged in their presentation. The results were mixed, and most of these seventies misfits did not last long in Hollywood. Paramount vice president Peter Bart said, "If another Elaine May type came along I would be dogged in derailing that movie, as I should have done with *A New Leaf*." He vowed "never again to advocate a project with a first-time director."[31] But in the early seventies, executives still permitted first-time directors like May to get behind the camera. And the brief marriage of commercial aesthetics and amateur aesthetics gave birth to some mischievous artistic accomplishments.

Before making a Hollywood movie, a director has generally received training in the competencies of professional film directing. Some Hollywood directors, however, are perhaps too competent, too good at delivering the goods, wasting their creative years on films that their commercial career goals require them to make. Films such as *Mikey and Nicky, Watermelon Man, Phantom of the Paradise, The Learning Tree, The Last Movie,* and *Badlands* showed us what Hollywood films could achieve when enthusiastic artists made them not for commercial purposes ("the maximum pleasure for the maximum number for the maximum profit") but for the love of making them.

4 MAKING, RELEASING, AND RERELEASING *MIKEY AND NICKY*

The picture is so good, I can't believe it will never be released.
PETER FALK, MARCH 1976, NINE MONTHS BEFORE
MIKEY AND NICKY'S THEATRICAL RELEASE

Mikey and Nicky had one of Hollywood's most troubled productions. It did not encounter the huge financial disasters that met *The Missouri Breaks* (1976), *Apocalypse Now* (1979), *Heaven's Gate* (1980), or, for that matter, *Ishtar* (1987), but cost overruns, extended shooting and editing periods, lawsuits, a theft accusation, and potential criminal contempt charges against Elaine May led journalist Andrew Tobias to label it "a truly monumental behind-the-scenes disaster."[1]

The story of making and releasing *Mikey and Nicky* has turns, reversals, and surprises all the way up to its reception today. I am going to tell the story in eight parts, beginning with May's script, which she started writing more than twenty years before filming began.

I. "A helluva story"

May conceived of dramatizing the story of Nicky and Mikey as early as 1953 or 1954, when she joined the Playwrights Theatre Club in Chicago (which later transformed into the Compass Players, then Second City).[2] She was in her early twenties. The club was looking for one-act plays, and she thought to herself, "What can I do with two guys and no scenery?"[3] Several of her fellow performers in Chicago later recalled seeing scraps of paper with pieces of the script and references to the title characters.[4] She never did the one-act, but later she thought, "Gee, this would be a good movie."[5] She told Peter Falk about the project during the production of *Luv* (1967). "In the course of one night," Falk said, "Elaine told me about this story. It was based on real people in a real neighborhood, people that were close to her, whom she had known when she was a child. She remembered it very vividly and it caused in her a need to write it. I thought it was a helluva story."[6] Shortly after the release of *Luv*, she had a complete script for the movie, with Falk committed to playing Mikey.[7]

As Falk says, real events inspired *Mikey and Nicky*. May grew up in a Mob-connected family in Chicago in the 1930s and 1940s. Her mother told her a story about two brothers, gangsters from the neighborhood, one of whom set up the other to be killed.[8] "I knew the widow of the Mikey character," May said. "And my mom told the story a lot because they were friends. And all of our friends were sort of, you know, gangsters. Not all of our friends. Some of them were just ordinary Jews."[9] In a prologue to her script that does not appear in the movie, May seems familiar with the internal mechanics of a Mob "hit." The prologue also demonstrates a novelist's flair for vivid description. This is how her script begins:

MIKEY AND NICKY
by
Elaine May

One of the oddest and, perhaps, most frightening characteristics of a "hit" is the behavior of the victim who is aware that he is slated to die.

He knows, almost as a certainty, that someone inside his organization, someone whom he considers a friend, will be used to set him up for the kill. This is done for obvious reasons. It is easier to kill a man who has been set up, and he can only be set up by a friend, because who else will he trust? The friend must also be known and accepted by the organization, because who else can they trust?

> There is also a flavor of ritual about the procedure, as primitive as the Cosa Nostra's ritual kiss of death. Perhaps it is because of the ritualistic response of the intended victim. Knowing the custom of the set-up as well as he does, and sometimes having actively participated in it, he will, almost invariably, call on someone inside the organization for help.
>
> Why he does this is a matter for speculation. That he does do it is a matter of fact. That he seldom escapes is a matter of record.
>
> But he does, in some instances, escape.[10]

May's prologue sets up the essential dramatic conflict of her story: when the bosses put out a contract on a mobster, he will rely on another mobster, a friend he trusts, for help, and that friend will either betray him or not. This conflict engaged May's imagination from the time she was a child in Chicago in the 1940s, through her time at Playwrights Theatre Club and Compass in the 1950s, through the production and release of *Mikey and Nicky* in 1970s, up until her 1978 reedit of the film, "because I never forgot it; it was such a terrible tale."[11]

II. "Elaine wrote it and you're going to be in it. That's all I need to know."

Before *Husbands* (1970) and *A Woman Under the Influence* (1974), before May had a studio deal to make the movie, before they all became friends, May cast Peter Falk and John Cassavetes as Mikey and Nicky. She cast Falk first, in 1967, and together they determined that Cassavetes ought to play Nicky.[12]

Falk met Cassavetes in 1968, on the set of *Machine Gun McCain* (1969), and approached him about the part over lunch in the Paramount commissary. He began telling Cassavetes about their characters, but Cassavetes interrupted him: "I'll do it." This response irritated Falk, who thought that Cassavetes was too flippant, so Falk told him how much the project meant to May and him and that he wanted Cassavetes to ask some questions before agreeing. This response set off Cassavetes, who stood up, yelling, "You think I'm like you—worried?!—anxious! Is it going to be a hit? Will the critics like it? Is my part good? Is your part better?" Cassavetes ranted like that for two minutes and finished with, "Elaine wrote it and you're going to be in it. That's all I need to know." And he sat down.[13]

May filled in the rest of her cast between 1969 and 1973. Famed acting teacher Sanford Meisner played Mob boss Dave Resnick ("I wanted someone who was in charge who nothing could throw," May said).[14] She cast Joyce Van Patten as Jan, Nicky's wife. Rose Arrick, a fellow Compass player, played Mikey's wife, Annie. Arrick had played a rich socialite in *A New Leaf* (1971), but she could also convincingly play marital domesticity.

May also made some unusual casting choices, ones that violated expectations established by previous gangster films. She cast Carol Grace as Nellie, Nicky's girlfriend. Gun molls traditionally look glamorous, like Rita Hayworth in *Gilda* (1946), or dangerous, like Ava Gardner in *The Killers* (1946). Grace, by contrast, is mousy and strange looking, older than the gangster girlfriend stereotype. She talks in an unusually soft and deliberate manner, poised and fragile.[15] In *Gangster Story* (1959), she had played a librarian. May offered her the part of Nellie in 1969 when Grace and her husband, Walter Matthau, had May and May's husband to their home for dinner. When Grace opened the front door for them, the first thing May said was, "My God, I have a part in a script that I'm working on that you would be perfect for."[16] The part of the hit man, Warren Kinney, went to Ned Beatty after principal photography began. (A draft script lists Robert Duvall as Kinney, but I have seen no evidence that Duvall was even approached.) One expects a tough actor to play a hit man—Falk played one in *Murder, Inc.* (1960)—but Beatty is the opposite of a tough guy. His most prominent role at that point was Bobby in *Deliverance* (1972), whom mountain men force to "squeal like a pig" as they rape him at gunpoint. According to May, Beatty "said to the costume person, 'I'd like my pants to be a little too short.' And I thought, he knew exactly who this guy is."[17]

Hollywood filmmakers typically favor typecasting, which eases viewer understanding. With typecasting, we can grasp a character's function in the plot simply by how they look and behave. In her casting decisions, May focused on each character's individuality, rather than thinking of a character solely as having a narrative role to fulfill. Her gangster moll is not like other gangster molls: she is meek, bookish, unusual. And her hit man is not like others we have seen: he is anxious, awkwardly dressed, socially inept. The deviation from type gives these characters a feeling of authenticity precisely because they are unfamiliar versions of familiar roles. They stand out as realistic because they violate expectations and genre norms.[18]

III. "An ironclad deal"

The deal to finance and distribute *Mikey and Nicky* went through two production firms and two studios before it ended up with Paramount. May first sold the project to producer Joe Manduke and United Artists in 1969, while she was still in production on *A New Leaf.* Scheduled for release in spring 1970, *Mikey and Nicky* was budgeted at $1.8 million, with Cassavetes and Falk already cast as leads.[19] After that deal fell through, the project was sold to Palomar Pictures International and Twentieth Century–Fox, which dropped it when the budget reportedly climbed to $2.2 million. Paramount picked it up in March 1973 at the initial budget of $1.8 million.[20]

Producer Howard Koch could not believe that Paramount would make another film with May after the difficulties the studio had with her on *A New Leaf.* Stanley Jaffe had replaced Koch as May's producer on *A New Leaf* after Koch tried to have her removed as director. Jaffe found her easy to work with at first, but a few weeks later he called Koch to say, "She's a —ing maniac!" So, when Koch heard that Paramount had signed with her again, he called studio head Frank Yablans in disbelief. Yablans told him, "Howard, what happened to you happened to you; it's not going to happen to me. We've got an ironclad deal."[21] The Paramount contract stipulated that if the cost of the film ran over $1.8 million, then the overages would come out of May's salary. The studio inserted other clauses to protect its interests and assert control over the project in case it went off the rails. If she ran 15 percent over budget, the studio could take over the film. The stipulated delivery date was no later than June 1, 1974. In return, May would have final cut.[22]

We know now that the film ran 139 percent over budget and missed the delivery date by two and a half years. Yablans assumed that his deal with May was "ironclad" because he thought he was dealing with a businessperson, someone motivated by money and careerism, the "rational agent" of neoclassical economic theory. He could not imagine a film director who cared about her art more than her salary, her studio contract, or her career in Hollywood.

IV. "It all went fucking over"

According to numerous accounts, May loved shooting *Mikey and Nicky.* She may have driven the executives crazy, and her producer, Michael Hausman, worked day and night to accommodate her ("I'm a director's producer. Anything within reason, I'll deliver").[23] Her cinematographer, Victor Kemper, quit the production twice. But she herself seems to have had her most rewarding experience as a film director. Carol Grace said about May's directing, "Something emotional happens and she leaves the real world. She can't say, 'That's it. We're finished.' . . . And she's so happy when she directs that she doesn't care about time."[24] These were not compliments. Grace thought that May did not have the temperament to direct—"It was hell," she said about the shoot—and was pleased that no one saw the film when it came out.[25]

If Grace was in hell, May, Cassavetes, and Falk were in heaven. "Both John and Peter were in great awe of her," wrote Grace.[26] Actors and crew were normally called for eight o'clock in the evening and worked nine or ten hours, sometimes shooting until eight in the morning. Falk and Cassavetes also attended dailies with May at five or six o'clock each evening.[27] As we saw when we examined May's directing methods on *A New Leaf, The Heartbreak Kid* (1972), and *Ishtar* (1987), May would not tell the actors on *Mikey and Nicky* what to do. Journalist Dan Rottenberg observed:

> Unlike most directors who tell their actors, "you go here, you go there, you stand on this spot," May gives her cast tremendous freedom. The actors simply run thru rehearsals and shootings again and again until they have something that satisfies them and her. She lets them stand wherever they want, to the dismay of her cameramen. Between rehearsals and shootings she may huddle for half an hour with Falk and Cassavetes, on a side of the street where no one else can hear them.[28]

May's failure to "care about time" or follow standard practices of principal photography created headaches for the crew, who thought she had no clue what she was doing. When Tom Miller, the film's publicist, raised the issue with Cassavetes, the actor corrected him, "She knows. Believe me."[29] The crew did not realize that she was following a different method, one that only she, Cassavetes, and Falk understood.

In her directing, May also neglected to maintain spatial continuity in filming, which is important for the editing process. If actors are in different positions during different takes, the editor cannot seamlessly cut together the various shots. For that reason, Hollywood directors must obey certain rules of cinematography on set (180-degree rule, 30-degree rule, etc.).[30] But the rules require that actors perform from the same marks during each take. "Peter and I played it every possible way," Cassavetes said about the hotel room scene. "One take we'd be on this side of the bed, another take on that side. It's hard as hell on the focus cameraman, the camera operator—the gaffer, the man who lights the set; it must drive them up the wall . . . and don't even mention John Carter, the film editor!"[31] May compensated for allowing actors to go anywhere by filming scenes with two or three cameras simultaneously.[32] Multicamera shooting allows editors to cut together different angles from a single take, but directors normally reserve multicamera shooting for action scenes and stunts that can be performed only once. Directors generally film dialogue scenes with one camera because dialogue scenes are easy to repeat with the camera at different angles for coverage. But not May's dialogue scenes. Her actors might change their locations, their deliveries, or the order of the lines. She wanted three cameras so that she could show a single take from various angles on the two actors, but the practice added difficulty and expense to the production.

The production team had a sixty-night shooting schedule for the entire film, but they spent fifteen nights just shooting the hotel scenes.[33] May eventually brought Carter to the hotel set to help match footage. "The scene had already been shot from every corner of the room as well as been played in those same corners," wrote Miller. "She now wanted to match this wildly improvisational footage with footage she was now going to shoot . . . and she wanted Carter to tell her how to do it. He returned to me with a headache."[34] For another scene at the hotel, May didn't like the placement of the stairs the crew had constructed in the lobby, and she had them rebuilt, delaying production for an additional day or more. Miller suggested to Cassavetes that another director would simply restage the scene. "And with another director you could conceivably get a hack piece of work," Cassavetes replied.[35]

Other creative decisions generated further delays. When Carol Grace got to Philadelphia for the shoot, the production wasn't ready for her. Falk and Cassavetes, according to Grace, were still shooting the graveyard scene and "didn't seem to be able to get out of the graveyard."[36] It took two more weeks before they started Grace's scenes in Nellie's apartment. For the subsequent fight scene, the actors were initially scheduled to leave the apartment on South Street and then turn onto Front Street for the fight. The crew had spent days setting up fake storefronts on South and timing streetlights for the action. On the night of the shoot, however, May decided to film the whole scene on Front, requiring the crew to repave the street because it was too bumpy, causing further delays.[37] Going over the film's budget sheet years later, Hausman said, "It all went fucking over."[38]

After sixty days, the entire scheduled shooting period, the team had shot only about half the film. In August 1973, they took a hiatus so that Falk could film an entire season of his *Columbo* television series. Paramount agreed to fund extra shooting days, provided that May shoot the remainder of the film in Los Angeles to save money. So production resumed in Los Angeles in January and, after another fifty days of shooting, ended in March 1974, ten months after photography began.[39]

From one perspective, it is plain to see why May exasperated Grace, Kemper, the crew, and the executives at Paramount. She was not professional in the way they expected. But it is just as easy to see why other people she has worked with—not just Falk and Cassavetes but also Mike Nichols, Charles Grodin, Warren Beatty, her editors, and many others—have been so devoted to her. She is creative, uncompromising. Many people describe filmmaking as both a business and an art form and point to the essential tension between the two identities. For Elaine May, there is no tension because it is only an art form.

V. "The third way was best"

After the evening's shoot ended at around eight in the morning, May would edit with John Carter for three and a half hours.[40] Later, during the hiatus between the Philadelphia and Los Angeles shoots, they edited the film at 130 West Fifty-Seventh Street in New York City, but they had a sound problem. May, who always had two or three cameras running, would occasionally pause one or another camera in the middle of a scene, which fouled up the sound coding. The film and sound would be slated at the top of the scene but would get out of sync at the point when the camera paused.[41] The filmmakers also recorded Falk and Cassavetes on separate audio tracks, both in stereo (four tracks total), which further complicated syncing and cataloging.[42] "Elaine and John Carter discovered that basically the whole film was out of sync," explained assistant sound editor Patrick McMahon, whose sole job during that four-month period was to put the film back in sync by going through it manually, "frame by frame." Once he completed a scene, he would hand it off to May and Carter to edit, while McMahon set about syncing another scene.[43] Assistant editor Vaughn Hazell described cataloging problems created by May's experimental editing process: May continually lifted lines from different takes and looped them into scenes in various combinations, and Hazell had to keep track of everything (code numbers, original tracks, and duplicates) so that, in the event they used one of those cuts, the lab could make a final print from their work print.[44]

When principal photography completed in March 1974, editing became more intensive. May set up an editing facility in a two-room suite at the Sunset Marquis Hotel in West Hollywood with two full-time editors—Carter and Sheldon Kahn—working in different bedrooms. The living room and other rented rooms stored film.[45] Falk and Cassavetes would sometimes help with the edit. In all, the production employed about a dozen people during editing, including a full-time librarian. They worked in two shifts, six days a week, often until two or three in the morning; May worked both shifts.[46]

In the editing room, May was a natural. She understood film editing intuitively and would see scene possibilities that a professional editor might not see. Of her two editors, Carter was the professional. She brought in Kahn to assist with editing for four weeks but ended up hiring him for almost eighteen months. A relative novice, Kahn did not know what a film editor could not do. "I was learning so much from Elaine about how to put something together that shouldn't go together necessarily."[47] Like many who have worked with May, Kahn quickly got on her schedule and wavelength. Hazell, also a novice at the time, said he looked forward to working with May to see what she was going to create: "This is going to be a master class today."[48] Kahn called working with her "an advanced course in editing."[49]

For May, the editing room provided another place for artistic experimentation. She seemed to relish the editing process as much as the shooting process and was just as obsessive about it. According to one source at the time, "We think she didn't want to finish it because she had worked on it so long it had become her whole life. She loved editing it. She would take a scene and have it cut every way possible."[50] According to Kahn, he and May would cut scenes sixteen or seventeen different ways.[51] "Her ideas moved so fast through her mind that she would not complete one thought before going on to the next thought."[52] She would see numerous possibilities for a scene and would give the editors instructions for cutting it a new way, "Now let's do that scene from John's point of view."[53] While Kahn was recutting a scene, she would work with Carter on a different scene and return to see Kahn's results. Then she would have him cut it from another point of view. "Elaine has a photographic memory," according to Kahn. "If we cut a scene thirteen ways, she'd go, 'The third way was best.' She'd then recall it frame by frame."[54]

The film was due to Paramount on June 1, 1973, and in July industry reporters were already questioning the lengthy editing period.[55] But postproduction was not completed until almost the end of 1976. May's editors estimated that they had over 1 million feet of film, perhaps even 1.5 million (between 200 and 275 hours), which they had to cut down to 10,000 feet, the standard length of a feature.[56] According to Kemper, May had even printed outtakes, footage discarded at the time of shooting, often because of some problem with photography.[57] She went over every line of dialogue "looking for the best readings," according to McMahon, and would grab off-camera lines and add them during cutaways in an effort to make them match the picture.[58] Because of the constant tinkering with dialogue, she had "boxes and boxes" of lifted sound clips from various takes that she might use, according to Hazell. "The log book was four inches thick of different code numbers for each scene."[59] Before nonlinear digital editing, this kind of postproduction tinkering took teams of people, and each little editorial change might take several hours to complete. "The studio didn't want to give her that kind of time," Hazell said, but she took it anyway.[60]

When asked why editing was taking so long, May would blame the sound. "Do you really want to know why *Mikey and Nicky* has taken six-and-a-half years to complete?" May asked an audience at the New School in October 1975, over a year before the film's release. "I wish I could say I was probing for artistic truths. Actually, I'm just trying to get it so you can hear it."[61] But sound clarity problems would not have delayed editing for years: it was her editing process. She continued to make changes up until the end, according to McMahon, who spent five or six months working on the final mix with May and sound editor John Strauss in New York. The delay, McMahon said, "wasn't because she wanted [the film] to sound better."[62] She was indeed probing for artistic truths; she was obsessed with it.

VI. Paramount Pictures v. Elaine May v. Paramount Pictures

When one reads about the lawsuits and countersuits between Paramount and May, it is hard to take a side. From a business perspective, Paramount executives seem perfectly reasonable. They paid for *Mikey and Nicky* (more than twice over before they sued her) and funded and accommodated her for years. They wanted their film. But from an artistic perspective—and the perspective, perhaps, of film history—Elaine May is the meritorious party. She was only trying to make the film she set out to make, and, compared to Paramount's blockbusters, *Mikey and Nicky* did not cost much. So I will lay out the story as objectively as I can and let readers determine fault.

Barry Diller replaced Frank Yablans as head of Paramount in 1974, and he had had enough of May and *Mikey and Nicky*, which was already over a year past its contractual delivery date. Diller arranged a screening of the film, such as it was. May invited a host of famous people to attend, including Ellen Burstyn, James Coco, Paddy Chayefsky, and Terrence McNally, presumably for backup.[63] But, at the screening, a problem quickly became evident: at various points, the sound disappeared. For some reason, May had removed the sound mix and replaced it with the work track, even though McMahon and Strauss had worked for months to complete the final mix. During silent moments, May stood up and described what characters were saying. McMahon was flabbergasted ("It was the most self-destructive thing I saw her do"), and Diller and the other executives at the screening were not happy.[64]

Afterward, at a meeting with Diller, May agreed to deliver the completed film by September 15, 1975, but on September 26 she asked Diller for another $180,000. Perhaps she figured that, since the studio had already sunk millions into the project, Paramount executives were unlikely to pull out. Up until then, that had been true. Paramount had continued to fund *Mikey and Nicky*, despite the overages, and had done the same with *A New Leaf*. But Diller refused to let the production go unchecked any longer. He demanded that May bring the film to the studio, where she could supervise the final cut using Paramount editors.[65] May must have recalled her experience on *A New Leaf*, when executives took the film from her and recut it their way. Distrustful and forever looking for an advantage with the studio, May "sold" *Mikey and Nicky* to a company called Alyce Films for $90,000. Alyce Films, it turned out, was a front established by Falk and other friends of May. So the studio sued her and she sued it, both claiming breach of contract.

Paramount sued first, in New York Superior Court, alleging that May had no right to sell its film. It had invested $4 million and demanded possession of all the footage, which May now held in an editing studio in New York.[66] May, the suit claimed, would not finish the film. May countersued in Los Angeles Superior Court, alleging $8 million in damages. She claimed that she had been within a few days of finishing when Paramount refused to put up completion funds. She further claimed that she had a right to sell the film once Paramount refused the additional funding. On October 27, 1975, New York judge George Stark ruled that Paramount had demonstrated its ownership and granted the studio possession.[67] But May didn't give up. She broadened her suit in Los Angeles, now claiming that Paramount had committed perjury in New York.

The chances of a resolution to the standoff looked bad. May was not going to give up her film just because she lost in court.[68] Paramount sent New York sheriff's deputies to May's editing studio to collect the film, but reels were missing. So the studio went back to court and, in September 1976, accused May and her husband, David Rubinfine, of violating the court's order not to move the footage. In deposition, Rubinfine admitted that he had removed eight to twelve cartons of film, hidden them in his trunk, and driven them to the home of a fellow psychiatrist in Connecticut. Justice Martin Stecher considered the action serious enough to pursue criminal contempt charges against May and Rubinfine.[69]

Still, May did not return the missing reels. Warren Beatty called

Diller to convince him to give May the $180,000 in completion money, but Diller refused. "She is a brilliant woman, and a wonderful woman," Diller said within earshot of a reporter, "but she can go to jail or the madhouse for *ten years* before I will submit to blackmail!" May and Diller finally talked on the phone. "Look, Elaine, return the film," he said to her. "This has gone on long enough. If you return it, I give you my word that things will go right for you. But I won't be blackmailed, and I won't put anything in writing. You have to trust me." Shortly afterward, May called back and told him, "Someone will come with the film." Within minutes, the missing reels had been returned in a box to Diller's outer office.[70] The lawsuits were dropped, including the criminal contempt charge. According to May, Diller didn't want Paramount "to be the only studio that jails a director for going over budget."[71] In the end, May supervised final editing at Paramount for the film's December 10, 1976, release.

VII. "An odd, biting, grinning, sideways-scuttling rodent of a picture"

Reviews were scathing. Almost all the major publications—*New York Times, Los Angeles Times, New York Post, Philadelphia Inquirer, New York* magazine, *Wall Street Journal, Saturday Review, Playboy, Newsweek, Time,* and many others—panned *Mikey and Nicky*. John Simon considered it one of the year's worst movies, calling it "Elaine May's current debacle."[72] Charles Champlin wrote, "In a long lifetime you are not apt to find more intelligence and good acting expended on a lost cause than in Elaine May's 'Mikey and Nicky.'"[73] Desmond Ryan called it "a movie without perceptible purpose."[74] Vincent Canby wrote, "It's nearly two hours of being locked in a telephone booth with a couple of method actors who won't stop talking, though they have nothing of interest to say, and who won't stop jiggling around, though they plainly aren't going anywhere."[75] Marie Brenner wrote, "There are no scenes as such, just rambling conversations, mumbled posturings, grunts, and moans."[76] Judith Crist said that May's "long night's tale is as dull, dreary, and unlikable as her stars."[77] The negative reviews kept coming: "two dull hours"; "dull, confused, plodding and sometimes unbearably pretentious"; "numbing"; "ambling" and "slight."[78] Frank Rich may have written the most devastating review. He called it an "almost unendurable mess" and the "work of an artist who's so wrapped up in her personal obsessions that she seems to have lost touch with her audience and, worse, with her talent." He said that the film "shouldn't be reviewed so much as quietly buried and forgotten."[79]

Some reviewers fixated on distractions, such as the film's lengthy production and cost overruns or the fact that it was not a comedy like *A New Leaf* or *The Heartbreak Kid*, which critics had loved. *Variety* wrote, "The stormy and costly production history of the project is the most interesting facet to this Paramount release."[80] Crist said that *Mikey and Nicky* proved that "anything John Cassavetes can do [May] can do more expensively" and, like many other reviewers, expressed disappointment at May's "total abandonment of the comedic but compassionate vein that has been her hallmark."[81] Ruth Batchelor wrote, "It is not only not a comedy, it is almost not a film."[82] Joy Gould Boyum called it "tedious and humorless, so heavy-handed and so lacking in artistry, one is almost driven to revise totally one's feelings about May's gifts."[83] Canby wrote, "Miss May is a witty, gifted, intelligent director. It took guts for her to attempt a film like this, but she failed."[84] For Canby and many others, May crashed when she got out of her lane.

Reviewers singled out the film's uncommercial look. Rich said that it "must be the mangiest-looking picture to be released by a major movie studio this year—and, from a technical standpoint, it's often not operating at a professional level."[85] Simon considered the editing and continuity "thoroughly shocking in a major film."[86] *Newsweek* criticized May's "technical raggedness . . . erratic framing and emphysemic editing."[87] Molly Haskell wrote, "Elaine May hasn't come any closer to mastering the basics of filmmaking." About the editing, Haskell said that you could throw the shots "up in the air and they would settle down in some form that as much resembles a pattern or progression as this one does."[88] Ryan wrote, "Entire segments of the sound track are far below professional quality" and "parts of the film bear the mark of an incredibly slapdash hand."[89] That "slapdash" comment might have infuriated May, if she read it, given the years she had spent working on each moment of the film.

Several reviewers suggested that May simply did not know what she was doing. Champlin criticized May's "indecisive" camera technique and suggested that May "has not yet got the hang of making movies."[90] Boyum said that the movie looked like it was "shot by an eight-year-old with his first Brownie (shoulders keep blocking our vision and people keep losing their foreheads)."[91] Crist bewailed the fact that "so provenly gifted a filmmaker should suddenly turn amateur."[92] *Mikey and Nicky* lacked the professional polish—centered frames, actor frontality, crisp focus, burnished sound design, perfected continuity—that one expects from a Hollywood production, and critics weren't having it.

The film, however, was designed to appeal to viewers looking for something less orderly and refined from Hollywood. In fact, appreciative viewers might have used some of the same terms to praise the film that we find in those negative reviews. The film is indeed "mangy" and "ragged," and it does feature "rambling conversations, mumbled posturings, grunts, and moans" and characters "who won't stop jiggling around." In a scathing review for *Time*, Jay Cocks called *Mikey and Nicky* "fractured, disorienting, out of control"; he added that "watching the picture is an unsettling and eventually oppressive experience" and compared the film to "a nervous breakdown."[93] One's opinion of *Mikey and Nicky*, I am thinking, depends on whether one appreciates a fractured, disorienting, unsettling, and oppressive filmgoing experience, the aesthetic equivalent of a nervous breakdown.

Indeed, in the few positive reviews the film received, we find some of the same impressions recorded in negative reviews, but the attitude is different. Writing for the *New Republic*, Stanley Kauffmann called *Mikey and Nicky* "an odd, biting, grinning, sideways-scuttling rodent of a picture," and that was a *positive* review. He concludes: "And out scurries a little furry film that first interests, then amuses, then bites you, then scurries away again, leaving you a bit sickened. But authentically sickened."[94] I have never seen the word *sickened* used in a positive way about a movie or anything else, but, if you liked *Mikey and Nicky*, you could see what Kauffmann was getting at. In 1978, he named *Mikey and Nicky* one of the ten best films of the previous decade, and, in 1982, "the best film that I know by an American woman."[95] Over the years, Kauffmann touted the film many times in his column upon its various rereleases.[96] David Sterritt, too, championed the film, using language that might otherwise have appeared in a negative review, calling it "the most grimly fascinating, if deliberately unpleasant, character study to hit the screen this year." For him, this "deliberately unpleasant" film planted May "on the map of budding first-class directors."[97] Jonathan Rosenbaum's glowing review described the film as "misanthropic, pitiless, bleak," another sentiment one finds in negative reviews.[98] Admittedly, other reviews were not entirely negative; several praised the performances by Falk,

Cassavetes, Grace, or Van Patten, and more than a few remarked on the film's powerful ending.[99] But, other than positive reviews by Kauffmann, Sterritt, and Rosenbaum, as well as Gene Shalit's praise in a 1977 interview with Peter Falk, I have found no other fully laudatory reviews at the time of the film's initial release.[100]

In the mid-seventies, bad reviews could sabotage the box office of just about any movie; however, even if the film had received more positive reviews, I doubt that *Mikey and Nicky* would have succeeded commercially. By 1976, the moviegoing public had lost the appetite for complex character studies. May may have taken too long to finish her film; she had barely caught the tail end of a wave. In any case, the initial returns were dismal. In its first run, it took in only $29,500 at the box office in its first three weeks, and it never again made enough to warrant reporting in *Variety*'s weekly summary of box office returns.[101] With literally dozens of scathing reviews, and not even a handful of critical champions, combined with almost total failure at the box office, Paramount executives stopped promoting it and pulled it from theaters. There was no point in spending any more money on this debacle. The film, in their minds, was a lost cause.

VIII. "The return of Elaine May's bitterly wonderful and almost unseen *Mikey and Nicky*"

May wanted her film back. She believed that the studio had not promoted it correctly and that, with a proper release, it might do well.[102] In a surprising turn, May, the artist, understood the market for the film better than the Paramount suits.

At a restaurant in Los Angeles in 1978, May, Falk, and Julian Schlossberg (a former Paramount vice president) met with Dick Zimbert, Paramount's vice president in charge of business affairs, to persuade him to sell *Mikey and Nicky*'s distribution rights. At the meeting, Schlossberg noted that Paramount had not given the film a "first-class" release, as required by May's contract, and he reminded Zimbert that May had already sued the studio. So they came to an agreement to transfer the rights from Paramount to Schlossberg and May for an undisclosed amount. After all the trouble the studio had faced with May and *Mikey and Nicky*, Schlossberg said, "they were happy to get rid of it."[103]

Schlossberg and May prepared *Mikey and Nicky* for a rerelease. To improve the pace of the film, May trimmed twelve minutes. *Mikey and Nicky* may offer the only instance of a director's cut that is shorter than the original theatrical release. The original version is not available and has, as far as Schlossberg knows, never screened publicly since he acquired the distribution rights; however, a comparison of Paramount's transcript of the 1976 final print to May's reedited version indicates that May mostly trimmed the first half of the movie, cutting several lines of dialogue from various scenes and some interactions with incidental characters. She also removed a scene with a desk clerk before Mikey visits Nicky's hotel room.[104]

Schlossberg prepared a new publicity campaign. For the new poster, he abandoned Paramount's tagline, "don't expect to like 'em," which he hated, in favor of a series of quotations from the few positive reviews the film had received, as well as a few choice quotes from mixed reviews by Kathleen Carroll in the *New York Daily News* and Howard Kissel in *Women's Wear Daily* (figure 4.1a–b).[105] The poster also included a few positive phrases from Jack Kroll's shattering review of the film in *Newsweek*, which had also called May "one of the great unresolved potentials of American movies."[106] At that time Schlossberg did not have much else to work with.

And here the story of *Mikey and Nicky* takes another turn. Together, Schlossberg and May embarked on a successful rerelease of the film that began in 1978 and has lasted nearly fifty years.

The most profitable and lengthy theatrical rerelease came in 1984–1985, when the film played in Los Angeles, Chicago, and New York City.[107] On May 15, 1985, *Variety* reported that *Mikey and Nicky* grossed $32,000 during one week in two theaters, exceeding in that one week the grosses of the film's entire initial run, and it remained on *Variety*'s weekly chart of 50 top-grossing films for four weeks.[108] Moreover, the film played in first-run theaters, including the eminent Cinema 1 in New York City, even though *Mikey and Nicky* was now eight years old. According to Schlossberg, *Mikey and Nicky* has played continually—in the United States, Canada, and especially Europe—since he acquired the rights, and he still satisfies screening requests at least once a month, more when May wins an award or some other honor.[109] The film received a DVD release in 2004, and, in 2019, the prestigious Criterion Collection released a Blu-ray of the film and featured on its website apprecia-

FIGURE 4.1A–B. The original 1976 *Mikey and Nicky* poster and the 1978 rerelease poster.

tive commentary from filmmakers and film commentators. Schlossberg eventually sold all the movies in the distribution catalog of his Castle Hill Productions (which included important works by John Cassavetes, Elia Kazan, Orson Welles, John Ford, and many others), except for *Mikey and Nicky,* which he holds on to for May and for his own sentimental reasons. "I will never sell the movie," he told me. "It's the little engine that could."[110]

Just as surprising as the film's newfound theatrical and video success, *Mikey and Nicky* started to earn increasingly positive reviews from critics. The turnaround in critical opinion is like none other that I have researched—perhaps more dramatic, even, than the famous reevaluation of *Bonnie and Clyde* (1967). It began slowly, with the eighties rerelease, at which point critics were still giving the film mixed reviews, although much better reviews than those of the previous decade. In general, critics who had hated the movie in 1976 still hated it. Desmond Ryan wrote in 1985, "the passage of time has not improved May's movie," which he regarded as "beyond retrieval."[111] Michael Blowen wrote, "Unfortunately, films don't improve with age."[112] However, the *New York Times*'s Vincent Canby (who, you remember, originally considered the film a failure) recommended it to his readers in 1985: "The film, about which I had major reservations when it originally opened here in 1976, has many articulate supporters who may now prove the rest of us wrong."[113] Apparently, some films do improve with age.

A new generation of critics found the film exhilarating. Sheila Benson wrote in the *Los Angeles Times*, "When a film gets too far ahead of its time, it can get lost. The return of Elaine May's bitterly wonderful and almost unseen 'Mikey and Nicky' (Cineplex) is a case in point."[114] Julie Salamon wrote in the *Wall Street Journal*, "With its tough, fevered inventiveness, 'Mikey and Nicky' keeps setting off little explosions of edgy excitement. I'm glad it's getting a second chance."[115] In 1984, Michael Ventura named it as an *LA Weekly* "Pick of the Week" and listed it among his "Top 20 Films of the 1970s," writing, "we are lucky to be given a second chance to experience it."[116] And in 1985, Ray Carney compared the film to "the essays of Emerson, one of the essential documents of the American imaginative predicament."[117]

Today, the almost universal pans of the 1970s have turned into almost universal praise of the film, and it is difficult to find negative reviews written after 1985. In the *New York Times*, Dave Kehr, writing about the 2004 DVD release, called *Mikey and Nicky* a "neglected wonder among the finest American movies of the 1970s, and perhaps of all time."[118] In 2006, J. Hoberman wrote for the *Village Voice*, "Among other things, *Mikey and Nicky* is the greatest Cassavetes film Cassavetes never made."[119] And the film's ragged camera technique earned praise in, of all places, *American Cinematographer*, which called the DVD "a classic that belongs on the shelf of any serious movie fan," an astonishing turnaround for a film that earlier reviewers had considered erratic, slapdash, technically unprofessional, amateurish, and "the mangiest-looking picture to be released by a major movie studio this year."[120] In recent years, the film has earned praise in the pages of the *Guardian* ("5 stars"), *Sight and Sound*, and the *New Yorker* ("hard-nosed masterpiece"), as well as just about any other publication that has evaluated the film in the past thirty years.[121]

It is difficult to explain *Mikey and Nicky*'s commercial and critical reversal, but we can speculate.

For one thing, recent interest in Elaine May and other female filmmakers in Hollywood has drawn attention to the film. May has been racking up awards since the 2010s, including the National Medal of Arts (2013), the Writers Guild of America's Laurel Award for Screenwriting Achievement (2016), a Tony Award for Lead Actress (2019), the PEN/Mike Nichols Writing for Performance Award (2022), and an Honorary Academy Award (2022). She has been the subject of several books and retrospectives and, over the decades, has transformed from an artistic rebel into an icon. Moreover, the previous antipathy toward May among feminist scholars (who, as I have discussed, either ignored her or blasted her) has shifted as well. Because her movies focused on male characters and often portrayed women as various types of pathetic, some feminist scholars looked at her work as a betrayal of feminism. But many scholars now regard May as one of Hollywood's female pioneers. This explanation for the critical reevaluation of *Mikey and Nicky*—that people are now paying more attention to May as a filmmaker—is supported by the fact that screenings increase whenever she wins another award.

Still, the argument that the film's acclaim results from the newfound attention to May and other female directors goes only so far and, to some extent, conflicts with my belief that the film has earned aesthetic appreciation for its own sake. No one has called any of May's other films a "masterpiece" or one of "the finest American movies of the 1970s, and perhaps of all time."[122] So I want to entertain two other possibilities that I believe better explain the changing status of the film.

Mikey and Nicky in some ways follows the reception pattern of cult films like *Freaks* (1932), *Seconds* (1966), *Harold and Maude* (1971), *Phantom of the Paradise* (1974), *The Warriors* (1979), *Labyrinth* (1986), *Bottle Rocket* (1996), *Donnie Darko* (2001), and *Primer* (2004). Cult films attract a niche audience rather than a mass audience. Indeed, what distinguishes a cult film (from just any film with a limited audience) is that the very features that alienate the mass audience exhilarate the niche audience. Cult audiences do not look *past* a cult film's weird, confusing, perverse, outrageous, or otherwise challenging features; those features attract the cult audience. As I noted about the initial critical response to *Mikey and Nicky,* positive and negative reviews often sounded surprisingly similar (remember Kauffmann's "odd, biting, grinning, sideways-scuttling rodent of a picture"), suggesting that, although critics came to opposing evaluations of the film, they often had similar impressions of it.[123] The mangy, bleak, disorienting, uncontrolled, spontaneous, and unsettling qualities of *Mikey and Nicky* alienated a mass audience (along with most critics in the seventies) but exhilarated viewers who were attracted to those sorts of challenges. But cult audiences have to find a film before they can appreciate it, and cult films, because they flop in the mainstream, can be hard for viewers to find. *Mikey and Nicky* had its champions from the beginning, but it took decades of theatrical rereleases and video releases before its audience became sizable enough to warrant a full-scale reappraisal. You had to know about *Mikey and Nicky* before you fell in love with it.

Finally, and most persuasively, I believe, it can take time, multiple viewings, and critical distance from a film's initial negative reception and troubled production history before masses of people come to appreciate challenging movies like *Mikey and Nicky*. Other Hollywood films have similarly undergone reevaluations over time, including *Citizen Kane* (1941), *Vertigo* (1958), *Touch of Evil* (1958), *Apocalypse Now* (1979), *Raging Bull* (1980), and *Blade Runner* (1982). These films were too complex or too novel for masses of viewers to grasp initially. Repeated exposure offered opportunities for viewers to manage the films' more challenging features.[124] The films' complexity, novelty, and artistic audacity caused them to suffer theatrically, but those very features also explain the films' enduring appeal among devoted fans. After almost fifty years of theatrical rereleases, cable television showings, video releases, and recent showings on streaming services, viewers have now had plenty of opportunities to experience and reexperience *Mikey and Nicky*. And with a movie like *Mikey and Nicky*, which rewards repeat viewings, the opportunities tend to snowball: as more people watch and rewatch the movie, it gains more attention, which warrants another release.

May had been working on *Mikey and Nicky* since she was a teenager, and now more people than ever are appreciating and contemplating her movie. The story of its production and reception, as I have laid it out here, is itself worthy of contemplation and appreciation.

Some of May's production difficulties resulted from bad luck, including a change in leadership at Paramount from Frank Yablans, who supported the film, to Barry Diller, who did not. She dealt with actor delays, technical fiascos, lawsuits, and criminal charges, all of which threatened the production of a film that she nearly did not complete and that, upon completion, almost wasn't released. Most of these difficulties, however, resulted from May's obsession with the project—the very obsession that enabled her to work on it for decades. Then, after screening for only a few weeks, her film almost died in Paramount's vault because the critics and the public hated it.

But May also enjoyed some good fortune and, because of her talent and obsession, managed to persuade key people to help her at key times. She found two leads, Peter Falk and John Cassavetes, whom she regarded as "perfect for the part" and who were also astonishingly good actors, good improvisers, and good friends.[125] They furthermore appreciated her unorthodox directing style and became about as devoted to the project as she was, working on it for years to see it done right. She had a producer, Michael Hausman, who accommodated just about every artistic decision, no matter how unreasonable it seemed or how much it cost or delayed production. She persuaded a former Paramount vice president, Julian Schlossberg, to wrestle the rights to her film from the studio (which would have allowed *Mikey and Nicky* to languish) and to work for decades to give it a proper release. And, after all of that, it turns out that she was right all along. It really was a brilliant film, and decades after she finished it, critics lauded it and the movie found its audience.

It is a helluva story. It would make a good movie.

We know the history of *Mikey and Nicky* as well as the context in which the film was made, so we can now examine the film itself in light of its historical background. The next part of this book analyzes the film's narrative, style, and performances in an effort to understand what makes *Mikey and Nicky* so exhilarating for the viewers who love it.

PART III

MIKEY AND NICKY'S ARTISTIC DESIGN

5 NARRATIVE

None of *Mikey and Nicky* was improvised because you can't improvise something that's that tight a story.

ELAINE MAY, 2023

Many commentators assumed that Peter Falk and John Cassavetes largely improvised *Mikey and Nicky*, provoking Falk to say to one interviewer, "Do they think anybody could get up and improvise a story like this here?! Are they crazy?!"[1] May, Cassavetes, and Falk all insisted that the film had almost no improvised dialogue, and a comparison of the shooting script to the film itself mostly bears out their statements. The film, however, clearly gives the impression of improvisation, and in this chapter we examine the way May created a narrative that feels at once tight and unified but also spontaneous, nuanced, and real. The chapter also investigates thematic issues, genre issues, characterization, narrative structure, and the aesthetic effects of *Mikey and Nicky*'s narrative.

Narrative is a broad term that refers to all the ways in which artworks connect events and tell stories. The academic study of narrative (known as *narratology*) offers analytic tools for understanding different aspects of a narrative. Three distinct approaches have emerged, each of which examines a separate aspect. David Bordwell identifies them as representation, structure, and narration.[2]

First, when we study *representation*, we endeavor to understand the content and meaning of a narrative—what Bordwell calls narrative "semantics." This aspect of narratology includes, for example, most studies of characterization, realism (how closely the work seems to represent the real world), themes (male friendship, betrayal, etc.), or other denotative components of a narrative.

Second, one can examine narrative as a *structure*—what Bordwell calls the "syntax" of narrative—the ways in which plot elements "combine to create a distinctive whole."[3] Examples include studies of act structures and scene structures, the organization of central and peripheral story information, or the formal relationships between separate plot elements.

Finally, we can study *narration*—what Bordwell describes as the "dynamic process of presenting a story to a receiver." When studying narration (the technical term for storytelling), we examine narrative as a temporal process that cues viewers to perform mental activities (make connections between scenes, generate expectations and hypotheses, or feel curiosity, surprise, or suspense).[4] This third approach to the study of narrative attempts to understand the function of a narrative's individual moments and their cognitive effects on audiences.

This chapter takes all three approaches—studying representation, structure, and narration in turn—because each illuminates important features of *Mikey and Nicky*'s narrative design. We will see the ways in which May's script offered more than just a blueprint for shooting, which is the traditional function of a shooting script; it afforded her actors performance opportunities. That is, it gave them opportunities to add nuance, complexity, and density to the moment-by-moment telling of the story.

Representation and Narrative Meaning

The scenario, one friend setting up another to be killed, offers a heightened version of the emotional conflicts that can plague relationships between men who knew each other as children—not just the aggression, rivalries, and resentments but also the affection, familiarity, intimacy, and fun that men share, and the way in which they mix in an emotional cauldron of loyalty, excitement, history, hurt, and hatred. May's script captured all of that, an impressive artistic accomplishment in itself. As a female scriptwriter, she observed things about men and male friendship that we do not normally see in movies. Cassavetes said about her, "Being a woman, Elaine can be more objective about the relationship between Mikey and Nicky. She can bring more insight to it."[5] Mikey, we come to understand, feels so hurt by years of slights and petty betrayals that he is willing to help the bosses kill Nicky. It is a daring concept for a story, potentially far-fetched, yet plausible within the context of May's complex portrayal of male friendship.

May's story also enables us to see what attracts Mikey to Nicky and why, after the cemetery scene, he seems determined for a while to help his friend escape. Over the years, the two men may have been close only sporadically, but the story depicts them as deeply connected. In the cemetery, Nicky reminds Mikey of their long history and shared memories: "I wish my mother was alive, and I wish your mother was alive, and I wish your father was alive, and I wish my father was alive, and I wish your brother Izzy was alive." Several throwaway lines further reveal their deep, long-standing connection, such as, "What way am I gonna see you I haven't seen you before?" and "Everyone we knew when we were kids is dead." Their memories help justify, in the minds of the audience, Mikey's years of loyal friendship to a man who seems mostly to aggravate and upset him.

When we see Mikey with the two other key people in his life—his boss, Dave Resnick (Sanford Meisner), and his wife, Annie (Rose Arrick)—we understand his connection to Nicky even better. With Resnick, Mikey seems apprehensive: "Dave, you know I'm sorry you don't like me, and I'm sorry I make you nervous." Resnick scoffs, but Mikey's line introduces an emotional vulnerability with his employer that we are not used to seeing in gangster movies. As for his wife, Annie lacks basic knowledge about him. She does not know the meaning of Mikey's watch, which she refers to simply as "your good watch," and does not even know that Mikey had a brother who died. When we witness Mikey with these other characters, we understand better how much his relationship with Nicky might mean to him. Nicky is his only friend.

May clearly worked hard to enrich the characterizations of her two leads. Mikey, despite limited self-understanding, has a complex emotional life that seems ill suited to the gangster world he lives in. He reveals his insecurity with lines like "because I'm stupid" and, when telling the story about his father giving Izzy the watch, "But that was just because he was sick that he gave it to him. He meant it for me." Each scene with Mikey adds complexity to his feelings toward Nicky. On the one hand, he is so angry at Nicky that he wants him dead ("he's crazy and a prick"), but on the other, he is so distraught by his role in the hit that he desperately tries to leave the hit man's car when he thinks the man is about to shoot Nicky.

Nicky, too, has a complex psychology that is both inconsistent and plausible. May could have made Nicky a stereotypical sociopath, manipulating others for his own benefit, but at times Nicky seems more self-destructive than self-serving ("stupidly mischievous," May called him),[6] squandering Mikey's help by humiliating him with Nellie (Carol Grace). May gave Nicky sympathetic qualities, too, including a desire to see his wife and child before he leaves town. She also gave him moments of self-insight. Nicky seems to know how badly he has treated his friend ("I did too much to him") and says to Nellie, "Hell, I don't know what's wrong with me. I guess I just like to show off." Such lines reveal surprising introspection for a character whose main traits are guile and impulsiveness. Nicky, in a way, knows himself.

Aside from *Mean Streets* (1973), Hollywood had never released a gangster film so focused on the emotional lives of its characters. The gangster genre situates the story of Nicky and Mikey within a familiar scenario, but the film does not follow any of the gangster film formulas that Hollywood developed in the studio era, such as the rise-and-fall saga seen in *Scarface* (1932) or the gangster-tries-to-go-straight variation featured in *The Roaring Twenties* (1939).[7] Both *Scarface* and *The Roaring Twenties* depict a gangster who betrays his partner, but neither film explores the interpersonal tragedy of the scenario.

The same may be said of gangster films that featured storylines more similar to *Mikey and Nicky*, in which a gangster, or undercover cop, sets up his friend. Undercover policeman Hank Fallon (Edmond O'Brien), after pretending to befriend gangster Cody Jarrett (James Cagney) in *White Heat* (1949), sets him up to be arrested and, without a second thought, shoots him repeatedly with a long-range rifle. (*Donnie Brasco* [1997] later explored the emotional consequences on the policeman who betrays a gangster he has befriended.) In *On the Waterfront* (1954), Terry Malloy (Marlon Brando) sets up his neighbor Joey Doyle (Ben Wagner) for a Mob hit but does it unknowingly ("I thought they was gonna talk to him"). Michael Corleone (Al Pacino) sets up his brother-in-law in *The Godfather* (1972) and watches the execution without remorse. Unlike these earlier crime films, *Mikey and Nicky* centers on the human tragedy of the scenario (troubled friendship, betrayal, feelings of guilt, knowledge of impending death), a tragedy not just for the condemned man but for the friend who fingers him.

Quotidian details, moreover, add genre-inappropriate nuances to the gangster plot. Unlike the glamorized killers of *The Godfather*, these gangsters have prosaic concerns. The Mob boss gets annoyed by bickering between his employees. The hit man misses his mark because he gets lost and can't find parking. He later worries that he won't make money on the job after expenses. Combined with a focus on the gangsters' complex emotional lives, such details add psychological realism and humanize characters that gangster films normally depict in stereotype.

Narrative Structure

The film relies on the structural properties characteristic of tight Hollywood scripts, including obstacles (fights between the lead characters, Nicky's erratic behavior and paranoia), deadlines ("When the hand hits 9:25, I'm gonna be back"; "When you hear the phone ring, I want you out of the bar on the street"), and solid causal connections between scenes. More so than most Hollywood movies, *Mikey and Nicky* obeys Aristotle's three unities: unity of *time* (the movie takes place over one night without noticeable temporal breaks), *place* (it features contiguous settings around Philadelphia), and *action* (the planned hit on Nicky unifies and motivates all the main narrative actions). The hit also provides May with a through line that her script can return to in order to prevent narrative detours (such as an interlude in a candy store) from derailing the plot.

One can observe the care May devoted to script structure by noting various motifs in her plotting. Mikey's watch serves as a unifying device from the first scenes in Nicky's hotel room until the final scenes in Mikey's home. Mikey gives Nicky the watch before he dashes to the coffee shop for cream. When Nicky later wants to hold on to the watch "for luck," Mikey swaps it for Nicky's gun. He later tries to swap back, but Nicky smashes the watch to thwart his friend's effort to leave, and they proceed to pick up the pieces on the street. Mikey then laments the loss when talking to the hit man and, toward the end of the film, tells Annie the story of receiving the watch from his father after the death of his brother, Izzy.

Other motifs generate connections between scenes outside of the narrative's causal logic. At various times, for instance, the characters hold conversations through doors (at Nicky's hotel room, his mother-in-law's apartment, Nellie's home, and Mikey's home at the end) and ultimately attempt to break down the doors in frustration, sometimes succeeding. The door motif creates scene harmonies that exist outside causality: Nicky doesn't bang on Mikey's door *because* he banged on Nellie's door, but it is the kind of action that happens in this movie. The effort to bang down a door also serves as a framing device, connecting an early scene, when Mikey first tries to get into Nicky's hotel room, to the end, when Nicky desperately tries to get into Mikey's home before he is killed. Such motifs unify the film, connecting scenes, settings, characters, and actions from beginning to end.

Judging from critical responses, however, viewers do not experience *Mikey and Nicky* as all that unified. The fact that many critics assumed the film was improvised suggests a more haphazard structure. We can attribute that impression, I believe, to two characteristics of *Mikey and Nicky*'s plotting: its unusual density and its emphasis on peripheral story information. Both characteristics complicate the classical Hollywood storytelling structure and clutter the film's neat causal design.

Let us first consider the narrative's density.

Elaine May writes scenes in which several things happen at once. According to Phillip Schopper, who supervised the restoration of *Mikey and Nicky* for Criterion, May said to him several times that every scene in a movie must concern more than one thing.[8] May's scenes might have five or ten different things going on. Schopper gave as an example the two-minute scene in which we first meet the hit man, Warren Kinney (Ned Beatty), talking on the telephone. This brief scene confirms the hit on Nicky, but consider how much additional narrative information it reveals: that the hit man has a hotel room and needs a street map, which tells us that he comes from another town, justifying a later scene in which Kinney gets lost; that the person on the other end of the line (who might be Mikey) is setting up the hit and has access to Nicky's location; that Kinney has up-to-date information about Nicky's clothes, even though Nicky changed his coat and jacket moments earlier; and that there is a time limit ("I figure fifteen, twenty minutes from here") and a signal for his arrival ("I'll let the phone ring three times"). All these details motivate later narrative events. The scene delivers much of this crucial information simultaneously—"instead of step-by-step in an exposition dump," Schopper explained—layering the scene with narrative meaning.[9]

Almost every scene in *Mikey and Nicky* has that sort of density. Early scenes in Nicky's hotel room establish the scenario, the reasons for the hit, Nicky's ulcer, the watch motif, the door-banging motif, Nicky's suspicions of Mikey, the long-term friendship between the two leads, their profession, the characters' mental states, and countless subtleties of characterization that come into play later in the movie. The scenes in the B&O bar overtly establish that Mikey is setting up Nicky and that Nicky is growing more suspicious of his friend, but we also learn about their marriages and children, including Nicky's concern about seeing his wife ("I've gotta say goodbye") and newborn ("If they don't see you for a while, they forget your face"). We learn about the mechanics of the hit, Mikey and Nicky's plans to escape, and the fact that, despite Mikey's efforts to remain in the bar, Nicky is restless. Much of this information enters the scene by the way (some of it seems like mere dialogue chatter), but all of it proves crucial to the story and becomes a hinge in the narrative structure: remove one hinge, and later events won't connect so tightly.

Now let us consider the film's emphasis on peripheral story information—that is, information that does not provide a hinge in the narrative structure but rather pulls our attention away from the main storyline.

Unlike most Hollywood films, which focus viewer attention on a central narrative (making a drug bust, fighting the Galactic Empire, killing a shark), *Mikey and Nicky* sometimes fixates on events that surround the central narrative, mostly character nuances. May's memorable population of side characters illustrates the film's preoccupation with narrative peripherals. In chapter 2, I noted that side characters in May's *A New Leaf* (1971) seem designed merely to serve narrative functions, holding little interest in themselves. In *The Heartbreak Kid* (1972), I said, she developed some more nuanced side characters, particularly Kelly's father and mother. In *Mikey and Nicky*, however, May seemed determined to exploit any opportunity to create viewer interest in each character that her leads encounter.

She exploited those opportunities everywhere the two men go, creating an entire world of personalities—a malcontented hit man, a distracted counterman, a pugnacious bus driver, a snarky bus rider—out of roles that other scriptwriters would afford no distinctive characterization at all. Her paranoid candy store owner (Martin Wolfson) casually reaches for a handgun while talking to Nicky, a surprisingly ominous gesture for an old man who barely moves. Although unpleasant at first ("What you see there is what I've got"), the man later seems to want to compensate for his earlier rudeness by making conversation ("I don't think they make Necco anymore"). He has a droopy bottom lip that suggests he has had a stroke. Unlike the side characters we typically encounter in Hollywood cinema, each one of May's characters is individuated and interesting, not one of them a type.

May avoids the clichés of a "Black bar" that pervaded films of the seventies, such as *The French Connection* (1971), *Shaft* (1971), and countless so-called Blaxploitation movies, which featured dingy-looking bars populated with pimps, strippers, and drug dealers. By contrast, May's bar is middle class, with well-dressed patrons, a wholesome atmosphere, and appealing music and decor. It looks like a real community. Mel (Eugene Hobgood), whom Nicky provokes, shows both politeness and nerve during their confrontation. The other patrons' efforts to mollify Nicky suggest their extensive experience handling racists.

Subtleties in the dialogue contribute to the interest of the side characters by making each of them more nuanced. When Kinney explains to Resnick why he was late to the B&O bar, the hit man says, "So any estimation of time which I may have given him is dependent on the fact that he knows what I've got to get through." Kinney's laborious phrases ("estimation of time which I may have given him," "dependent on the fact") sound stiff and official, suggesting the character's insecurity as he attempts to compensate for Mikey's criticisms and his own failure to complete the hit. Nellie normally speaks with poise ("I'm very interested to see what happens in Indochina") and often sounds prim ("Oh please, stop it Nicky"), but when Nicky infuriates her, her entire style of speech changes. She screams, "I never laid Moe Schatz, you liar!" Such a vulgar line would only come out of Nellie when she has lost her composure, and her speech at that point reveals a raw, less refined side to her character.

The peripheral characters do not just draw our attention away from the central storyline; they also contribute to the density of the narrative. May establishes Mikey and Nicky's home lives in very little screen time, hinting at rich backstories. The scene between Nicky and his wife, Jan (Joyce Van Patten), signals not just a troubled marital life but their specific troubles ("Is this the way your girlfriends treat you?" "Is everybody else busy tonight?") and their long-standing efforts to deal with them. Jan's response to Nicky's statement that the bosses are going to kill him—"I'm not interested," she says, "Why are you telling this to me?"—indicates a determination to rid herself of caring about her husband after years of false promises and hurt. Other lines suggest the intimacy of their marriage. Her line, "People get angry when you steal their money," tells us not only that Nicky did indeed steal from Resnick but that he told his wife about it. Nicky's efforts to hug, kiss, and appease her ("I did this for you") show us the behaviors that have helped win her back in the past. When she softens at the end of the scene—kissing him, crying, and blocking his exit—we witness the lifetime pattern of their marriage.

Even Jan's mother (Virginia Smith), who has no lines, has a personality and a relationship with her son-in-law. She shows distrust and concern as she sheepishly spies on Nicky and Jan's conversation from the hallway. When Nicky walks past her to see his infant daughter, the mother appears frightened at first, stiffening her back and eyeing him suspiciously, yet when he gently cups her chin, she cannot help but soften her gaze and touch his arm in what looks like an involuntary gesture, an instinctive penchant to show him tenderness. Their behavior together, which lasts mere seconds, suggests a history of affection between them.

May could have made Mikey's wife, Annie, a comfortable stereotype—knowing, kind, and loyal, like Vito's wife in *The Godfather*. But Annie's responses to her husband seem strangely off base. Unlike Nicky and Jan, Mikey and his wife seem disconnected, their scenes together lacking any display of intimacy. Annie acts overly polite, as though the long-married partners are still having first dates. She treats their toddler with more natural politeness ("Harry, would you bring me a crayon? Crayola?"), but her interaction with Mikey seems stiff and affected. When she says to Mikey about his father, "I'm sure he liked you, too," she misses the whole point of Mikey's story, offering him bland, and inappropriate, reassurance. After less than two hours with Mikey, we know him better than she does.

In designing *Mikey and Nicky*'s narrative, May combined a classical Hollywood structure—featuring protagonists with clearly defined goals and obstacles and various narrative deadlines, unities, and running motifs—with dense plot details, some of which have only peripheral relevance to the main storyline. The classical structure provides a solid foundation for the film, a jumping-off point for what is most interesting about it: nuances within the film's depiction of characters, incidents, relationships, and backstories—nuances that add complexity, subtlety, and density to the classical plot patterning.

Narration

Whereas the analysis of *representation* and meaning articulates what *Mikey and Nicky* is about, and the analysis of *structure* studies the film's narrative composition, the analysis of *narration* explains the moment-by-moment experience of the plot. Narration looks at narrative as an act, a series of pragmatic cues that spark responses from viewers.

We can study, for example, the way in which the film doles out story information in intervals, causing viewers to continually generate and revise hypotheses about what has happened, what will happen, and what is happening at the moment. Let us analyze *Mikey and Nicky*'s moment-by-moment narration to see how the film cues viewers to construct various hypotheses about story events.

During the first twenty-five minutes of the film, audiences are likely curious to answer two key questions: is there indeed a hit on Nicky, and is Mikey trying to help his friend avoid it? The narration cues us to construct more- or less-probable hypotheses in answer to each question by carefully restricting our access to story information. When we first meet Nicky, for instance, he seems paranoid, perhaps delusional, which suggests that the bosses may not have contracted to kill him after all. But eventually Mikey starts to believe him, making the hit more credible. Although Nicky seems suspicious of Mikey, Mikey's behavior signals that he sincerely wants to help his friend avoid the hit. Mikey, after all, brought Nicky ulcer pills and even eats one himself to show Nicky they are not poisoned. And he desperately rushes to bring Nicky milk and cream. When Mikey says, "I'm gonna get you outta town," he sounds sincere. By the time they leave the hotel (about nineteen minutes into the movie), we have two highly probable hypotheses: there is a hit on Nicky, and Mikey will try to help him escape.

Later scenes confirm one hypothesis and upend the other. The film dispels any doubts about the hit when we see a hit man with pictures of Nicky (21 minutes), explaining to someone we do not see the plan to complete the hit at the B&O bar. But the moment the film settles our question about the hit on Nicky, it raises doubts about Mikey. When shots of the hit man on his hotel phone cut to Mikey on a telephone in a bar (22 minutes), the editing suggests that the two characters are having a conversation. We now have reason to believe that Mikey is in on the hit. But that hypothesis contradicts our earlier understanding that, despite Nicky's suspicions, Mikey is genuinely concerned about his friend. Discussing this moment from the movie on his podcast, Quentin Tarantino called the prospect that Mikey is fingering his friend "unfathomable."[10] So perhaps the cut from the hit man to Mikey on the telephone was just an unintended implication, or perhaps the film is mischievously raising unfounded doubt. Mikey, after all, does not behave as though he was just talking to a hit man, casually explaining to Nicky the airline information he has gathered on the phone. Still, we now have two hypotheses in conflict—Mikey is trying to help Nicky escape, and Mikey is setting up his friend—and reasons to believe each one.

The scene in the B&O bar confirms the second hypothesis, but the narration does so in stages, doling out story information in bits. First, Mikey tries to delay leaving the bar, then drinks his beer for an awkwardly long time, then grows nervous about the clock, then thinks he heard the phone ring, as though waiting for the hit man's call (27 minutes). Although we have, since the opening scenes, relied on the understanding that Mikey is working as hard as he can to help Nicky, we can no longer confidently maintain that hypothesis. What had seemed "unfathomable" now seems incontrovertible: it has all been a setup, even in the hotel room and the diner, when Mikey seemed so determined to get his friend to safety.

But the film maintains our curiosity by withholding key story information about Mikey's motivations. Again, May manipulates our understanding so that we generate hypotheses that help us make sense of story events. We might hypothesize, for instance, that Mikey does not want to finger his friend. His strangely distracted behavior toward Nicky on the bus (38 minutes) reinforces that hypothesis. Another scene on a bus, after the cemetery, leads us to believe that Mikey is so loath to help the bosses kill Nicky that he now intends to help his friend escape. "Yeah, you sonofabitch, I'm coming with you!" (54 minutes). Mikey won't go through with the setup after all; their friendship is too strong.

But the hypothesis that Mikey will not help the bosses grows less probable during the argument on the street (67 minutes). We learn the history of Nicky's malicious behavior toward Mikey, which justifies Mikey's previous efforts to help get him killed and his later efforts to help Kinney find Nicky (77 minutes). We finally understand Mikey's conflicted attitude toward the hit, a conflict further revealed when he wants to get out of Kinney's car before the hit (90 minutes), when he tries to convince Resnick not to allow the hit man to wait for Nicky near Mikey's home (94 minutes), and when Mikey bars Nicky from his house before Nicky is shot at the film's end (105 minutes).

The narrational analysis above indicates the ways in which May's script precisely controls viewer comprehension, causing viewers to generate or revise both curiosity hypotheses (there is or isn't a hit on Nicky; Mikey is or isn't setting up his friend) and suspense hypotheses (Mikey will or won't go through with it; Nicky will or won't be killed) until the end, when the narration answers all of our key questions. Each hypothesis seems more or less probable depending on the information the narration has given us at a given moment. The film periodically surprises viewers, keeping us on guard for some new revelation that alters the plot trajectory or that explains in retrospect what we have already witnessed. The characters themselves do not change much, but our understanding of them changes and grows increasingly complex.

Mikey and Nicky deftly handles viewer comprehension, but all Hollywood movies, we can say, conceal or reveal story information in a controlled manner in order to cue viewers to form curiosity and suspense hypotheses.[11] This tight control of story information affords Hollywood movies a feeling of omniscience—the movie knows all but is telling us only in bits. *Mikey and Nicky*, however, feels more unpredictable than other Hollywood movies, leading reviewers to call it "rambling" and "confused." It lacks the cool control that we expect from Hollywood movies in part, I want to argue, because May tends to deliver story information obliquely. Most Hollywood movies convey events and character intentions directly, through visible character action, exposition, or explicit dialogue (*Gone with the Wind*'s "I'll never be hungry again"). *Mikey and Nicky*, by contrast, often conveys key story information through subtext and performance. The film invites viewers to make inferences based on indirect plot cues and subtleties in the actors' behavior. Hence, the movie inspires active observation and inferential reasoning.

May developed her oblique storytelling skills creating comedy routines with Mike Nichols, where much of the humor resulted from the things their characters do not say. When a boss compliments his secretary's expert photocopying ("Your average girl isn't going to care, you see"), we understand that he really just wants to get her into bed. When a female doctor asks her attractive male patient, "Does your wife cook for you?" we know that she is really trying to determine whether he is married. When one of May's characters says on the phone, "This is your mother. Do you remember me?" we understand that she feels overlooked and wants her son to know it. Humor, in these scenes, results from the incongruity between what characters say and what we infer. Characters beat around the bush, revealing their motives not directly but through subtext, leaving audience members to infer the real meanings behind the dialogue.

Mikey and Nicky conveys meaning in much the same way. The characters rarely articulate their motivations directly. Mikey never says, for instance, "I'm going to help kill that guy for how he's treated me all these years," but when he says to Nicky, "You make me out a joke to Resnick, just like you made me out a joke to that girl, and I'd do anything for you," we can infer the reasons he is helping the bosses. This is a key piece of plot information—it explains the primary motivation for everything Mikey has done so far—but no one in the movie articulates it; we figure it out.

In scene after scene, the movie cues us to deduce character motivations and mental states from subtext rather than direct articulations. In the cemetery scene, Nicky's line, "Things that happened when we were kids that no one else knows about but us, it's in our heads," suggests that he is thinking about his own death, or that he wants to express closeness to Mikey, or perhaps that he is manipulating Mikey so that Mikey will continue to help him. Mikey replies, "What are you talking about? I know what really happened when I was a kid. . . . And I tell Annie about a lot of things that happened to me when I was a kid, and she enjoys listening to that." Mikey's line leads us to infer that he is trying to distance himself from Nicky, that he wants to believe that he has others in his life who are just as important to him as Nicky, and that Mikey feels uneasy about setting him up. And later, when Mikey says to Annie, "Do you enjoy hearing stories about when I was a kid?" we make the connection to the cemetery scene and infer, perhaps, that Mikey is now trying to justify his earlier statement to Nicky or else justify the loss of the one person in his life who knew him as a child. When later, in the same scene, he says to her, "Nick Godolin knew Izzy. Nick Godolin knew my mother from my father. And my Aunt Rose," we infer a whole new set of unarticulated emotions. Someone like Mikey would never say explicitly, "This man, who is going to die, is an important person in my life." He is too immature for that kind of insight, and May knows it. So instead she has him say, "Nick Godolin knew Izzy." We do the rest.

So far, I have focused on indirect dialogue, but we find some of the most expressive examples of oblique storytelling in the performances. *Mikey and Nicky* relies on actors to deliver story information through intonation, body language, and facial expression. When you read Hollywood movie scripts, it often seems that the writers are struggling to make a script *actor-proof* by conveying story information with utmost clarity. It is a reasonable approach to script writing. Scripts are not novels. Readers must convert the script into moving images in their head, which is tricky. Scripts are read by agents, executives, and their assistants, who may not understand a story told obliquely. Scripts, moreover, must serve as blueprints for production, a set of instructions for the creative participants. Actors may not understand their characters if dialogue is ambiguous. The director may not understand parts of the story unless the writer ensures that every important piece of story information is articulated in the script through either overt action or dialogue. Action and dialogue are the primary ways in which scriptwriters exert control over a production that, in most cases, will fall out of their hands as soon as they submit their final draft.

An accomplished actor herself, May knew what actors could bring to a scene that a script may only hint at. Commentators describe Elaine May as an "actor's director," but she is also an actor's writer; she constructs scenes so that actors have interesting things to do. In *Mikey and Nicky*, her actors deliver some of the most important story information through their performances, information that other scriptwriters would deliver through character action, lines of dialogue, or some other overt narrative device.[12] Indeed, most Hollywood screenwriters look at scenes primarily as opportunities for story development—moving the story from A to B. May seems to look at scenes as performance possibilities—opportunities for actors to do something exciting. So she allows the actors' performances to move the story forward.

As an example, let us consider the scene in the B&O bar when we learn that Mikey is setting up Nicky. The moment completely upends the story, but their dialogue (almost identical in the script and movie) is innocuous:

MIKEY: Hot in here, huh?
NICKY: Yeah.
MIKEY: Are you okay? Your stomach okay?
NICKY: Fine.
MIKEY: Eat some crackers. Was that the phone?
NICKY: I don't know. You expecting a call?
MIKEY: What?
NICKY: Nothing.
MIKEY: That would be funny, wouldn't it? Some guy using a bar as an office.
NICKY: Let's get out of here.

The performances, not the dialogue, convey the meaning of this key scene. Mikey eyes Nicky intently, looks up at the clock, wipes sweat from his forehead. As he says, "Some guy using a bar as an office," he scratches his face, takes a deep breath, crunches his mouth; he is nervous. Nicky stares at Mikey suspiciously. Mikey, we now understand, is setting Nicky up, and Nicky seems to know it. And how do we know Nicky knows it? His line, "Let's get out of here," merely hints at the realization, but before the line we see it in Cassavetes's slowly changing facial expression (figure 5.1a–d).

May not only lets the actors' performances bear the weight of the storytelling; she relies on her actors to find the emotional interest of each scene. Consider the very end of the film, when the hit man shoots Nicky in front of Mikey's home. It is a dramatic scene, and commentators, even some who hated the movie, regularly remarked on the extraordinary ending, calling it "harrowing," "brilliant," "a powerful wallop of an ending," and "one of the great final scenes of any American film from the 1970s."[13] In 2021, *New York* magazine listed it among the "101 Greatest Endings in Movie History."[14] Shooting a man trying to escape does not itself make a scene powerful; we find similar scenarios throughout film history. *Mikey and Nicky*'s ending is powerful because May's script gave

FIGURE 5.1A–D. *Mikey and Nicky* conveys Nicky's suspicion of Mikey not through dialogue but rather through Cassavetes's changing facial expression in a single shot.

the actors opportunities to fill in their characters' emotional experience of the moment.

The following excerpt from the shooting script shows us what May gave the actors to work with. It depicts the moment right before Nicky is shot, as he tries to convince Annie to let him into the house.

MIKEY
(Softly) Run, schmuck. Why won't you run.

NICK
Honey, I think you better let me in. Annie! Annie let me in. ANNIE!

(He begins hurling his body against the door. The door trembles and MIKEY quickly bolts it and then begins pushing furniture in front of it. He nods to ANNIE and, without speaking, she helps him.)

NICK
Annie? Could you open the door? Oh, PLEASE, Annie, open the door. Annie? I don't feel good. Annie I'm gonna be sick. Oh, PLEASE Annie. Annie . . . Annie . . . Annie . . .
(He breaks off and there is the sound of retching)
Oh no, oh no, oh no, oh, no! Oh, please! Get me a doctor! Please get me a doctor! Wait, please! Mikey, get me a doctor. I'm perforating. Mikey! Wait, you got to wait. I don't feel good. Mikey! Get me a doctor.

(There is the sound of a shot, then another.)[15]

There are several things to say about the effect on the audience of this scene, which looks so blank on the page but in performance is gut wrenching.

For one thing, staging Nicky's murder outside Mikey's home, with Mikey and Annie inside, adds emotional complexity to the scenario. We contemplate the scene from the perspective of all three characters: Nicky desperately trying to get into the house, Mikey desperately trying to keep him out, and a baffled Annie trying to help her husband. The scene cuts between Nicky's panic outside to the stress inside, Mikey leaning his head on the door, aghast at Nicky's wailing, Annie looking to her husband for guidance. Mikey's facial expression shows how distraught and angry he is and the devastating impact on him of witnessing his friend's inevitable murder, which he has helped cause. His line, "Run, schmuck," suggests furthermore that he still cares about his friend. And what must Annie be thinking? She does not know about the hit on Nicky, but after having worked so hard to convince him to leave, she helps her husband bar the door. Each character's perspective is interesting in itself, and together they generate a complex scene of growing desperation—Mikey and Annie ultimately shoving furniture against the door, Nicky banging his whole body against it, the door rattling with each thrust—all climaxing at the instant that Nicky is shot.

The emotional core of the scene is Nicky's panicked effort to stay alive. The script signals that panic with lines that indicate the character's fixation on getting in the house by convincing Annie that he is sick. The lines give the actor an overall strategy for the scene but leave it to the actor to flesh out the scene's emotional development. Nicky, the script suggests, has committed to a losing strategy and cannot seem to change it, even when death is imminent. In an earlier scene, after Nicky breaks Mikey's watch, he deftly shifts tactics in an effort to keep Mikey from leaving: he jokes ("You don't have the time, do you?"), pacifies ("I think I know a guy who can put it together again"), bargains ("You want another one?"), apologizes ("I'm sorry about the watch"), minimizes his own bad behavior ("What's the difference? I was kidding"), contradicts ("Mikey, you're wrong"), pleads ("Please don't walk out on me"), antagonizes ("Screw you"), delays ("Wait a minute"), berates ("What other friends have you got?"), belittles ("You get on his nerves"), and reasons with Mikey ("I'm the one who lent you two hundred dollars when you needed it"). Moments like this suggest a limber mind improvising its way out of trouble.

In his murder scene, however, Nicky gets stuck onto one track and cannot get off. When Nicky sees the hit man's car, Cassavetes rhythmically chants, "Annie, Annie, Annie," but then amps up the energy as his desperation grows: he coughs, then pretends to retch, then wails that his ulcer is perforating. And how does Cassavetes deliver May's line "Wait, please!" which is buried in Nicky's dialogue? He turns directly to the hit man himself and pleads with him, as if to say, "Hold on because I'm going to get through this door any second now," a gesture so irrational that I am awed the actor pulled it off.

For most of us nonactors, May's script gives little indication of the scene's power—a panicked Nicky tries to escape a hit and gets killed—but her script gave the actors the material to build each character's emotional experience, which generates the scene's exhilarating effect.

May's oblique storytelling techniques in *Mikey and Nicky* do not violate classical Hollywood narrative norms, but they do make the film more indirect than typical Hollywood movies, and they require spectators to make a series of inferences based on mere hints in the plot. They also, I suspect, led reviewers to falsely assume that the film was largely improvised. The actors, not May, must have made the movie. In their minds, if May had made it, we would see her telling the story: it would be explicit in the dialogue, action, and exposition, just like in other Hollywood movies. But instead we see the actors convey story information through subtext, behavior, facial expression, pacing, and inflection. Whatever interest the film has, those reviewers believed, comes from what the actors did, not what she did. Reviewers did not realize that May's script handed the actors the story to tell. Whereas most Hollywood screenwriters endeavor to make their scripts actor-proof, May wanted to give her actors opportunities to invent. One chief talent of a screenwriter is the ability to know how much of the story to give over to the actors. With the right actors, it turns out, you can give over a lot, but in doing so the writer effaces herself.

6 STYLE

Her technical raggedness is exasperating—the erratic framing and emphysemic editing are an inadvertent parody of Cassavetes's own earlier films without their raw power. Elaine May remains one of the great unresolved potentials of American movies.

JACK KROLL, REVIEW OF *MIKEY AND NICKY*, *NEWSWEEK*, 1976

Initial reviews of *Mikey and Nicky* hammered the film's uncommercial look and sound. In chapter 4, I quoted some of the harsher judgments, but I will refresh your memory: May, they said, was an "amateur" with "an incredibly slapdash hand" who was "not operating at a professional level," had "not yet got the hang of making movies," and had not mastered "the basics of filmmaking."[1] In this chapter, we try to figure out what these reviewers were responding to and to what extent we can say that May created the film's style deliberately. But first I will define what we mean by *style*.

Style denotes the distinctive manner in which a work is presented, shaping our experience of artworks. According to David Bordwell, "Style is the tangible texture of the film, the perceptual surface we encounter as we watch and listen."[2] We analyze style by noting patterns of techniques, either in a single artwork or artist (individual style) or in a collection of works by many artists (group style). The Hollywood group style—which comprises standard practices in cinematography, mise-en-scène (the arrangement of objects put in front of the camera), editing, and sound—gives the movies their commercial appearance. Such practices eliminate or minimize technical imperfections, obvious continuity failures, and anything shoddy or murky in the presentation. Filmmakers working

FIGURE 6.1A–B. A sequence in which shots of Cassavetes are in focus and reverse shots of Falk are out of focus.

in Hollywood generally subordinate their individual style to the group style. May did so on her three other films but not *Mikey and Nicky*. Her perfectionism with regard to the dramatic and performance aspects of production contrasted with a looseness in technical areas that Hollywood filmmakers are normally very strict about, such as focus, continuity, and synchronized sound.

Let us first consider aspects of the film that we can identify as "mistakes," where May is obviously making do with technically imperfect footage.

Style "Mistakes"

Among the first things one observes about *Mikey and Nicky*'s style are the many technical errors. The cinematography does at times come off as "slapdash." The camera shakes, not in the way traditional handheld cameras shake but like it was jostled. Several shots appear out of focus.

Out-of-focus shots could indicate a deliberate stylistic choice, but these are clearly errors. In one part of the hotel room scene, for instance, when Nicky is sitting on the floor, the shots of John Cassavetes are in focus but the reverse shots of Peter Falk are not (figure 6.1a–b). With each cut between the two shots, the contrast is jarring. I suppose one could come up with some interpretation that explains why shots of one actor should be in focus and the other out of focus, but it would be a stretch.

In many scenes, the continuity is off. *Continuity* refers to the continuous presentation of space and time, which involves avoiding noticeable temporal gaps, mismatched mise-en-scène elements, and jarring cuts. In mainstream cinema, continuity is considered a technical rule. *Mikey and Nicky* sometimes violates it. Actors appear in different positions in consecutive shots, or the way they wear their clothing has changed. In the hotel room, Nicky sometimes looks very unshaven and other times only slightly unshaven. In Jan's mother's apartment, sometimes the chain on the front door is broken (suggesting that, in some previous take, Cassavetes must have broken it when he banged on the door) and at other times it isn't. Moreover, things appear in the frame that viewers should not see. In one shot, we can see a camera operator moving in a hotel mirror. Later, when Mikey and Nicky head to the elevator, someone is peeking out of it, presumably a crew member or elevator operator who thought he was out of frame (figure 6.2). In the cemetery scene, you can see a lavalier microphone pinned to Cassavetes's shirt.

Sound and image do not always sync. At various times, May was obviously using the sound from one take and the visuals from another, when characters mouth one thing, but we hear them say something different. The editor sometimes covered up the discontinuity by cutting away from the character who is speaking, cutting to a long shot, or showing a character from behind so that the viewer cannot see how the character's mouth is moving. At other times, the editor relied on the darkness of the image to conceal a mismatch with the soundtrack. Still, it is often fairly obvious that the editor is fudging. In other instances, the editor just accepted the mismatch and did not attempt to cover it up. For instance, at times we see the actors' mouths moving but don't hear them say anything. At other times (including the last two shots of the movie, when Mikey says to Annie, "Would you go to bed?"), we hear the line but the actor's mouth never moves.

FIGURE 6.2. When Mikey talks to Nicky about taking the elevator downstairs, a man is seen peeking out of the elevator at the left side of the frame.

So, how should we think about these "mistakes"? Commentators have explained them in two opposing ways, both unconvincing.

We find one explanation in the film's initial reviews: May doesn't know what she is doing. She hasn't "got the hang of making movies." This explanation would be plausible if not for the fact that her two earlier films do not have such problems. She had a professional crew on *Mikey and Nicky*, just as she did on her other movies, including professional cinematographers, camera operators, editors, and sound technicians. They knew Hollywood's standard practices.

Another explanation is that these are not mistakes at all; they are deliberate stylistic choices. Upon the film's rerelease in the 1980s, the *Wall Street Journal* wrote that the "jerky close-ups" and "unsettling visual exaggeration suits these characters."[3] When the DVD came out in 2004, *American Cinematographer* wrote that the style serves "as the perfect visual corollary to the characters' emotions."[4] IndieWire wrote that the film's style "gives it an almost unbearably naturalistic feel."[5] Justifying the out-of-focus shots, Jeremy Carr wrote, "the camera's erratic focus reflects [Nicky's] own touch-and-go coherence."[6] And Julian Schlossberg said in an interview on the 2019 Criterion Blu-ray, "Elaine did not want a pretty movie."[7] I think in some cases we can regard the "erratic" presentation as a stylistic choice: the style does indeed reflect the hyperactive spirit and spontaneity of the plot and performances. But if all these so-called mistakes are in fact stylistic choices, then May has deliberately alienated a lot of viewers and reviewers for no evident reason. It is not as though she broke new ground stylistically by having a jostling camera, out-of-focus shots, or out-of-sync dialogue. It is not as though a visible crew member or a visible microphone makes *Mikey and Nicky* stylistically innovative. The film, furthermore, is not a Brechtian experiment in spectator alienation; it is a realist drama. If these were deliberate stylistic choices, then I don't know what May was up to.

I want to offer a third idea that I think better explains what we are observing: what if these are indeed mistakes (not deliberate stylistic choices), and what if May knew they were mistakes (she is not incompetent), but she didn't care? Perhaps she included those particular shots and dialogue tracks because she liked something else about them. With all that footage and a professional crew, I find it hard to believe that she could not construct an entire film out of takes that had no technical imperfections or continuity failures. Assistant sound editor Patrick McMahon told me about just such a version of the movie, a "slick" cut composed over several weeks by editor Eric Albertson.[8] May saw that cut and discarded it. Clearly, she did not like those takes and chose different ones. Another director might say, "I love that facial expression, but the focus is soft, so we can't use it," or "I love the way he delivered that line, but we didn't catch him on camera, so it won't sync." In the editing room, May first designed each scene's narrative and emotional development, then made the combination of takes work as best she could, even if technical imperfections remained.[9]

Rather than conceiving of the shot as the central unit of the film's construction, May put the performance at the center. The actors performed the hotel scene "every possible way," according to Cassavetes.[10] After two years in editing, I think that May could have cut a version of the hotel scene in which Falk and Cassavetes were both in focus in every shot, but perhaps she preferred the take with Cassavetes on the floor. So what if the focus on Falk was soft? And she evidently wanted to end the film with that shot of Falk's face, even though he wasn't delivering the film's last line in that take. According to McMahon, "every place where something is out of sync, there was a sync line" that May could have used. But if May "could find a reading of [an] off-camera line that was better than what was happening when the camera was rolling, she would use it."[11] Assistant editor Vaughn Hazell said that May did not like Falk's pronunciation of the word *kaddish* in the graveyard scene and wanted to dupe the word from another take. Hazell explained to her that the background sound would not match, but she proceeded anyway, leaving it to her editors to make it work as best they could, all so that she could get one word performed the way she wanted it.[12] The performance came first, then she figured out a way to make the selected takes work together technically as best she could.

I do not mean to suggest that May did not care at all about continuity. She worked for years in the editing room, matching shots and syncing dialogue. But she seemed willing to surrender a commercial appearance for the combination of dialogue tracks, moving images, and scene design that she preferred. This willingness to neglect Hollywood's standard stylistic practices for the sake of a preferred performance may make her look like an "amateur" filmmaker, but that just means that she was willing to sacrifice continuity and other indicators of technical professionalism for the sake of something she considered artistically more important.

May's willingness to include technical mistakes in her film underscores Hollywood filmmakers' slavish obedience to technical perfection. She is obviously not the only Hollywood filmmaker who has had to choose between a technically commercial take and a preferable take that contained some flaw (soft focus, mismatched mise-en-scène, dialogue out of sync, a microphone or crew member in the shot). Again, we see how May's unorthodox approach to Hollywood filmmaking calls into question the industry's artistic priorities. Indeed, her approach raises what should be an obvious question: why should the more "commercial" take always win the competition between the preferred performance and technical perfection? It may seem obvious that movie studios should not accept technical flaws in their films, but that is only because we are accustomed to Hollywood movies that exert strict control over the medium. Rather than regard technical perfection as a sign of quality, we could look at it as a hang up. Albertson's "slick" cut of *Mikey and Nicky* might have better pleased critics exasperated by May's "erratic" style, but I doubt it was a better movie.

We have no way to know how many otherwise strong takes Hollywood filmmakers have discarded because of technical flaws, but I suspect it happens lots of times. And we don't know how many performances might have been improved if the director had allowed actors to move about a set spontaneously rather than requiring them to hit marks set solely for the benefit of camera operators, gaffers, focus pullers, grips, and editors. Why don't we call those choices "mistakes"? Consider how many movies might have been improved by a willingness to include a flawed outtake or an accident in the shooting process that added something delightful to a scene. An emphasis on flawless technique has led film commentators to valorize Hollywood filmmakers such as Alfred Hitchcock, Martin Scorsese, and Stanley Kubrick, whose films show technical mastery. By the same token, commentators have underrated filmmakers like May, whose style is more unruly, or, to use their term, more *amateurish.*

Deliberate Style

If you make a mistake, repeat it. Jazz theorists call this a "musical save."[13] "If a wrong note comes out, you have to make something out of that note," explains jazz trumpeter Art Farmer. "You can't just let the solo fall apart."[14] Musician Tommy Turrentine says, "Man, you hit a wrong note, and just go to your chromatic." Chromatic notes do not belong to the scale being used, but they embellish a musical piece. Musicians often use chromaticism deliberately to add tension, but chromatic notes can also help a musician recover from mistakes. "Your chromatic will bail you out," says Turrentine.[15] If you continue playing notes chromatically, they start to sound like they belong. What started out as a mistake can become a deliberate style.

Once May permitted technical imperfections in her film, she could let others in, including obstructed camera angles, excessively dim scenes, and disorienting cuts. We will readily notice such things in a Hitchcock film because they would stand out, but in *Mikey and Nicky* they become normal through repetition. We get used to the ragged technique, which becomes the style of the film.

The argument I questioned earlier—that May's erratic technique was not a mistake but a deliberate stylistic choice—has a degree of truth. The technique does imbue her film with a spontaneous, disordered energy similar to what we witness in her lead characters. The style is also naturalistic (true to life, serious, unadorned) and suits the drab ambience of mid-level gangsters who spend the night traipsing from a dingy hotel room through Philadelphia's streets, bars, shops, buses, and apartments. Sound devices contribute to the naturalism. Rather than a musical score, which rarely appears in the film, we hear the sounds of people and spaces—car horns and bus engines, clinking glasses and barroom chatter, a television, a jukebox, a radio.

The camerawork, which is often handheld, also adds to the naturalism, not because shaking cameras are more realistic (they are not) but because we associate a shaking camera with observational documentaries, which record events that have not been staged for the camera. The impression of unstaged action also results from our limited access to characters' faces and physical behavior, as though viewers are watching events from an imperfect vantage, the camera capturing whatever it can at the moment. Hollywood movies generally use highly communicative cinematography. Director Alexander Mackendrick called the viewer "the Invisible Imaginary Ubiquitous Winged Witness."[16] He meant that at each moment filmmakers position the viewer in the most ideal place—to receive story information and anticipate future events—even if the camera defies the laws of physics. *Mikey and Nicky*'s viewers are invisible and imaginary but neither ubiquitous nor winged. The framing may be off, or an object might obscure the actors (figure 6.3a). Sometimes the filmmakers have positioned the camera so that we see neither of the main characters frontally, refusing us access to their faces and making it more difficult to infer their mental states (figure 6.3b). At times, the camera cannot find an ideal position and might even miss part of an action. Hence, *Mikey and Nicky*'s camera is not always fully communicative (it sometimes conceals what we want to know) or fully omniscient (it does not always know what's going to happen next).

Like the cinematography, the lighting is naturalistic. Naturalism does not necessarily mean avoiding artificial techniques. The filmmakers must have used additional lights, for instance, in several scenes in order to illuminate actors' faces—we would have difficulty seeing the fight on the street or faces inside the hit man's car if the filmmakers had used only available street lighting—but May clearly aimed for a naturalistic effect. Except for the last scene, the film takes place entirely at night as the characters move from brightly lit spaces (such as the bus or the B&O

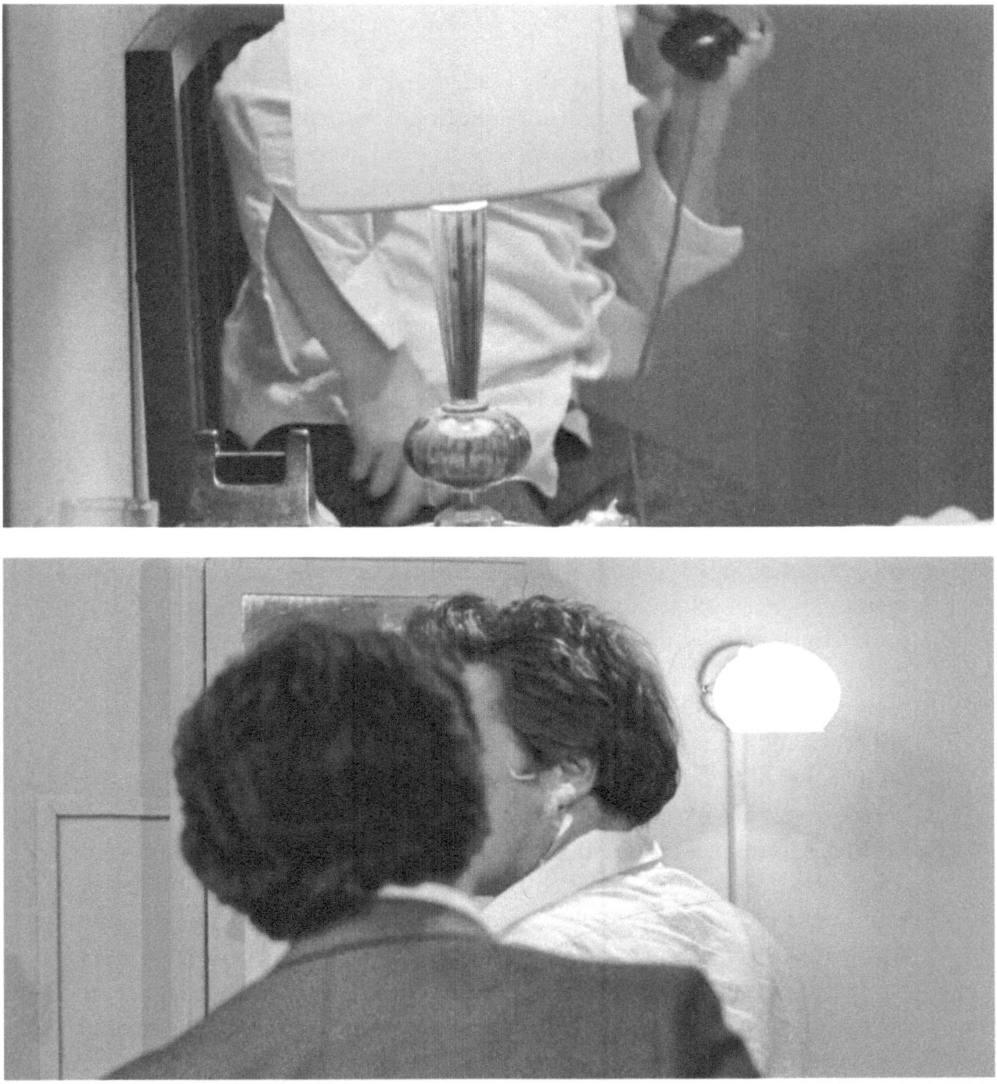

FIGURE 6.3A–B. Framing sometimes denies the viewer access to characters' faces, where we might find information about their mental states.

bar) to dim ones in which one can hardly see the actors (such as the cemetery or Nellie's apartment after Nicky turns out the lights). I considered including images from the cemetery scene for illustration, but they were too dark to print, mostly black frames with outlines of human shapes. This style of cinematography and lighting emblematizes the narration as a whole. It shows the same naturalism and spontaneity that we see in the performances, dialogue, and character behavior—an effort to capture human impulse, lifelike detail, and emotional volatility.

We can observe the same aversion to explicitness and exposition in May's visual style that we saw in the previous chapter on narrative. I would not describe her style as enigmatic—as it is in many art films, like *Odd Obsession* (1959), *Persona* (1966), and *Vagabond* (1985)—but it can be oblique, revealing story and character information indirectly rather than through the camera's focused attention on objects of narrative importance. Camera positioning, for instance, may conceal some of the action (figure 6.3b). We learn some details about the characters (their personalities, mental states, economic status, and situation) indirectly through costuming and set design, which furthermore create a rich ambience for the film: a bent cigarette in Nicky's mouth (figure 6.4a), newspapers strewn on his bed, a table crowded with beer cans and glasses of milk (figure 6.4b). Each time I watch the film, I admire the men's expensive clothing, including Nicky's monogrammed shirt, and grow concerned by their cavalier attitude toward their clothes as they tumble through Philadelphia's dingier settings, particularly in the fight scene, when Mikey's silk suit is tousled as they wrestle on the wet street. We learn all sorts of things about Nicky and Mikey through incidental features of the mise-en-scène and through their attitude toward the objects in their surroundings.

May's loose production methods no doubt contributed to the sometimes obscure and disorganized presentation, particularly in the hotel room scene, when she refused to provide marks for Falk and Cassavetes and instead told the camera operators to follow the actors. Operators have difficulty keeping actors in frame, lit, and in focus when actors have no marks. Furthermore, May's decision to use multiple cameras and multitrack audio, and her tendency to periodically start and stop the camera, led to discontinuities between the image and the dialogue track. But May developed an oblique and disorderly style that suited her production methods, her storytelling technique, and her artistic goals.

Readers familiar with the directorial work of John Cassavetes will recognize a similarity between the style of his independent films and that of May's *Mikey and Nicky*. When people note Cassavetes's influence on *Mikey and Nicky*, I gather they are responding mostly to the dialogue and performance styles, the emphasis on performance itself (combined

FIGURE 6.4A–B. Objects in the mise-en-scène (a bent cigarette, a table crowded with beer cans and glasses of milk) create a rich ambience and add detail to the story and characterizations.

with the presence of Cassavetes and Falk), and the cinematography. Carr notes that *Mikey and Nicky*'s haphazard camerawork and tightly framed shots are unlike those in May's other films. "Here, more like a Cassavetes film," he says, "the camera's position is occasionally extraneous, often obscured (as in *Faces*), and moving in and out of close-up with portions of the action repeatedly obstructed by the backs of people's heads or inanimate objects."[17] May's director of photography, Victor Kemper, also shot Cassavetes's *Husbands* (1970).

But we should not exaggerate the extremity of May's style. May's technique in *Mikey and Nicky* rarely subverts Hollywood's stylistic norms and is certainly less subversive than Cassavetes's technique in *Faces* (1968), *Husbands*, and *A Woman Under the Influence* (1974). May provides establishing shots toward the beginning of each scene—shots that establish the setting, the characters' spatial relations and mental states, and the scene's temporal relationship to the previous scene. Her scenes invariably fall into the shot/reverse-shot pattern typical of Hollywood dialogue scenes, offering us a two-shot of both characters, followed by closer views of each one. And her film style is generally subservient to narrative patterning. When a character pulls a gun, we see the gun. When the narrative requires the characters to make phone calls, we see them on the phone. Cassavetes's films, by contrast, reject many of Hollywood's stylistic imperatives, including the imperative that film style should serve narrative purposes. Cassavetes's camera, unlike May's, will sometimes train on characters who have only peripheral relevance to the main narrative action at the moment, eliding crucial plot information. Whereas Cassavetes's film style often functions independently of whatever story events his films may be depicting, May's style generally serves the telling of her story.

In the last chapter, I noted that May's narrative design is fairly tight and conventional. Although *Mikey and Nicky* has an unusual number of narrative digressions, a focus on character interiority rather than action, and a more oblique and dense form of storytelling than we find in more typical Hollywood cinema, nothing about the film's narrative design violates Hollywood's classical norms. The same is largely true of the film's stylistic design. The argument that some have made, that "*Mikey and Nicky* is the greatest Cassavetes film Cassavetes never made," points to Cassavetes's influence on May but neglects the fact that May was working in a more conventional mode of filmmaking.[18] Within that mode, however, May challenged some of Hollywood's artistic priorities, resisting in particular the pressure to discard a technically imperfect shot in favor of a technically perfect one. As an editor, May, it seems, did not want to reject any takes that would help her create the most engaging scene design. So rather than bind herself to principles of stylistic control that govern most Hollywood filmmaking (and that she followed on her previous films), she embraced a ragged style that gave her license to include shots and sounds "far below professional quality."[19] Admitting so many technically flawed takes into a Hollywood film was her one truly subversive stylistic decision.

7

PERFORMANCE

You experiment, and you fall on your ass.

ELAINE MAY, 1975

In my introduction, I argued that *Mikey and Nicky*'s delights do not stem from any bold or eccentric artistic devices, making it difficult to trace the source of the film's artistic success to anything singular or readily observable. Elaine May's achievement, I argued, derives instead from the moment-by-moment interest of the movie and her efforts to make each scene dense, subtle, and complex. But so far we have barely touched on the acting, the only aspect of the film that earned consistent praise. Great acting is not a bold or eccentric artistic device. Understanding great acting requires close analysis. In this chapter, I analyze the ways in which the performances emerged from May's unorthodox directing techniques and the individual performance styles of John Cassavetes and Peter Falk.

For a film so reliant on performance, *Mikey and Nicky* has no obvious actor showcases. It has nothing like the opening of *Patton* (1970), or the "Attica" scene in *Dog Day Afternoon* (1975), or the "You talkin' to me?" scene in *Taxi Driver* (1976), scenes that broadcast the stars' acting talents and charisma. Instead, *Mikey and Nicky* offers enthralling bits of character interaction—moments of spontaneity, nuance, or unexpected behavior. Except for the scene of Nicky's murder, none of the moments are really clip worthy (We are unlikely to see one in a retrospective of great moments in acting from the American Film Institute or the Oscars), but together they make the film enthralling because they invite viewers to reevaluate a situation, observe something curious in a character's demeanor, or integrate some new behavior into their understanding of a character or a relationship. Such moments did not appear by chance. May and her leads worked night after night over months of shooting to make a moment as minor as ordering cream or riding a bus a performance event.

An Actor's Director

An accomplished actor and improviser herself, May knew how to elicit authentic and spontaneous moments of interest from her actors. According to Cassavetes, "She provides the props, the set, having worked it all out in advance with the prop guys, the art directors and so forth. And she has a concept of character and direction that allows for flexibility in the actor's development of his characterization."[1] In his brief time on set, publicist Tom Miller witnessed May's efforts to get the most out of her performers for even minor scenes. Miller observed May shoot an early scene at a diner in which Mikey tries to get a cup of cream for Nicky, who is having an ulcer attack. Mikey, already hurried and unsettled, has just ten minutes to return to Nicky's hotel room. May convinced her assistant director Peter Scoppa to take the part of the diner counterman who refuses to sell Mikey the cream, which, the man explains, only comes with the purchase of coffee. It is a one-minute scene, not crucial to the plot, but May did fourteen takes, plus five close-ups, and shooting took all night.

Miller's description is worth reprinting at length because it might be the only detailed, firsthand observation of May's working methods. For the diner scene, May sought to create an environment in which Falk might do something spontaneous. She gave no directions to Falk or Scoppa,[2] but when setting up the first take, she looked around vaguely for something the actors could work with.

> And there they were. . . . Doughnuts. . . .
>
> She felt, selected, rejected, and transferred doughnuts for a period of fifteen minutes. Why some were rejected as unfit for camera and others chosen to make their wild cinematic debut was never revealed to those of us who were watching. . . .
>
> I asked Pete Scoppa what had been the point. . . . "For Falk to work with, if he wants. . . . She'll never tell him how to use them.

> . . . Then again he may ignore them. We'll just have to wait and see." . . .
>
> Certainly Peter Falk had been given something to work with. He had his choice of an individual doughnut, the collective doughnuts, the doughnuts and the box together in a cataclysmic orgasm of business, or portioning this wealth of material, first the doughnuts and then the box. Also provided for him were a crumpled napkin, a coffee cup with dregs of coffee remaining, and silverware lying about. Somehow it all came together in my head as confirmation of what John Cassavetes and Peter Falk had both told me about Elaine May: that she is the best actor's director in the business, always giving the actor something to work with. . . .
>
> In his contretemps and frustration with the counterman, Peter Falk attacked the doughnuts in every conceivable way, all on the first take.
>
> He slung them, spit on them, threw them, kicked them, and stomped them. . . . The level of anger and violence exhibited by Falk was totally unexpected. . . . Everyone was watching spellbound, Elaine visibly ecstatic. Falk's performance was totally mesmerizing. . . .
>
> The scene was shot fourteen times that night. And that was the master shot alone. Then came the same scene with close-ups. The doughnuts disintegrated. In some takes, Falk merely threw and broke plates and stayed on his side of the counter. In others he used doughnuts like grenades. When the doughnut supply ran out, the prop man was reduced to Scotch-taping doughnut pieces together for subsequent takes.[3]

Little of Falk's work with the doughnuts appears in the finished film, which merely shows Scoppa moving doughnuts and Falk pushing them onto the floor; viewers might miss the whole action if they aren't looking for it. The entire scene is just one shot, so nothing from any of the other takes appears in the film. So were those other thirteen master shots and five close-ups just wasted time and footage? From a financial standpoint, yes. If May had planned to present the scene in one long take—as Yasujirō Ozu, Orson Welles, or Jacques Tati would have—she could have skipped over the close-ups and other angles and moved on to the next scene after the first take. But any of those other takes *might* have appeared in the film, had Falk done something with the doughnuts that May liked better. "You experiment, and you fall on your ass," May said about directing.[4] The diner shoot was all an experiment, and something may or may not come out of an experiment.

When we talk about an "actor's director," we are normally referring to a director who supports the actors' craft and actively enlists their cooperation in the filmmaking. May regularly consulted with her actors and looked for ways (such as doughnuts) to inspire their creativity. But she was not always trying to please her actors. Indeed, you could say that she was using her actors in order to get the performances she wanted for her film. Carol Grace, who played Nellie, felt that May was too fixated on getting what she wanted for her movie at the expense of her actors' well-being. During one take, Grace said, Cassavetes slapped her so hard in the face that she burst into tears "from shock and hurt and confusion" (figure 7.1); May continued to shoot even though Grace could not continue the scene.[5]

May could be mischievous and goad her actors. Miller describes an outtake in the diner scene in which May secretly tried to frustrate Falk by telling Scoppa to say the wrong lines. "Let's rattle him a little," May said to Scoppa, who "thought Falk might be rattled enough as it was," but he did it:

> Falk enters and speaks his first line. Scoppa replies with something totally out of left field but still in character. Confusion and anger flood Falk's face as he tries to continue the scene as written while Scoppa continues playing it as though the script were foreign to him, stepping on some cues, oblivious to others.
>
> Again Falk jumps the counter, this time with a fork raised in his hand. It is raised to stab Scoppa, who knows he's in heavy-duty danger. He runs from behind the counter and swings around two female extras having coffee and pastry and disappears behind a stanchion, yelling as he went, "This guy's out of his head!" All the while Falk is pursuing him brandishing the fork, Elaine yelling, "You're getting out of camera range!" and Scoppa replying, "And that's where I intend to stay!"[6]

FIGURE 7.1. John Cassavetes actually slapped Carol Grace when filming *Mikey and Nicky*.

The street scene offers another example of mischievous directing. The scene takes place immediately after Nellie bites Mikey's lip, but it was filmed ten days later, and May was not getting the intensity she wanted from Falk. After two or three takes, she called him over to whisper something. He leaned in to listen, Falk says, and May "suddenly, savagely, sank her teeth as deep as they could go into my lip. I was in the middle of my scream when I heard Elaine in her small voice say to the cameraman, 'Action.'"[7]

Miller describes another incident in which May told an assistant to close a door in the hotel that Cassavetes expected to be open. Cassavetes banged into the door, "furious, certain that some luckless crew member had screwed up. He threw his gun at the door and kicked it, then banged his head against the door. Elaine May, a shy grin on her face, said quietly and sweetly, 'Cut.'"[8] This take does not appear in the film, either, but May was always looking to create moments of spontaneity on camera, and it is the nature of spontaneity that you never know when it might appear.

My point is not that May was a tricky director but rather that she wanted to see what her actors would do when unprepared. No moment in the movie was too small to work on—ordering cream, moving through a doorway. Every moment deserved some toying with, which helps account for the fact that, for fans of this movie, every scene offers something exciting and memorable. For May, there were no mere exposition scenes, easy scenes, or "pickup" shots. May refused to shoot pickups, which fill gaps in continuity, preferring instead to shoot an entire scene again. Every take offered an opportunity to add something to the film.

We find rough equivalents to May's style of directing with some American avant-garde directors (Andy Warhol, for example), New American Cinema directors (Shirley Clarke), and art house directors (Henry Jaglom), who also relied heavily on actors' spontaneous behavior. But those filmmakers worked with small, even micro, budgets and tiny crews. Hollywood movies require too much on-set crew for repeated on-camera experimentation just to see what might happen. A low-budget Hollywood film like *Mikey and Nicky*, in particular, cannot afford the time, but May did it anyway.

May's approach to directing actors not only got her in trouble during her shoot but made her an object of scorn (and eventually a pariah) in Hollywood. Miller asked an assistant director on set about May's refusal to shoot pickups. "She wants to reshoot the entire scene," the assistant director said despairingly. "She doesn't edit in her head." Her refusal to treat any shot as minor, according to Miller, cost the production "incalculable time and money."[9] Journalist Dan Rottenberg wrote about the production, "If [May] had more of a managerial mind, she might be able to know in advance that certain people wouldn't be needed on a particular night, but the only game plan for this movie exists in Elaine May's head, and even she isn't sure what she wants."[10] Her unorthodox style of direction provoked a lot of furious and frustrated people on the crew and in the offices at Paramount, who regarded her as unprofessional and inept.

A professional Hollywood director understands the financial pressures of photography and plans accordingly. Nobody complains when a filmmaker experiments during the script-writing process. Script writing encourages experimentation; it is cheaper to rewrite than reshoot. And nobody considers a director inept if she tries out fourteen different costumes, or scouts fourteen different locations, or tries fourteen new ideas in rehearsals just to see what might happen. Movies are, after all, artworks, and making art involves exploring possibilities. But if a film director experiments on camera with fourteen different takes of a one-minute scene and "isn't sure what she wants," then she is unprofessional.

May might not disagree with that assessment. "You're supposed to be crisp," she said about directing *A New Leaf*, "You're supposed to say, 'Cut! Print! Beautiful! Next setup!' You're supposed to say it for the morale of the crew, like a captain on a ship. I couldn't say, 'Cut! Print! Beautiful! Next setup!' I couldn't even say, 'Action!'"[11] For her first film, she developed her own process, which defied Hollywood's strict procedures for shooting scenes. Years later on *Mikey and Nicky*, her process did not conform any better to standard practices. Indeed, her investment in on-camera experimentation had grown more extreme. She treated principal photography as an extension of the creative writing process. Author Toni Morrison described that process as, "Write, erase, do it over."[12] May seems to have taken that approach to photography: shoot, erase, do it over. Her approach may not fit a movie like *Gone with the Wind* (1939), but a movie like *Mikey and Nicky*, which relies so heavily on actors' creative contributions on set, might benefit if the production approached photography with the same spirit of experimentation that we traditionally expect during script writing and preproduction.

This alternative model of filmmaking puts much of the weight of the film on the performances. If the performers bomb, so does the film. But even reviewers who blasted *Mikey and Nicky* often appreciated the acting. "The performances by Cassavetes and Falk are strikingly good. Cassavetes, in fact, has rarely been better," wrote a critic for the *Independent Film Journal*, before going on to say, "Unfortunately, the story is slight and the reverberations from what transpires, intended as shock waves, emerge more like ripples."[13] In the *Los Angeles Times*, Charles Champlin praised the acting but called the film a "lost cause."[14] The *Los Angeles Free Press* also panned the movie, except to say that "Falk and Cassavetes are both wonderful."[15] In his scathing review for the *Philadelphia Inquirer*, Desmond Ryan wrote, "Miss May was fortunate or wise enough to recruit two actors of high improvisational skills in John Cassavetes and Peter Falk and what moments of acuity and sense 'Mikey and Nicky' enjoys appears entirely due to them."[16] Many reviewers seemed to assume that Cassavetes and Falk made the movie almost on their own through sheer acting talent, that May herself had little to do with whatever artistic value the film has. But Cassavetes and Falk did not draw such consistently effusive praise for their performances in other movies, though they had both worked with a lot of good directors. May got performances out of her two leads that other directors had not.[17]

Next, we examine what she got.

John Cassavetes and Peter Falk

By the time they began filming *Mikey and Nicky* in 1973, John Cassavetes and Peter Falk already had a history of artistic collaboration and friendship. They worked together on a studio film, *Machine Gun McCain* (1969), then two of Cassavetes's films, *Husbands* (1970) and *A Woman Under the Influence* (1974), and a 1972 episode of *Columbo*. Their close off-screen relationship no doubt helped them develop the sense of intimacy we see between their characters in *Mikey and Nicky*, the actors having spent many months together on their various shoots. May attributed the improvisational feeling of the film to the fact that "A, they were friends, and, B, they were perfect for the part."[18] Playing old friends, like playing siblings, poses a special challenge for actors: for the characters' interactions to come across as natural, the actors must achieve a level of familiarity that normally takes time to grow. Cassavetes and Falk already had that familiarity.

They had similar personalities, too—both New Yorkers, born two years apart, children of European immigrants, one Jewish and the other Greek. As actors, they exuded physical energy, sometimes to the point of mania. Falk earned his first Academy Award nomination playing a violent hoodlum in *Murder, Inc.* (1960), and Cassavetes earned his as a rebellious convict in *The Dirty Dozen* (1967). About seeing Cassavetes repeatedly on television in the 1960s, Falk said, "I kept thinking 'We're the same height; why don't I get some of those roles?"[19] Normally, the pairing in a buddy film emphasizes contrasts between the actors—one calm and the other energetic, one from the city and the other from the country, one white and the other Black, one violent and the other gentle, one goofy and the other cool. Consider the pairings of Dustin Hoffman and Jon Voight in *Midnight Cowboy* (1969), Richard Pryor and Gene Wilder in *Silver Streak* (1976), Eddie Murphy and Nick Nolte in *48 Hours* (1982), Mel Gibson and Danny Glover in *Lethal Weapon* (1987), or Robert De Niro and Charles Grodin in *Midnight Run* (1988). By contrast, in *Mikey and Nicky*, the actors charge through various Philadelphia settings and share a propensity for violent outbursts. The actors could calm their natural energy, as Falk did in *Columbo* and Cassavetes did in *Whose Life Is It Anyway?* (1981), but *Mikey and Nicky* gave them plenty of opportunities to amp it up. At various points in the film, they both attack strangers, slap Nellie in the face, try to break down doors, and engage in all sorts of roughhousing. They eventually end up in a physical fight.

Their fight in the middle of a wet Philadelphia street might be the most nuanced and authentic-looking fight in Hollywood cinema, largely due to the actors' buzzing performances and the scene's unpredictable energy and general messiness. The fight, for one thing, has no clear beginning or end. It starts as an extension of Nicky's effort to keep his friend from leaving and ends when Mikey saunters off, disheveled and exhausted. In between, we see shoving, wrestling, slapping, slipping on wet pavement, along with heads pinned to the ground, feet wrapped around bodies, headlocks, and tossed coats. There is never a moment when we think one of them might be winning or losing, and the fight has no clear development, no build in suspense or emotional energy, no climax. The characters fight, roll on the ground, stare at each other, fight a bit more. It has none of the typical rhythms and actions of a movie fight scene. May said about it, "I had noticed that when men fight, they never punch, they push."[20] So she had them push and wrestle, as in the real fights she had seen. The whole event looks like a spontaneous physical outburst, sloppy and unstaged.

Although the actors are well matched in terms of natural physical energy, they expend it in different ways across the film. Falk's outbursts seem more controlled, issuing from the character's anxiety and frustration. Think of Mikey first pounding Nicky's hotel room door with his open palm, then slamming his body into it, and finally trying to kick in the door because Nicky won't open it. Or think of Falk attacking poor Peter Scoppa because the counterman won't sell Mikey cream. Mikey's energy builds and bursts forth. You can start to predict his outbursts, physical and verbal, when the actor tenses his jaw. By contrast, Nicky's energy looks more unhinged. He suddenly attacks a bus driver out of juvenile competitiveness, maybe just for the fun of it, or maybe from boredom. He slaps Nellie so hard and unexpectedly that Grace wrote about the moment in her memoir (figure 7.1).[21] When Nicky later slaps

Mikey in the fight scene, Cassavetes is so unbalanced that he slips and falls in the street (figure 1.7). Whereas Falk imbues Mikey with a restrained anger that displays the character's insecurities, Cassavetes gives Nicky an impulsive physical energy that reflects the reckless behavior that got Nicky into trouble with the Mob in the first place. Nicky acts without thinking.

Throughout the film, Cassavetes imbues Nicky with excessive bodily energy that appears restless and out of the character's control. Jeremy Carr writes of Nicky's "sweaty grimaces, his wild, wide-eyed paranoia, his pained fretfulness, and his mischievous grin, hinting at what may dwell beneath the simmering insanity. Cassavetes' expressions divulge a recklessness and a teeming energy just waiting to burst forth."[22] Indeed, Nicky seems incapable of staying still. He starts running suddenly, punches his open palms, snaps his fingers, twists his ring, whistles, exaggerates his facial expressions, tosses crackers at Mikey, pretends to tap-dance, and sometimes talks, coughs, snorts, and laughs all at the same time. In the B&O bar, instead of just settling down for a drink, he looks around impatiently, blows smoke rings (figure 7.2a), and jumps out of his chair. When he eats a cracker, he doesn't do it in the normal way. He lets the cracker dissolve in his mouth, brings his hand to his throat as if feeling the cracker, and gives a sinister "look how funny" expression for his friend (figure 7.2b). The actor is always up to something physically curious. When Nicky does calm down, the pause in his general fidgetiness suggests a moment of poignance or recognition, as when his slowly changing facial expression indicates his suspicion that Mikey is setting him up (figure 5.1a–d).

From the very start of the film, Nicky's behavior and emotions fluctuate in unpredictable ways. In the first dialogue exchange between the two leads, as Mikey stands outside the hotel room door, Nicky screams "Mikey!" His voice bellows more than we expected and sounds more desperate, and he puts an odd emphasis on the second syllable, "mi-KEY!" Mikey's pained expression when he hears it suggests that it surprises him, too. Nicky says the name two more times in the same way. We have already seen Nicky pacing around the room in anguish, but the energy behind the line is still inexplicable and suggests a mind under greater duress than we thought. The character even calms down unpredictably. Later in the scene, for instance, he says, "You know, I don't shave," in a way that is so unruffled (compared to his immediately previous wail-

FIGURE 7.2A–B. John Cassavetes imbues Nicky with restless energy; his character rarely stays still.

ing of "I'm gonna die") that he seems to have suddenly moved on to an entirely new mental track, a different emotional register altogether from that of the bawling Nicky we heard one second earlier.

His fear also comes and goes unpredictably. At the start of the scene, Nicky is clearly terrified, but he settles down when he shaves and cleans himself up. He looks cogent and controlled as he tries to convince Mikey

FIGURE 7.3. In the hotel room scene, Nicky's fear comes and goes.

of the hit ("I got a better one for you. How do you know it's *not* true?"). But when Mikey finally appears to believe him, Nicky suddenly grows frightened again, as though convincing Mikey of the hit made it more real. He hunches his shoulders, lies back on the bed in discomfort, and looks up at his friend pleadingly ("You said they *weren't* looking for me") (figure 7.3). We get the impression of a racing mind, filled with conflict and multiple facets—rational and irrational, confident and terrified, combative and gentle—depending on the thoughts that flash through his head at the moment.

Cassavetes finds unexpected ways to deliver his lines, varying his intonations, attitudes, and energies, thereby conveying his character's dynamic mental state. In the cemetery scene, when Nicky stands at his mother's headstone, we register the character's changing thoughts and emotions mostly through the actor's vocal inflections, not the lines themselves. At one point he whimpers to Mikey, "I was talking to my mother," but later he says a similar line, "I'm talking to my mother, here," with forceful anger. The actor gives his characteristic wheezy laugh when he says, "Now that I'm here, I don't know what to do," chuckling and snorting uncontrollably. The line "I don't want to die, Ma," which another actor might deliver with pathos, completely cracks him up. Yet when the script gives Cassavetes a real Elaine May punch line—"It's very hard to talk to a dead person, there's nothing in common"—he delivers that line seriously. Part of Cassavetes's charisma as an actor came from his ability to give unusual meanings to lines that seem otherwise straightforward, suggesting a personality that never behaves in the expected way or follows the social scripts that govern most daily interactions. This contrarian quality gave Cassavetes a career playing misfits and nonconformists. In *Mikey and Nicky*, the actor's unpredictable manner seems to come from Nicky's tumultuous inner life, one in which every interaction is fraught with competition, anger, fear, cruelty, passion, or nervous excitement—emotions heightened by the extremity of a scenario in which the character thinks a hit man might kill him at any moment.

With all of Cassavetes's dynamism and charisma—combined with the emotionally heightened scenario that May wrote for his character—it would have been easy for Cassavetes to overshadow his acting partner in the film, but Falk delivered an equally compelling performance, loaded with subtleties that suggest Mikey's busy mind and rich inner life. The actor peppered his performance with incidental behaviors that add shadings to his interactions with other characters. In the B&O bar, for example, when Nicky plays the Andrews Sisters' "Beer Barrel Polka" on the jukebox, Mikey looks over at him and raises his eyebrows, as if to ask, "This is the song you want to listen to?" It is a friendly, unspoken bit of kidding, absent in the script, that gives the audience some narratively unnecessary business to observe. Later, Mikey is so upset and frightened by Nicky's sudden appearance outside his home that he approaches Annie with his fist clenched, as if saying to her, "If you answer that door I'll punch you" (figure 7.4). It is an irrational gesture—she wasn't even moving in that direction—that seems to come out of Mikey's desperation and anger toward Nicky. Still, it is the kind of gesture we would expect from a hoodlum like Mikey, given the propensity for frustrated violence that we saw in earlier scenes. Brief incidental gestures like these permeate Falk's performance, myriad details that make Mikey's personality and his interactions with other characters dense and multifarious.

Falk displays another kind of nuance when he alters his character's demeanor, sometimes just slightly, depending on whom the character is interacting with. We can compare Mikey's ease with Nicky, for instance, to his demeanor with other characters. Even though he might hate the guy, Mikey clearly engages more intimately with Nicky than he does with anyone else, a connection that makes the long-term friendship

FIGURE 7.4. Falk instills Mikey with frustrated anger, clenching his fist at his wife when Nicky shows up at the door.

depicted in the film strikingly believable. They hug, grapple, grab each other's shoulders, and seem so loose together that they could be mistaken for brothers. In an interview about the film, Falk said, "An evening with Nicky is more fun than an evening with my wife. Nicky can make me laugh."[23] With Annie, Mikey seems impatient, easily irritated. When he tells her the story of his brother, Izzy, he corrects her too insistently ("No, he was ten"), like he is scolding a child. He displays outright contempt when he says, "I just told you he lost all his hair because of a fever," rolling his eye, touching his temple, visibly exasperated, a routine gesture that suggests a life together of miscommunications and annoyances and that helps account for their stiff interactions as a couple (figure 7.5). Narratively minor gestures like these suggest an entire history of marital interactions.

We can also observe subtle changes in Mikey's demeanor, which we have gotten to know well during the ninety minutes we have already spent with him, in a scene between Mikey and Mob boss Dave Resnick (Sanford Meisner). Mikey now seems slightly nervous, like someone making an effort to behave with poise. He holds his cigarette in a more formal way, sits up, and speaks more deliberately with Resnick than he did with Nicky. He smiles when he tells Resnick, "He said you didn't like

FIGURE 7.5. Falk indicates Mikey's impatience and irritation with his wife by touching his temple and looking away from her.

me," as though joking, but he looks intimidated, fidgeting with his cigarette in a nearly successful effort to appear relaxed.

Falk layered additional meanings within scenes that might otherwise seem straightforward. In the first bus scene, as Mikey and Nicky are heading to an all-night theater, where Mikey knows that a gunman will shoot Nicky, Falk's performance suddenly turns strange: the character looks distracted, his mouth contorted, his reactions to Nicky delayed. He angles his body away from Nicky and seems stuck in his own head (figure 7.6). Falk delivers his lines without the same naturalness and familiarity that the character normally shows with his old friend. When he looks at Nicky, he seems to be studying him. This brief interaction takes only two minutes of screen time, but in a 1984 interview about the film's rerelease, several dozen film and television performances later, Falk vividly remembered performing the scene in 1973. He also remembered his confusion about how to say the banal lines that May had given his character. And he remembered May helping him get to that performance.

> I didn't know what to do. What are we talking about? I'm saying to him he shouldn't smoke on the bus. I think I say to him, "Don't

FIGURE 7.6. Mikey looks distracted on the bus.

> I owe you two hundred?" And he says, "Yeah, but you don't have to pay me now." "I'll pay you now," I say. Then [Nicky] gets into a beef with the woman in back over the smoking. And then all of a sudden out of the blue. . . . I say something about his hands, and he just makes a joke about learning to play the piano when he was a boy, whatever the hell it is.
>
> How do you plan the scene? Talk about preparing! How do you prepare? What in your life have you ever gone through to prepare you for this?
>
> All right, in a regular gangster picture you're supposed to set this guy up and you do away with him, so you go in there and you just *behave*, you talk about the races. . . . Talk sports, whatever the hell it is, and you walk off the bus, and the guy does him in, and you tell the hit-man, "Jesus Christ, I gotta get home. Oh no, fuck it, let's play a game of pool," or something like that. And the audience will think it's terrific, they'll enjoy this character. But that kind of scene—that doesn't tell you anything about *people*.[24]

Falk here contemplates the way an actor in a "regular gangster picture," the kind with cold-hearted gangsters, would perform the bus scene. We can imagine that another actor playing Mikey might deliver the same lines as a way of distracting Nicky ("You got big hands. You coulda been a piano player with those hands"). Make Nicky feel relaxed, prevent him from realizing he is about to be killed. A scene from *The Godfather* (1972) follows that formula, when Clemenza (Richard Castellano) casually teases Paulie (John Martino) before a hit man shoots him. The movie follows up the cold-hearted murder with the cold-hearted line, "Leave the gun. Take the cannolis." According to Falk, "the audience will think it's terrific, they'll enjoy this character." Falk had himself played that kind of character in *Murder, Inc.*, earning him an Oscar nomination.

In *Mikey and Nicky*, however, Falk rejects the gangster film cliché as inhuman ("that doesn't tell you anything about *people*"). Still, he did not know what to do with May's lines about hands and pianos, until May nudged him toward another approach to the scene. She told Falk to fixate on Cassavetes's interesting physical features:

> She starts talking about death. The fact that people defecate before they die. The fact that there is such a thing as a death rattle. You can wet your pants. And she says, "Try playing how interesting something is. Become fascinated with something. The size of the pores on his face. Just get interested in that, or anything."
>
> So I'm playing this scene, and that's all I'm thinking about. I'd choose different things [with different takes]. How John would smile—whatever. And one time I did that without self-consciousness, unaware of what the next line was. And at one point, then, in that scene, I had a fresh thought. And the thought was that this bus—maybe it *was* a bus, but it wasn't in Philadelphia, it was in the Balkans. And maybe it was a hearse. And I wasn't sure whether or not this was a dream. And I wasn't sure whether this person next to me was alive. Because, you know, John has high cheekbones. So I saw a skeleton. But he would laugh, and then I knew it wasn't a skeleton . . . and this strange creature was sitting next to be [*sic*] that I knew but I *didn't* know, but that sometimes was *fascinating*. I didn't always *like* him, but I didn't *dislike* him—he was just fascinating.[25]

A strong performance, like Falk's performance in the bus scene, seems somehow inevitable, as though only one way of performing the scene would tell the story correctly. We can easily forget that the performance came out of a process and that a different process might have led the actor to a different interpretation of the scene. Rejecting gangster film clichés, Falk was desperate to find a human way to perform the bus scene, and May, casually and without much instruction, offered him one: focus on how "just fascinating" his acting partner was. Through that process, he expressed qualities of his character's mental life—denial, remorse, fascination, an ability to dissociate—that we had not seen in the character before and that added variety to the performance and complexity to Mikey's interactions with his friend. From that scene on, our understanding of Mikey includes his unusual behavior on the bus, which we integrate into whatever understanding we had of the character prior to the scene.

I have argued that we should broaden our conception of improvisation to include moments like the bus scene, in which the actor is having spontaneous thoughts, "unaware of what the next line was," even as he continues to deliver the dialogue in the script. An actor's training often includes improvisation games precisely because they encourage the creative attitude toward performance that Falk showed in the bus scene. "The energy released to solve the problem," Viola Spolin writes in *Improvisation for the Theater*, "being restricted by the rules of the game and bound by group decision, creates an explosion—or spontaneity—and as is the nature of explosions, everything is torn apart, rearranged, unblocked."[26] Falk was bound by rules (the bus driving Nicky to his death, the lines of May's script, the face of the actor with whom he is performing, his resolve to avoid gangster film clichés), he had a problem to solve (how should Mikey behave with his friend at this moment?), he engaged in a spontaneous moment of creativity (entering a dream state, imagining his friend already dead), and out came a performance so striking that eleven years later he remembered his entire working process ("everything is torn apart, rearranged, unblocked").

May engaged in countless hours of on-camera experimentation not because she wanted the actors to improve the lines of her script. Her script was, in Cassavetes's description, "one of the tightest I've ever read."[27] Indeed, after all that experimentation, May's shooting script is nearly a transcript of her finished film. So why shoot hundreds of hours of footage just to film the lines of her script? May wanted to capture the actors' moments of spontaneity, when they worked out something in real

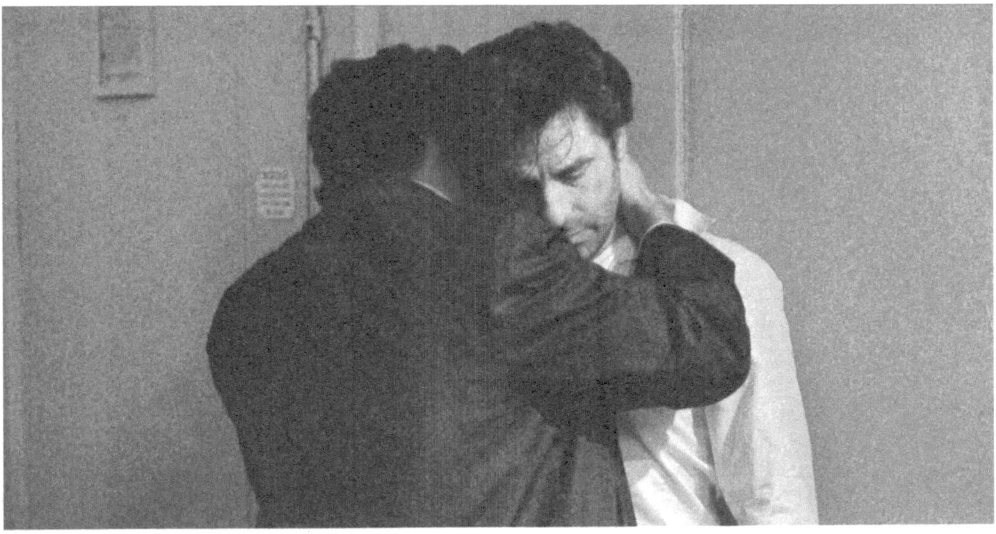

FIGURE 7.7. Mikey rubs Nicky's stiff neck and turns the gesture into an embrace.

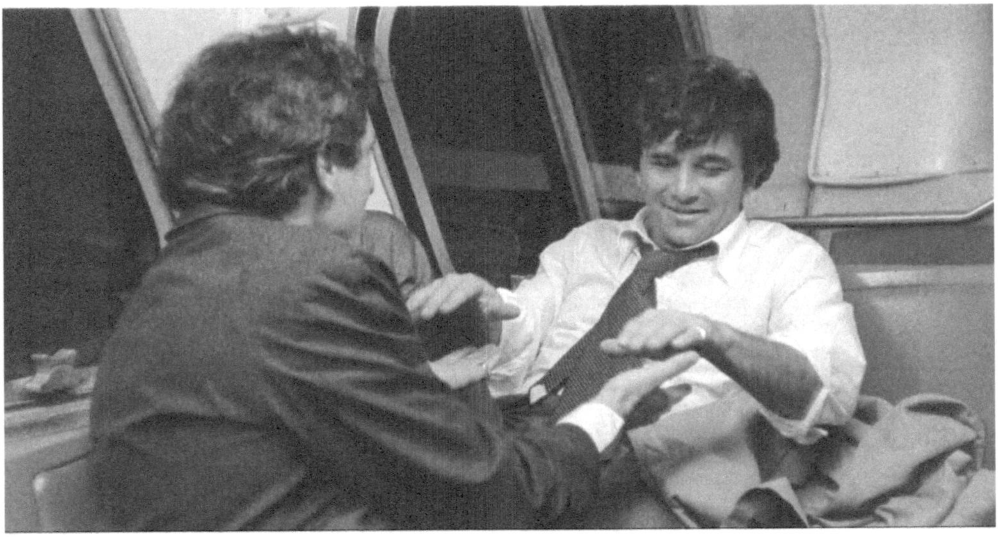

FIGURE 7.8. Mikey and Nicky play slap hands on a bus.

time. She understood the excitement of improv and felt that excitement watching Falk and Cassavetes, even as they delivered her scripted lines. And to capture as many of those spontaneous moments as she could, she needed them to perform scenes again and again, and she needed to shoot a lot of film. To catch lightning in a bottle, you need a lot of lightning and a lot of bottles.

FIGURE 7.9. Nicky tries to tuck in his shirt before letting Mikey in the hotel room.

The story of a man setting up his friend to be killed by the Mob has inherent interest. It captivated May for decades. But the filmmakers were not content merely to ride the crest of a good story and a tight script, qualities that do not necessarily make a movie interesting moment by moment. That degree of sustained interest required them to work at a granular level. I have selected a handful of granular moments to analyze in this chapter, moments that, to my mind, add interesting detail to a character, an interaction, or a situation. I could have selected countless others: Mikey rubbing Nicky's stiff neck and turning the gesture into an embrace (figure 7.7); the two of them blithely playing slap hands on a bus (figure 7.8); Nicky half-tucking in his shirt before letting Mikey into his hotel room, as though doing so made him look any better (figure 7.9). Remove one of these performance moments and not only would the story be just as tight, but the movie would be almost as good. None of them puts a crucial hinge in the narrative structure, and none of them is a performance triumph. But each of these moments makes the scenes in which they appear more subtle (we might observe a character nuance we had not noticed before), dense (the scenes offer a lot more to observe than just plot information), and complex (characters exhibit all sorts of inconsistent feelings and behaviors). May spent 110 days on set so that each moment of *Mikey and Nicky* could offer viewers something "just fascinating."

CONCLUSION

When making *Mikey and Nicky*, Elaine May challenged Hollywood's artistic priorities. Whereas Hollywood filmmakers, in order to safeguard their budgets, typically make their most consequential creative decisions before principal photography begins, May refused to decide such things ahead of time. She delayed key creative decisions until each day's shoot, which drastically slowed production and transformed a scheduled sixty-day photography period into a ten-month process. An improviser by training and an experimenter by artistic temperament, she waited to see how things looked when the actors were performing and the cameras rolling. "Do it again," she would say, and let the camera run a full reel, looking to her actors to do something that she did not plan on.[1]

In this way, she is the artistic antithesis of filmmakers like Stanley Kubrick and Jacques Tati, whose excessive takes resulted not from experimentation but from a precise preconception of how they wanted their films to look. Kubrick and Tati were pictorialist directors, like Alfred Hitchcock and Yasujirō Ozu, who concentrated on cinema's visual properties. They molded actors' performances so that each shot conformed to the images in their head. Few shots in *Mikey and Nicky* serve a mere pictorial effect. For May, film cameras existed to record performances. She worked more in the tradition of naturalist filmmakers like John Cassavetes, Arthur Penn, Robert Altman, Shirley Clarke, Sidney Lumet, and Hal Ashby, all of whom inspired unscripted moments of actor creativity.

In postproduction, May again extended the period of experimentation. Editing in Hollywood means piecing together the best takes in order to realize blueprints laid out in the script. May, however, wanted to cut each scene multiple ways ("Now let's do that scene from John's point of view").[2] As a consequence, a film that would typically take ten weeks to edit took two and a half years. I don't think May intended to reconceptualize Hollywood's production process. I doubt she understood when she started shooting that she was going to spend the next three years and seven months in photography and postproduction. Rather, I think she relied on a working process she knew from her earlier films and skills she had developed as a student of Paul Sills and Viola Spolin in improvisational theater.

Throughout the production, May resisted pressures to conform to Hollywood's notion of professionalism. Her crew told her, *You don't know what you're doing; you need to follow the production practices we know.* Paramount executives told her, *You're spending too much money; you need to hurry up and finish.* May shot and edited not in the normal way and not on the schedule she was given but in the way that she wanted and for as long as she felt she needed— willfully antiprofessional. Professionalism gets you the respect of your crew and gets your film finished on time and on budget, but it cuts off options. May's process generated an abundance of creative possibilities. I imagine that other versions of *Mikey and Nicky* could be edited from her footage, all with the same dialogue and action but with different characterizations, different interactions, different moments of emphasis, poignance, and emotional resonance, each version complex, dense, and subtle in a unique way. That one shoot might have generated a dozen movies just as ambitious and just as exhilarating.

Mikey and Nicky also calls into question how a Hollywood movie must behave. May's plotting was tight enough that she could fill it with incidental moments and characters that enriched the narration. Apparently, for many viewers and reviewers, these incidentals signaled a haphazard narrative design, but May did not squander any opportunity to "get the most out of any scene," as one of her assistant editors put it.[3] She created complexity by fixating on extraneous story events and peripheral characters that might compete with the main storyline for the audience's interest. She created density by adding (and encouraging her actors to add) nuances to each scene, each character, and each interaction, not just the friendship between Mikey and Nicky but their interactions with their wives, families, colleagues, and people they encounter over the course of a night. And she achieved subtlety through a more oblique form of storytelling than we find in most Hollywood movies. Subtext and actor behavior, rather than explicit dialogue and character action alone, would tell the story, and she relied on her actors to generate each scene's emotional development.

May made stylistic choices that we almost never see in a commercial production, using shots in her finished film that many commentators regarded as "far below professional quality."[4] Aesthetic philosopher Jonathan Gilmore argues that we may evaluate an artwork favorably, even if it fails to satisfy the norms of its artistic category, if it successfully achieves its creator's aims.[5] May sacrificed technical perfection for the sake of aims she considered more important: obtaining the most compelling performances and emotional development for each scene. For May, the technical elements considered during editing—audio quality, continuity, focus, framing, unobstructed views, camera stability, and the synchronization of sound and image—would have to yield to the preferred performances.

Scholars often attribute an artwork's aesthetic worth to bold artistic decisions, but the difference between a good artwork and a great one can hinge on a series of minor artistic choices that end in only minute changes to the work. Little things in art, when added together, matter a great deal. Writing about artistic merit, philosopher Frank Sibley observes, "even a slight change might make all the difference."[6] We know, from studying *Mikey and Nicky*'s history, how much work went into each moment and how intentional Elaine May's working process was. The film's artistic achievements, I have tried to demonstrate, resulted from countless minute choices that May and her collaborators made throughout the film's lengthy production.

May's production process would never work as an alternative industry model. For one thing, the process introduces additional uncertainty into a business already filled with uncertainties. Her process is financially inefficient, with unpredictable box office results. A Hollywood film is expensive; a studio cannot just hope that it will end up commercially successful. Hollywood's standard filmmaking practices are designed to limit expenditures and increase the likelihood of a film's financial viability. For another thing, May's process depends on the creativity and personal investment of extraordinary actors, like John Cassavetes and Peter Falk. Not every actor can experiment on camera for months. Dustin Hoffman and Warren Beatty, both strong actors, could not do it. Few Hollywood actors, moreover, are willing to shoot for 110 days from eight o'clock in the evening until the early hours of the morning, attend dailies before shooting, and help with editing for another two years. What's more, Falk put up his own money for completion funds and helped publicize the movie for another decade to see that it received proper attention. May had lined up the right actors to play Mikey and Nicky, and she somehow managed to get a studio to finance her project.

But the early seventies were a special time in Hollywood, when studios were hiring untrained filmmakers like May, who could open up new markets and appeal to audiences looking for more unconventional movies like *Mikey and Nicky*, with its heightened realism and performance energy. She obtained funding for the film at the right time. She also exploited a business flaw in commercial filmmaking: once studio executives commit to a project, it is hard for them to get out of it. Even when a budget goes wild and a film falls years behind schedule, the executives generally see a project through to the end, rather than cut their losses. But unless a filmmaker ultimately conforms to Hollywood's notion of professionalism, anyone who exploits that flaw will not last long in the industry.

Journalists, Paramount executives, and May's own crew all thought she was incompetent—everyone except for the other artists, the actors and editors who worked alongside her for years to bring off this little gangster drama. They understood that the very qualities that made her appear incompetent also made her a great artist: her constant experimentation, a reliance on intuition rather than standard industry practice, an unwillingness to close off options even when she was months behind her shooting schedule or years past her contractual delivery date. Elaine May might have thrived better as an independent filmmaker, but she needed Hollywood money to fund her unorthodox production methods, which were expensive. She directed four Hollywood films, one of them, I have argued, a masterpiece. That may not sound so productive, but only a handful of Hollywood directors have managed to make a masterpiece.

ACKNOWLEDGMENTS

Several friends, colleagues, and institutions helped me with this project. Carlos Kase, Ted Nannicelli, and Dana Polan each read the entire manuscript and offered all sorts of excellent advice and criticism. Dana also arranged access to New York University's library resources. Vaughn Hazell, Patrick McMahon, Phillip Schopper, and Jeffrey Wolf helped me put together various pieces of *Mikey and Nicky*'s production history. Michael Kantor connected me with producer-distributor Julian Schlossberg, who offered me a wealth of information and support. Julian also helped me get information from his friend Elaine May, who would not meet with me. This is how that worked: I forwarded some questions to Julian, he asked May to answer them, on my behalf, then he called me with her answers.

The kind people in the Margaret Herrick Library of the Academy of Motion Picture Arts and Sciences helped me find archival documents on Elaine May and *Mikey and Nicky*. The University of North Carolina Wilmington (UNCW) afforded me several research grants to work on the book. My colleagues in the UNCW Department of Film Studies cheered me on. My editor, Jim Burr, encouraged me to write the book after I gave it a tepid sales job ("I'm thinking of writing a book about a movie you've never heard of, but I don't know that anybody will want to read it."). That is a true story, and he was truly supportive. Lynne Ferguson and I deliberated over commas, definite articles, and line breaks as though our reputations depended on the outcome, and Jessica Hinds-Bond appraised every word. I could not have dreamed up more caring editors.

Dana Sachs helped me so much with the manuscript that I plan to share book royalties with her, although I am guessing they won't amount to much. Anyway, she has my heart.

NOTES

Introduction

1. Andrew Tobias, "For Elaine May, a New Film—But Not a New Leaf," *New West*, December 6, 1976, 57.

2. Jack Kroll, "Elaine's Night Out," *Newsweek*, December 27, 1976, 56.

3. See, respectively, Lloyd Sachs, "In May's Screen Gem, Women's Albums, Genius Shines," *Chicago Sun-Times*, January 2, 2005, 2; J. Hoberman, "A Reclusive Auteur's Brilliant Career, from the Jewish New Wave to a Legendary Bomb," *Village Voice*, February 22, 2006, 48; Carrie Rickey, "Elaine May: Laughing Matters," *Sight and Sound* 28, no. 10 (2018): 43; David Blum, "The Road to *Ishtar*," *New York*, March 16, 1987, 42; Janet Coleman, *The Compass: The Improvisational Theatre That Revolutionized American Comedy* (University of Chicago Press, 1991), 295; Carrie Courogen, *Miss May Does Not Exist: The Life and Work of Elaine May, Hollywood's Hidden Genius* (St. Martin's Press, 2024), 159.

4. Dan Rottenberg, "Elaine May . . . or She May Not," *Chicago Tribune*, October 21, 1973, 56.

5. Quoted in Sam Wasson, *Improv Nation: How We Made a Great American Art* (Harper Perennial, 2018), 97.

6. David A. Cook, *Lost Illusions: American Cinema in the Age of Watergate and Vietnam, 1970–1979* (Charles Scribner and Sons, 1999), 2.

7. Patricia Rodden Zimmermann, *Reel Families: A Social History of Amateur Film* (Indiana University Press, 1995), 3.

8. John Cassavetes, *Cassavetes on Cassavetes*, ed. Ray Carney (Farrar, Straus and Giroux, 2001), 183.

9. David E. James notes that the use of the term *amateur* to mean "lover" in film criticism dates back at least to the 1920s, when C. Adolph Glassgold used the term in his essay "The Films: Amateur or Professional," *Arts* 15, no. 1 (1929): 56–59. Similar uses of the term, James writes, remained popular among avant-garde filmmakers in the 1960s. David E. James, "Amateurs in the Industry Town: Stan Brakhage and Andy Warhol in Los Angeles," *Grey Room*, no. 12 (Summer 2003): 81–93.

10. Stan Brakhage, *Essential Brakhage: Selected Writings on Film-Making*, ed. Bruce R. McPherson (Documentext, 2001), 142.

11. Maya Deren, *Essential Deren: Collected Writings on Film*, ed. Bruce R. McPherson (Documentext, 2005), 18.

12. Deren, *Essential Deren*, 17–18.

13. Deren, *Essential Deren*, 18.

14. Jake Wilson, "Dangerous Business—Elaine May as Existential Improviser," in *ReFocus: The Films of Elaine May*, ed. Alexandra Heller-Nicholas and Dean Brandum (Edinburgh University Press, 2019), 69–70.

15. Quoted in Rachel Abramowitz, *Is That a Gun in Your Pocket? Women's Experience of Power in Hollywood* (Random House, 2000), 66.

16. See, respectively, Cook, *Lost Illusions*, 76; James Naremore, *On Kubrick*, rev. ed. (British Film Institute, 2023), 7; Alexander Walker et al., *Stanley Kubrick, Director: A Visual Analysis*, rev. and enlarged ed. (Norton, 1999), 20.

17. Quoted in Thomas Thompson, "Whatever Happened to Elaine May?," *Life*, July 1967, 59.

18. John Cassavetes, interview, in Tom Miller's working notebook for *Mikey and Nicky*, 1973, Tom Miller Papers, Special Collections, Margaret Herrick Library, Academy of Motion Picture Arts and Sciences, Beverly Hills, CA.

19. Peter Falk, *Just One More Thing* (Da Capo Press, 2007), 228.

20. Quoted in Abramowitz, *Is That a Gun in Your Pocket?*, 66.

21. Quoted in Abramowitz, *Is That a Gun in Your Pocket?*, 66.

22. Quoted in Dick Lemon, "Movies: How to Succeed in Interviewing Elaine May (Try, Really Try)," *New York Times*, January 4, 1970, D13.

23. Maya Montañez Smukler, "Hollywood Can't Wait: Elaine May and the Delusions of 1970s American Cinema," in Heller-Nicholas and Brandum, *ReFocus*, 57.

24. Brakhage, *Essential Brakhage*, 145.

25. Quoted in Michael Rivlin, "Elaine May: Too Tough for Hollywood?," *Millimeter* 3, no. 10 (1975): 46. May has repeated the opinion that experience damages one's artistry in several interviews, including Mike Nichols, "Elaine May in Conversation with Mike Nichols," in *Nichols and May: Interviews*, ed. Robert E. Kapsis (University Press of Mississippi, 2020), 213.

26. Arthur C. Danto emphasizes the role of an artwork's contextual, historical, and institutional dimensions, in addition to its intrinsic features, in shaping aesthetic experience. Arthur C. Danto, *The Transfiguration of the Commonplace: A Philosophy of Art* (Harvard University Press, 1981).

27. Jonathan Gilmore proposes that we can "evaluate works with reference to their essential aims, ends and purposes." Similar to Gilmore, Noël Carroll argues that we should value artworks based on the worthiness of their aims and their success at achieving these aims: "The work is good, in part, if, or to the degree that, it realizes its purposes and imperfect to the degree that it fails to do so." And Andrew Klevan argues, likewise, that we can evaluate a film aesthetically by judging how successfully it achieves its objectives or how well its parts function "within the design or themes of the whole." He furthermore notes, "In the contemporary study of aesthetics, beauty is often employed as a synonym for excellence, or as an umbrella term that encompasses the wide array of merit qualities that exist (for example, graceful, subtle, eloquent, or intricate)." Jonathan Gilmore, "A Functional View of Artistic Evaluation," *Philosophical Studies* 155, no. 2 (2011): 290; Noël Carroll, "Forget Taste," *Journal of Aesthetic Education* 56, no. 1 (2022): 8; Andrew Klevan, *Aesthetic Evaluation and Film* (Manchester University Press, 2018), 42–43, 18.

28. Jerrold Levinson argues, "Pleasure that testifies to artistic value must go beyond a single encounter, must be experienceable by others, and at other times: it cannot be merely fly-by-night or flash-in-the-pan"; our satisfaction "may deepen and extend itself on successive encounters." Jerrold Levinson, *The Pleasures of Aesthetics: Philosophical Essays* (Cornell University Press, 1996), 2–3. See also Anthony Savile, *The Test of Time: An Essay in Philosophical Aesthetics* (Oxford University Press, 1982).

29. For some recent publications that call *Mikey and Nicky* a "masterpiece," see Jim Hemphill, "Mikey & Nicky (1976)," *American Cinematographer* 86, no. 4 (2005): 16–17; "The Week Ahead: Feb. 26–March 4; Film," *New York Times*, February 26, 2006; Richard Brody, "A Man's World: Elaine May's Feminist Angle on the Gangster Film," *New Yorker*, May 1, 2015, 10.

30. Tobias, "For Elaine May," 69.

31. Kroll, "Elaine's Night Out," 56.

32. Caryn James, "The Fireworks of Elaine May," *New York Times*, February 24, 2006, E1.

33. Manohla Dargis, "Film," *New York Times*, February 5, 2006, Late Edition, 35.

34. Jeremy Carr, "*Mikey and Nicky* (1976)—Elaine May and the Cassavetes Connection," in Heller-Nicholas and Brandum, *ReFocus*.

35. Kent Jones, "In the American Grain," *Film Comment*, March/April 2016, 53.

36. Ray Carney, "Pulp Affliction: The Sorry State of Contemporary Film," *Baffler*, no. 8 (December 1995): 46.

37. For other earnest efforts to describe *Mikey and Nicky*, see Chuck Stephens, "Chronicle of a Disappearance," *Film Comment*, March/April 2006, 46–48, 50–53; Brad Stevens, "Male Narrative/Female Narration: Elaine May's *Mikey and Nicky*," *Cineaction*, no. 31 (1993): 74–83.

38. David Bordwell, "Historical Poetics of Cinema," in *The Cinematic Text*, ed. R. Barton Palmer (AMS Press, 1989), 371.

39. Bordwell, "Historical Poetics of Cinema," 371.

1. Comedian

1. Julian Schlossberg, email to author, July 13, 2022. May tells the same story in Julian Schlossberg and Elaine May, *Try Not to Hold It Against Me* (Beaufort Books, 2023), xiii.

2. Tom Miller's working notebook for *Mikey and Nicky*, 1973, 30, Tom Miller Papers, Special Collections, Margaret Herrick Library, Academy of Motion Picture Arts and Sciences, Beverly Hills, CA.

3. Quoted in Janet Coleman, *The Compass: The Improvisational Theatre That Revolutionized American Comedy* (University of Chicago Press, 1991), 32.

4. Coleman, *The Compass*, 24.

5. May was so enamored with Spolin that, when the "High Priestess of Improvisation" left Chicago to return to Los Angeles, May called out to her waiting at a bus stop, "We need you, Viola. Don't go!" Coleman, *The Compass*, 94.

6. Mark Freeman, "Teenagers on Stage—The Comedy of Elaine May and Mike Nichols," in *ReFocus: The Films of Elaine May*, ed. Alexandra Heller-Nicholas and Dean Brandum (Edinburgh University Press, 2019), 28; Coleman, *The Compass*, 106.

7. Viola Spolin, *Improvisation for the Theater: A Handbook of Teaching and Directing Techniques* (Northwestern University Press, 1963), ix.

8. Spolin, *Improvisation for the Theater*, 3.

9. Spolin, *Improvisation for the Theater*, x.

10. Spolin, *Improvisation for the Theater*, x.

11. Several commentators have remarked on the resonance between the movie's title and the name of May's comedy partner, a resonance that seems to them preg-

nant with meaning. What it means, however, no one dares to venture, and I suspect that it is meaningless, especially since May seems to have had the title before she met Mike Nichols.

12. Freeman, "Teenagers on Stage," 29.

13. Richard Burton, *The Richard Burton Diaries*, ed. Chris Williams (Yale University Press, 2012), 368.

14. For a discussion of Nichols and May's bold anti-institutional material, and the way it got them labeled "sick" by the media, see Kyle Stevens, "Tossing Truths: Improvisation and the Performative Utterances of Nichols and May," *Critical Quarterly* 52, no. 3 (2010): 35–37.

15. Molly Haskell, "Woman Directors," *American Film* 1, no. 8 (1976): 18–23; Alison Butler, *Women's Cinema: The Contested Screen* (2002; Wallflower Press, 2019).

16. Annette Kuhn and Susannah Radstone, eds., *The Women's Companion to International Film* (University of California Press, 1994), 258.

17. Marjorie Rosen, *Popcorn Venus: Women, Movies, and the American Dream* (Avon, 1973), 386.

18. Molly Haskell, "A Long Day's Journey into Buddy-Buddy Land," *Village Voice*, January 3, 1977, 37.

19. Lynne Jackson and Karen Jaehne, "Eavesdropping on Female Voices: A Who's Who of Contemporary Women Filmmakers," *Cinéaste* 16, no. 1 (1987): 38–43.

20. Barbara Koenig Quart, *Women Directors: The Emergence of a New Cinema* (Praeger, 1988), 41.

21. Quart, *Women Directors*, 42, 43, 39.

22. Julian Schlossberg, interview with author, January 4, 2024.

23. "What makes this sequence so singularly discomfiting isn't just the spectacle of the woman's humiliation," writes Elizabeth Alsop; "it's the character's active complicity in that humiliation." Elizabeth Alsop, *Elaine May* (University of Illinois Press, 2025), 80.

24. Stephen Booth, *"King Lear," "Macbeth," Indefinition, and Tragedy* (Yale University Press, 1983), 84.

25. Quoted in Coleman, *The Compass*, 112.

26. Carrie Courogen, *Miss May Does Not Exist: The Life and Work of Elaine May, Hollywood's Hidden Genius* (St. Martin's Press, 2024), 88–89.

27. Spolin, *Improvisation for the Theater*, x.

28. Spolin, *Improvisation for the Theater*, 6.

29. Quoted in Barbara Gelb, "Mike Nichols: The Special Risks and Rewards of the Director's Art," *New York Times*, May 27, 1984, Late Edition, 42.

30. Quoted in Gerald Nachman, *Seriously Funny: The Rebel Comedians of the 1950s and 1960s* (Pantheon Books, 2003), 349.

31. Quoted in Coleman, *The Compass*, 232.

32. Quoted in Gelb, "Mike Nichols," 42.

33. Quoted in Sam Kashner, "Who's Afraid of Nichols & May?," *Vanity Fair*, January 2013, 104.

34. Quoted in Nachman, *Seriously Funny*, 349.

35. Actor Byrne Piven described May's direction of the Playwrights production

of *Miss Julie* by August Strindberg: "She was always trying to find the truth of the moment improvisationally," but in the end, Piven says, she always returned to the script. Quoted in Coleman, *The Compass*, 72.

36. Neil Simon, "Dialogue on Film," interview by James Powers, *American Film*, March 1, 1978, 38.

37. Peter Falk, "15 Questions," in Miller's working notebook for *Mikey and Nicky*.

38. Cassavetes said that May would "funnel you back to the script." John Cassavetes, interview, in Miller's working notebook for *Mikey and Nicky*, 24.

39. Cassavetes, interview, in Miller's working notebook for *Mikey and Nicky*, 24.

40. Falk, "15 Questions," in Miller's working notebook for *Mikey and Nicky*.

41. Elaine May and Julian Schlossberg, "Elaine May Chats with Julian Schlossberg About Her Comedy, Acting, and Directing Careers," 2023, posted June 4, 2024, by Turner Classic Movies, YouTube, 16:06, https://www.youtube.com/watch?v=p-4POuAW_iU.

42. Elaine May, "ACE [American Cinema Editors] Presents: *Mikey and Nicky* with Elaine May," interview by Phillip Schopper and Jeffrey Wolf, Metrograph Theater, New York, December 7, 2024.

43. Spolin, *Improvisation for the Theater*, 58, 96, 98, 120–128.

44. Patrick McMahon, interview with author, January 11, 2025.

45. Marshall Fine, *Accidental Genius: How John Cassavetes Invented the Independent Film*, reprint ed. (Miramax, 2006), 22.

46. Grover Lewis, *Academy All the Way* (Straight Arrow Books, 1974), 115.

47. Fine, *Accidental Genius*, 23.

48. Spolin, *Improvisation for the Theater*, 3.

49. Fine, *Accidental Genius*, 24.

50. May, "ACE Presents."

51. Peter Falk, *Just One More Thing* (Da Capo Press, 2007), 181.

52. Falk, *Just One More Thing*, 196.

53. Miller's working notebook for *Mikey and Nicky*, 26.

54. Quoted in Michael Hausman and Victor Kemper, "The Making of *Mikey and Nicky* (1976)," posted August 28, 2020, by Hollowshape, YouTube, 14:26, https://www.youtube.com/watch?v=qIXnPfJfy_I.

55. Miller's working notebook for *Mikey and Nicky*, 6.

56. David Blum, "The Road to *Ishtar*," *New York*, March 16, 1987, 42. The anecdote also appears, with slight variations, in Jeremy Carr, "*Mikey and Nicky* (1976)—Elaine May and the Cassavetes Connection," in Heller-Nicholas and Brandum, *ReFocus*, 131; Patrick Cooper, *"Aren't You Gonna Die Someday?": Elaine May's* Mikey and Nicky*: An Examination, Reflection, and Making of* (BearManor Media, 2019), chap. 41; and Chuck Stephens, "Chronicle of a Disappearance," *Film Comment*, March/April 2006, 46.

57. Dan Rottenberg, "Elaine May . . . or She May Not," *Chicago Tribune*, October 21, 1973, 56.

58. Miller's working notebook for *Mikey and Nicky*, 44.

59. McMahon, interview with author.

60. Todd Berliner, *Hollywood Incoherent: Narration in Seventies Cinema* (University of Texas Press, 2010), 188–189.

61. Quoted in Judith Crist, *Take 22: Moviemakers on Moviemaking* (Viking, 1984), 256.

62. Mike Leigh, *Mike Leigh on Mike Leigh*, updated ed., ed. Amy Raphael (Faber and Faber, 2022), 30.

63. Berliner, *Hollywood Incoherent*, 189.

64. One can observe the way in which Nichols and May polished a sketch by comparing the 1958 and 1959 television versions of "Teenagers in a Car." See Mike Nichols and Elaine May, "Teenagers," 1958, posted October 29, 2020, by Omnibus with Alistair Cooke, YouTube, 7:56, https://www.youtube.com/watch?v=XpYxH1BciHQ; Mike Nichols and Elaine May, "The Teenagers in a Car Sketch," 1959, posted March 17, 2015, by Cantara Christopher, YouTube, 10:39, https://www.youtube.com/watch?v=LJtUtF2gxK4.

65. Julian Schlossberg, conveying answers from Elaine May to author, September 10, 2024.

2. Filmmaker

1. Quoted in Michael Rivlin, "Elaine May: Too Tough for Hollywood?," *Millimeter* 3, no. 10 (1975): 16.

2. Rivlin, "Elaine May," 16.

3. A. N. Ryan to Eugene H. Frank, "Re: A New Leaf," interoffice communication, April 3, 1968, *A New Leaf* production records, Paramount Pictures Special Collection, file 180, Margaret Herrick Library, Academy of Motion Picture Arts and Sciences, Beverly Hills, CA; cited in Carrie Courogen, *Miss May Does Not Exist: The Life and Work of Elaine May, Hollywood's Hidden Genius* (St. Martin's Press, 2024), 115.

4. Quoted in Rivlin, "Elaine May," 17.

5. Quoted in Mike Nichols, "Elaine May in Conversation with Mike Nichols," in *Nichols and May: Interviews*, ed. Robert E. Kapsis (University Press of Mississippi, 2020), 212.

6. Maya Montañez Smukler, "Hollywood Can't Wait: Elaine May and the Delusions of 1970s American Cinema," in *ReFocus: The Films of Elaine May*, ed. Alexandra Heller-Nicholas and Dean Brandum (Edinburgh University Press, 2019), 48.

7. Courogen, *Miss May Does Not Exist*, 72, 76.

8. Quoted in Sam Wasson, *Improv Nation: How We Made a Great American Art* (Harper Perennial, 2018), 297.

9. Quoted in Courogen, *Miss May Does Not Exist*, 140.

10. Quoted in Rachel Abramowitz, *Is That a Gun in Your Pocket? Women's Experience of Power in Hollywood* (Random House, 2000), 66.

11. Andrew Tobias, "For Elaine May, a New Film—But Not a New Leaf," *New West*, December 6, 1976, 66.

12. Julian Schlossberg, email to author, July 13, 2022.

13. Schlossberg, email to author.

14. Quoted in Abramowitz, *Is That a Gun in Your Pocket?*, 68.

15. Quoted in Nichols, "Elaine May in Conversation," 214.

16. Jeanine Basinger, "Giving Credit—Pioneering Women," Directors Guild of America, Winter 2011, https://www.dga.org/craft/dgaq/issues/1004-winter-2011/features-giving-credit.

17. Dorothy Arzner, interview by Karyn Kay and Gerald Peary, in *Women and the Cinema: A Critical Anthology*, ed. Karyn Kay and Gerald Peary (Dutton, 1977), 158. Originally published in 1974, this interview remains the only comprehensive interview with Dorothy Arzner, who died in 1979.

18. Arzner, interview by Kay and Peary, 159.

19. Donna R. Casella, "What Women Want: The Complex World of Dorothy Arzner and Her Cinematic Women," *Framework: The Journal of Cinema and Media* 50, no. 1/2 (2009): 240–241.

20. William Donati, *Ida Lupino: A Biography* (University Press of Kentucky, 1996), 34, 114.

21. Michael L. Shuman, "Accidental Outlaw: Agency and Genre in *The Bigamist*," in *Ida Lupino, Filmmaker*, ed. Phillip Sipiora (Bloomsbury Academic, 2021), 99.

22. Tobias, "For Elaine May," 59.

23. Quoted in Abramowitz, *Is That a Gun in Your Pocket?*, 62.

24. "Elaine May's 'Bumpy Ride' on 'Leaf'; Manduke Sticks on 'Mikey & Nicky,'" *Variety*, August 27, 1969, 6.

25. Quoted in Peter Bart, *Infamous Players: A Tale of Movies, the Mob (and Sex)* (Grand Central, 2012), 146.

26. Abramowitz, *Is That a Gun in Your Pocket?*, 62.

27. Stanley Jaffe to Charles Bluhdorn, Martin Davis, Robert Evans, and Bernard Donnenfeld, October 7, 1970, 2, *A New Leaf* production records; cited in Smukler, "Hollywood Can't Wait," 48.

28. Bernard Donnenfeld to Charles Bluhdorn and Martin Davis, interoffice communication, May 16, 1969, *A New Leaf* production records; cited in Courogen, *Miss May Does Not Exist*, 127.

29. Courogen, *Miss May Does Not Exist*, 128.

30. Elizabeth Alsop, *Elaine May* (University of Illinois Press, 2025), 44.

31. "They needed to reframe the story as a quirky romantic comedy and shift it away from whatever homicidal tale Elaine was concocting." Courogen, *Miss May Does Not Exist*, 121.

32. Peter Bart to Robert Evans, "Subject: *A New Leaf*," interoffice communication, February 7, 1969, 3, *A New Leaf* production records; cited in Smukler, "Hollywood Can't Wait," 49.

33. Quoted in Rivlin, "Elaine May," 17.

34. Carol Robertson, *The Little Book of Movie Law* (American Bar Association, 2013), 223.

35. Robertson, *The Little Book of Movie Law*, 224.

36. Producer Howard Koch said, "The lights went down, and the judge sat there and he screamed and laughed and screamed and laughed, and the lights go up and he says, 'It's the funniest picture in years. You guys win.'" Quoted in Abramowitz, *Is That a Gun in Your Pocket?*, 62.

37. Phil Rosenthal and David Wild, hosts, *Naked Lunch* podcast, "Elaine May" episode, July 21, 2022, 1:22:05.

38. Quoted in Rosenthal and Wild, *Naked Lunch* podcast.

39. Roger Ebert, "The Movies: 'A New Leaf,'" *Chicago Sun-Times*, April 6, 1971, 47.

40. Vincent Canby, "Love Turns 'New Leaf' at Music Hall," *New York Times*, March 12, 1971, 28.

41. Quoted in John Brady, *The Craft of the Screenwriter* (Simon and Schuster, 1982), 330.

42. Charles Grodin, interview by Jenni Matz and Bill Dana, American Comedy Archives, Emerson College, Boston, February 23, 2005; cited in Courogen, *Miss May Does Not Exist*, 132.

43. Kim Hendrickson, "10 Things I Learned: *Mikey and Nicky*," Criterion Collection, January 31, 2019, https://www.criterion.com/current/posts/6160.

44. Cybill Shepherd with Aimee Lee Ball, *Cybill Disobedience: How I Survived Beauty Pageants, Elvis, Sex, Bruce Willis, Lies, Marriage, Motherhood, Hollywood, and the Irrepressible Urge to Say What I Think* (HarperCollins, 2000), 110.

45. Quoted in Ryan Gilbey, "From Improv to *Ishtar*: The Many Lives of Comedy Genius Elaine May," *Guardian*, November 18, 2018.

46. Vincent Canby, "'Heartbreak Kid': Elaine May's 2d Effort as Director Arrives," *New York Times*, December 18, 1972, 56.

47. Lee Beaupre, "Elaine May's 'Mikey' to Paramount; Palomar in Scratch When Budget Rises," *Variety*, March 21, 1973, 3; "Big Rental Films of 1973," *Variety*, January 9, 1974, 19.

48. Tom Stempel calls May "one of the legendary script doctors in the business." Tom Stempel, *Framework: A History of Screenwriting in the American Film*, 3rd ed. (Syracuse University Press, 2000), 222.

49. Quoted in Charles Champlin, "Warren Beatty: Two Sides to a Hollywood Story," *Los Angeles Times*, January 28, 1979, K37.

50. Quoted in Wasson, *Improv Nation*, 335.

51. Sam Kashner, "Who's Afraid of Nichols & May?," *Vanity Fair*, January 2013, 94–106.

52. Quoted in Wasson, *Improv Nation*, 264.

53. Sydney Pollack to Elaine May, Western Union Mailgram, December 22, 1982, *Tootsie*—New York Film Critics, file 1781, Sydney Pollack Papers, Special Collections, Margaret Herrick Library; cited in Courogen, *Miss May Does Not Exist*, 202.

54. Courogen, *Miss May Does Not Exist*, 203.

55. Elizabeth Alsop says about *Ishtar*, "The first sequence alone was easily one of the funniest things I had ever seen." Alsop, *Elaine May*, xi. We find similar efforts to celebrate *Ishtar* in Hendrickson, "10 Things I Learned"; Kashner, "Who's Afraid of Nichols & May?"; Brent Lang, "As Elaine May Turns 89, It's Time to Give the Filmmaking Giant the Credit She Deserves," *Variety*, April 21, 2021; "The Week Ahead: Feb. 26–March 4; Film," *New York Times*, February 26, 2006.

56. To read recent critics still complaining about against-type casting in *Ishtar*, see Charles Bramesco, "*Ishtar* at 30: Is It Really the Worst Movie Ever Made?," *Guardian*, May 15, 2017; Time Out, review of *Ishtar*, September 10, 2012, https://www.timeout.com/movies/ishtar; Brad Weismann, "*Ishtar* (Elaine May, 1987)," *Senses of Cinema* (blog), July 2019, https://www.sensesofcinema.com/2019/cteq/ishtar.

57. David Blum, "The Road to *Ishtar*," *New York*, March 16, 1987, 40.

58. See, respectively, Peter Falk, *Just One More Thing* (Da Capo Press, 2007),

225; Bruce Bennett, "Hope and Crosby They Were Not—Charles Grodin Recalls Making 'Ishtar,'" *Wall Street Journal*, May 16, 2011, Eastern Edition, A24.

59. Quoted in Blum, "The Road to *Ishtar*," 41.

60. Quoted in Blum, "The Road to *Ishtar*," 41.

61. Patrick McMahon, interview with author, January 11, 2025.

62. Quoted in Peter Biskind, "Inside *Ishtar*," *American Film*, May 1, 1987, 27.

63. Quoted in Wasson, *Improv Nation*, 297.

64. Quoted in Biskind, "Inside *Ishtar*," 26.

65. Quoted in Biskind, "Inside *Ishtar*," 66.

66. Quoted in, respectively, Guy Flatley, "Falk on 'Mikey': This Is No Romp in the Park," *New York Times*, December 17, 1976, 62; Michael Ventura, "The Passionate Art of Peter Falk," *LA Weekly*, November 23, 1984, 34.

67. Quoted in Biskind, "Inside *Ishtar*," 66.

3. Seventies Misfits

1. "Elaine May's 'Bumpy Ride' on 'Leaf'; Manduke Sticks on 'Mikey & Nicky,'" *Variety*, August 27, 1969, 6.

2. Tino Balio, "The Art Film Market in the New Hollywood," in *Hollywood and Europe: Economics, Culture, National Identity, 1945–95*, ed. Geoffrey Nowell-Smith and Steven Ricci (British Film Institute, 1998), 63; Douglas Gomery, *Shared Pleasures: A History of Movie Presentation in the United States* (University of Wisconsin Press, 1992), 188.

3. David A. Cook, *Lost Illusions: American Cinema in the Shadow of Watergate and Vietnam, 1970–1979* (Charles Scribner and Sons, 1999), 162.

4. Cook, *Lost Illusions*, 322–334.

5. Cobbett Steinberg, *Reel Facts: The Movie Book of Records* (Vintage Books, 1982), 371.

6. Cook, *Lost Illusions*, 162.

7. Cook, *Lost Illusions*, 499.

8. Cook, *Lost Illusions*, 2.

9. James Monaco, *American Film Now: The People, the Power, the Money, the Movies* (Oxford University Press, 1979), 20.

10. Cook, *Lost Illusions*, 23.

11. Richard Maltby, "'Nobody Knows Everything': Post-Classical Historiographies and the Consolidated Entertainment," in *Contemporary Hollywood Cinema*, ed. Stephen Neale and Murray Smith (Routledge, 1998), 24.

12. Monaco, *American Film Now*, 393.

13. Such directors included Robert Aldrich, Woody Allen, Robert Altman, Hal Ashby, Peter Bogdanovich, John Boorman, Michael Cimino, Francis Ford Coppola, Brian De Palma, Miloš Forman, Bob Fosse, William Friedkin, Arthur Hiller, Stanley Kubrick, Sidney Lumet, Terrence Malick, Paul Mazursky, John Milius, Mike Nichols, Alan Pakula, Gordon Parks, Ivan Passer, Sam Peckinpah, Arthur Penn, Roman Polanski, Bob Rafelson, Michael Ritchie, Nicolas Roeg, Paul Schrader, Martin Scorsese, Robert Towne, Melvin Van Peebles, and others. These filmmakers helped establish an American art cinema or, at least, helped make Hollywood movies more like art cinema.

14. David Thomson, "The Decade When Movies Mattered," in *The Last Great*

American Picture Show: New Hollywood Cinema in the 1970s, ed. Thomas Elsaesser et al. (Amsterdam University Press, 2004), 74.

15. I am referring to movies that film commentators regularly regard as characteristic of Hollywood in the seventies. For more on the "perversity" of 1970s cinema, see Todd Berliner, *Hollywood Incoherent: Narration in Seventies Cinema* (University of Texas Press, 2010).

16. Cook, *Lost Illusions*, 355–356.

17. Martin Scorsese, *Scorsese on Scorsese*, rev. ed., ed. Ian Christie and David Thompson (Faber, 2003), 54.

18. Berliner, *Hollywood Incoherent*, 43, 51, 173.

19. Patricia Rodden Zimmermann, *Reel Families: A Social History of Amateur Film* (Indiana University Press, 1995), 3.

20. Richard Maltby, *Hollywood Cinema: An Introduction*, 2nd ed. (Wiley-Blackwell, 2003), 15.

21. Maltby, *Hollywood Cinema*, 16.

22. Maltby, *Hollywood Cinema*, 14.

23. Quoted in Mike Nichols, "Elaine May in Conversation with Mike Nichols," in *Nichols and May: Interviews*, ed. Robert E. Kapsis (University Press of Mississippi, 2020), 212.

24. Peter Bart, *Infamous Players: A Tale of Movies, the Mob (and Sex)* (Grand Central, 2012), 145.

25. Maya Montañez Smukler writes, "May had come to Paramount as a reputable comedian with dazzling critical reviews and impressive ticket sales. . . . As common as it was during these years for young filmmakers to helm studio pictures without coming up through the ranks compared to previous generations, it was still expected that these lucky few would be hired with some previous filmmaking skills." Maya Montañez Smukler, "Hollywood Can't Wait: Elaine May and the Delusions of 1970s American Cinema," in *ReFocus: The Films of Elaine May*, ed. Alexandra Heller-Nicholas and Dean Brandum (Edinburgh University Press, 2019), 46.

26. Quoted in Phil Rosenthal and David Wild, hosts, *Naked Lunch* podcast, "Elaine May" episode, July 21, 2022, 1:22:05.

27. "Salute of the Week: Elaine May," *Cue*, September 20, 1969; cited in Carrie Courogen, *Miss May Does Not Exist: The Life and Work of Elaine May, Hollywood's Hidden Genius* (St. Martin's Press, 2024), 113.

28. Herman Raucher, interview by Preston Fassel, Cinedump, September 13, 2016, https://www.cinedump.com/interviews/2016/9/13/hermanraucher.

29. Film scholar Racquel Gates has written about the ways in which Van Peebles's approach to the project transformed *Watermelon Man* into a story of Black empowerment. See Racquel Gates, "Subverting Hollywood from the Inside Out: Melvin Van Peebles's *Watermelon Man*," *Film Quarterly* 68, no. 1 (2014): 9–21.

30. Like De Palma, several other seventies filmmakers abandoned some of their artistic eccentricity as they professionalized in Hollywood. George Lucas made avant-garde films at the University of Southern California School of Cinematic Arts and began his feature filmmaking career with the chilling, detached *THX 1138* (1971), before making the more romantic *American Graffiti* (1973) and *Star Wars* (1977). Bob Rafelson directed *Head* (1968), *Five Easy Pieces* (1970), and *The King*

of Marvin Gardens (1972), before turning to the more mainstream *The Postman Always Rings Twice* (1981) and *Black Widow* (1987). Before making the blockbuster *Alien* (1979), Ridley Scott directed an art film, *The Duellists* (1977).

31. Bart, *Infamous Players*, 148.

4. Making, Releasing, and Rereleasing *Mikey and Nicky*

1. Andrew Tobias, "For Elaine May, a New Film—But Not a New Leaf," *New West*, December 6, 1976, 57.

2. Janet Coleman, *The Compass: The Improvisational Theatre That Revolutionized American Comedy* (University of Chicago Press, 1991), 295.

3. Elaine May, interview by Haden Guest, November 12, 2010, Harvard Film Archive, Harvard University, Cambridge, MA.

4. Coleman, *The Compass*, 295.

5. May, interview by Guest.

6. Quoted in Marshall Fine, *Accidental Genius: How John Cassavetes Invented the Independent Film*, reprint ed. (Miramax, 2006), 314–315.

7. Dan Rottenberg, "Elaine May . . . or She May Not," *Chicago Tribune*, October 21, 1973, 56.

8. Elaine May, "ACE [American Cinema Editors] Presents: *Mikey and Nicky* with Elaine May," interview by Phillip Schopper and Jeffrey Wolf, Metrograph Theater, New York, December 7, 2024.

9. Elaine May and Julian Schlossberg, "Elaine May Chats with Julian Schlossberg About Her Comedy, Acting, and Directing Careers," 2023, posted June 4, 2024, by Turner Classic Movies, YouTube, 16:06, https://www.youtube.com/watch?v=p-4POuAW_iU.

10. Elaine May, "MIKEY AND NICKY—Script," circa 1973, 1, Special Collections, Margaret Herrick Library, Academy of Motion Picture Arts and Sciences, Beverly Hills, CA.

11. May, "ACE Presents."

12. Wayne Warga, "Falk—Many a Sinking Ship's Saving Grace," *Los Angeles Times*, December 16, 1968, G1, 13.

13. Quoted in Peter Falk, *Just One More Thing* (Da Capo Press, 2007), 185. A similar version of this story appears in John Cassavetes, *Cassavetes on Cassavetes*, ed. Ray Carney (Farrar, Straus and Giroux, 2001), 203.

14. May and Schlossberg, "Elaine May Chats with Julian Schlossberg."

15. Barbara Koenig Quart writes that Nellie, "with an odd looking, slightly beat, out-of-focus face . . . is no blond floozy, earth mother, or other usual cliche, but a distinctive person." Barbara Koenig Quart, *Women Directors: The Emergence of a New Cinema* (Praeger, 1988), 46.

16. Carol [Grace] Matthau, *Among the Porcupines: A Memoir* (Random House, 1992), 239. Grace used her birth name when making *Mikey and Nicky* and her married name when she published her memoir.

17. May and Schlossberg, "Elaine May Chats with Julian Schlossberg."

18. Kristin Thompson argues that "realism has often been perceived as a departure from the norm of popular, classical, familiar cinema." Kristin Thompson, *Breaking the Glass Armor: Neoformalist Film Analysis* (Princeton University Press, 1988), 200–201.

19. "Elaine May's 'Bumpy Ride' on 'Leaf'; Manduke Sticks on 'Mikey & Nicky,'" *Variety*, August 27, 1969, 6.

20. Lee Beaupre, "Elaine May's 'Mikey' to Paramount; Palomar in Scratch When Budget Rises," *Variety*, March 21, 1973, 3.

21. Quoted in Tobias, "For Elaine May," 59.

22. Tobias, "For Elaine May," 59.

23. Quoted in Rottenberg, "Elaine May . . . or She May Not," 556.

24. Matthau, *Among the Porcupines*, 243.

25. Matthau, *Among the Porcupines*, 243. Grace (Matthau) further wrote about the film: "Every once in a while, there was talk of its going to Cannes and I'd cringe a little bit, but by now [1992] I think the movie is quietly dead," 246.

26. Matthau, *Among the Porcupines*, 243.

27. Tom Miller's working notebook for *Mikey and Nicky*, 1973, 5, Tom Miller Papers, Special Collections, Margaret Herrick Library.

28. Rottenberg, "Elaine May . . . or She May Not," 56.

29. Miller's working notebook for *Mikey and Nicky*, 23.

30. The 180-degree rule maintains the screen direction of characters and objects in the frame by keeping the camera on one side of an imaginary line ("axis of action") during filming. The 30-degree rule instructs filmmakers to move the camera position by at least 30 degrees between consecutive shots of the same mise-en-scène elements so as to avoid a jump cut.

31. John Cassavetes, interview, in Miller's working notebook for *Mikey and Nicky*, 3.

32. Tobias, "For Elaine May," 62.

33. Miller's working notebook for *Mikey and Nicky*, 8.

34. Miller's working notebook for *Mikey and Nicky*, 25.

35. Miller's working notebook for *Mikey and Nicky*, 24.

36. Matthau, *Among the Porcupines*, 242.

37. Patrick Cooper, *"Aren't You Gonna Die Someday?": Elaine May's* Mikey and Nicky*: An Examination, Reflection, and Making of* (BearManor Media, 2019), chap. 40.

38. Cooper, *Aren't You Gonna Die Someday?*, chap. 7.

39. Tobias, "For Elaine May," 62.

40. Miller's working notebook for *Mikey and Nicky*, 6.

41. Patrick McMahon, interview with author, January 11, 2025.

42. Carrie Courogen, *Miss May Does Not Exist: The Life and Work of Elaine May, Hollywood's Hidden Genius* (St. Martin's Press, 2024), 169. Vaughn Hazell, assistant editor for John Carter, dealt with the complications of having four separate audio tracks. Vaughn Hazell, interview with author, January 17, 2025.

43. McMahon, interview with author.

44. Hazell, interview with author.

45. Sam Wasson, *Improv Nation: How We Made a Great American Art* (Harper Perennial, 2018), 199; Tobias, "For Elaine May," 62.

46. Tobias, "For Elaine May," 62; Rachel Abramowitz, *Is That a Gun in Your Pocket? Women's Experience of Power in Hollywood* (Random House, 2000), 66.

47. Quoted in Wasson, *Improv Nation*, 200.

48. Hazell, interview with author.

49. Quoted in Courogen, *Miss May Does Not Exist*, 166.
50. Quoted in Tobias, "For Elaine May," 63.
51. Abramowitz, *Is That a Gun in Your Pocket?*, 66.
52. Quoted in Courogen, *Miss May Does Not Exist*, 166.
53. Quoted in Wasson, *Improv Nation*, 199–200.
54. Quoted in Abramowitz, *Is That a Gun in Your Pocket?*, 66.
55. Marilyn Beck, "Presley to Encore Satellite Show," *Atlanta Constitution*, July 29, 1974, 13A.
56. McMahon, interview with author.
57. Quoted in Wasson, *Improv Nation*, 201.
58. McMahon, interview with author.
59. Hazell, interview with author.
60. Hazell, interview with author.
61. Quoted in Michael Rivlin, "Elaine May: Too Tough for Hollywood?," *Millimeter* 3, no. 10 (1975): 17–18.
62. McMahon, interview with author.
63. McMahon, interview with author.
64. McMahon, interview with author. Others, such as Carrie Courogen, report that the filmmakers had not completed the sound mix at the time of this screening. Courogen, *Miss May Does Not Exist*, 169.
65. Abramowitz, *Is That a Gun in Your Pocket?*, 67.
66. "Par, Elaine May Sue Each Other; Film Over-Budget and Incomplete," *Variety*, October 29, 1975, 5.
67. "Par, Elaine May Sue Each Other," *Variety*, 5.
68. While working on the film, assistant editor Patrick McMahon thought that it might never be released, or that the studio would simply dump it in a few theaters in order to satisfy its contractual obligation, which, ultimately, is what it did. McMahon, interview with author. Peter Falk, too, thought the film would never be released. Bob Thomas, "Goodby, Columbo," *St. Louis (MO) Post-Dispatch*, March 8, 1976, 6D.
69. "Par Charges Criminal Conduct in 'Mikey' Suit vs. Elaine May," *Variety*, September 15, 1976, 5.
70. Quoted in Tobias, "For Elaine May," 66.
71. May, interview by Guest.
72. John Simon, "May, Bogdanovich, and Streisand: Varieties of Death Wish," *New York*, January 10, 1977, 55.
73. Charles Champlin, "'Mikey, Nicky' Play Cat and Mouse," *Los Angeles Times*, December 25, 1976, D1.
74. Desmond Ryan, "'Mikey and Nicky' Returns, but It Shouldn't Have Bothered," *Philadelphia Inquirer*, May 20, 1977, C9.
75. Vincent Canby, "'Mikey and Nicky,' Film on Amity," *New York Times*, December 22, 1976, 34.
76. Marie Brenner, "The Coast of Living," *Texas Monthly*, March 1, 1977, 120.
77. Judith Crist, "Out of the Mouths of Admen . . . ," *Saturday Review*, January 22, 1977, 49.
78. Respectively: Joe Pollack, "At the Movies," *St. Louis (MO) Post-Dispatch*, September 23, 1977, 47; Clyde Gilmour, "Elaine May's *Mikey and Nicky* in Deep

Trouble," *Toronto Star*, May 3, 1977, F1; Edward Blank, "'Exorcist II: Heretic' Amuses, 'Mikey and Nicky' Half and Half," *Pittsburgh (PA) Press*, June 17, 1977, A9; E. P., "Buying & Booking Guide: *Mikey & Nicky*," *Independent Film Journal* 79, no. 1 (1976): 30.

79. Frank Rich, "'Mikey and Nicky' a Painful Mess," *New York Post*, December 22, 1976, 318.

80. Murf, review of *Mikey and Nicky*, *Variety*, December 22, 1976, 20.

81. Crist, "Out of the Mouths of Admen . . . ," 49.

82. Ruth Batchelor, "With Such Friends—Who Needs Enemies?," *Los Angeles Free Press*, January 7, 1977, 9.

83. Joy Gould Boyum, "Talented Artists, Dismal Movies," *Wall Street Journal*, January 17, 1977, 15.

84. Canby, "'Mikey and Nicky,' Film on Amity," 34.

85. Rich, "'Mikey and Nicky' a Painful Mess," 318.

86. Simon, "May, Bogdanovich, and Streisand," 55.

87. Jack Kroll, "Elaine's Night Out," *Newsweek*, December 27, 1976, 56.

88. Molly Haskell, "A Long Day's Journey into Buddy-Buddy Land," *Village Voice*, January 3, 1977, 37.

89. Ryan, "'Mikey and Nicky' Returns," C9.

90. Champlin, "'Mikey, Nicky' Play Cat and Mouse," D1.

91. Boyum, "Talented Artists, Dismal Movies," 15.

92. Crist, "Out of the Mouths of Admen . . . ," 49.

93. Jay Cocks, "Hit Men," *Time*, January 31, 1977, 59.

94. Stanley Kauffmann, review of *Mikey and Nicky*, *New Republic*, January 1 and 8, 1977, 20–21.

95. Respectively: Stanley Kauffmann, "Stanley Kauffmann on Films," *New Republic*, December 8, 1978, 18; Stanley Kauffmann, *Before My Eyes: Film Criticism and Comment* (Da Capo Press, 1982), 275.

96. See, e.g., Stanley Kauffmann, "Films Worth Seeing," *New Republic*, May 27, 1985, 24.

97. David Sterritt, "'Voyage' Proves 'a Rather Dull Cruise': Also, Connery in 'Next Man' and New Elaine May Study," *Christian Science Monitor*, December 31, 1976, 19.

98. Jonathan Rosenbaum, "Moving," *Film Comment*, July/August 1977, 2.

99. For mixed reviews of the film, see "Movie Guide," *Christian Science Monitor*, February 11, 1977, 18; Kathleen Carroll, "Et Tu, Mikey?," *New York Daily News*, December 23, 1976, 44; Murf, review of *Mikey and Nicky*, 20.

100. Gene Shalit, "What's Happening: Instant Interview with Peter Falk," *Ladies' Home Journal*, March 1977, 14.

101. "50 Top-Grossing Films," *Variety*, January 12, 1977, 41.

102. Julian Schlossberg, interview with author, September 7, 2024.

103. Schlossberg, interview with author.

104. Elaine May, "Mikey and Nicky Release Dialogue Script," 1976, Special Collections, Margaret Herrick Library.

105. Carroll, "Et Tu, Mikey?"; Howard Kissel, review of *Mikey and Nicky*, *Women's Wear Daily*, December 20, 1976, 5.

106. Kroll, "Elaine's Night Out," 56.

107. Julie Salamon, "Buddy Love," *Wall Street Journal*, May 16, 1985, 30.

108. "50 Top-Grossing Films," *Variety*, May 15, 1985, 9.

109. Schlossberg, interview with author, September 7, 2024.

110. Schlossberg, interview with author, January 4, 2024.

111. Desmond Ryan, "'Mikey and Nicky' Seeks a Second Opinion," *Philadelphia Inquirer*, May 27, 1985, C3.

112. Michael Blowen, "'Mikey and Nicky' Still Looking for the Right Formula," *Boston Globe*, October 4, 1985, 55.

113. Vincent Canby, "Film View; It's That Time of Year When Unusual Movies Blossom," *New York Times*, April 28, 1985, 17.

114. Sheila Benson, "Elaine May Film Reborn and Praised," *Los Angeles Times*, November 14, 1984, H1.

115. Salamon, "Buddy Love," 30.

116. Michael Ventura, "Pick of the Week: *Mikey and Nicky*," *LA Weekly*, December 30, 1984.

117. Ray Carney, "Mikey and Nicky," in *Magill's Cinema Annual 1985: A Survey of 1984 Films*, ed. Frank N. Magill (Salem Press, 1985), 579–580.

118. Dave Kehr, "Critic's Choice: New DVD's," *New York Times*, December 21, 2004, E3.

119. J. Hoberman, "May Days," *Village Voice*, February 14, 2006.

120. Jim Hemphill, "Mikey & Nicky (1976)," *American Cinematographer* 86, no. 4 (2005): 17; Rich, "'Mikey and Nicky' a Painful Mess," 318.

121. Respectively: Peter Bradshaw, "*Mikey and Nicky* Review—a Neglected Gem of 70s Cinema," *Guardian*, June 15, 2018; Kim Morgan, review of *Mikey and Nicky*, *Sight and Sound* 25, no. 10 (2015): 27; Richard Brody, "A Man's World: Elaine May's Feminist Angle on the Gangster Film," *New Yorker*, May 1, 2015, 10.

122. Kehr, "Critic's Choice," E3.

123. Kauffmann, review of *Mikey and Nicky*, 20–21.

124. For more on the ways in which exposure to a challenging artwork increases understanding and pleasure, see Todd Berliner, *Hollywood Aesthetic: Pleasure in American Cinema* (Oxford University Press, 2017), 171–172.

125. May, interview by Guest.

5. Narrative

1. Quoted in Michael Ventura, "The Passionate Art of Peter Falk," *LA Weekly*, November 23, 1984, 34. Many reviewers assumed that the actors improvised their lines, including Desmond Ryan ("May takes the screenplay credit but you have the sense of impromptu dialogue throughout the film, which is reminiscent of Cassavetes' 'Husbands'"), Clyde Gilmour ("the impression soon grows, however, that she encouraged actors Falk and Cassavetes to improvise their material with the cameras rolling"), and Joy Gould Boyum (Falk and Cassavetes "seem to be improvising their lines"). Desmond Ryan, "'Mikey and Nicky' Returns, but It Shouldn't Have Bothered," *Philadelphia Inquirer*, May 20, 1977, C9; Clyde Gilmour, "Elaine May's *Mikey and Nicky* in Deep Trouble," *Toronto Star*, May 3, 1977, F1; Joy Gould Boyum, "Talented Artists, Dismal Movies," *Wall Street Journal*, January 17, 1977, 15.

2. David Bordwell, "Classical Hollywood Cinema: Narrational Principles and

Procedures," in *Narrative, Apparatus, Ideology: A Film Theory Reader*, ed. Philip Rosen (Columbia University Press, 1986), 17.

3. Bordwell, "Classical Hollywood Cinema," 17.

4. Bordwell, "Classical Hollywood Cinema," 17.

5. Tom Miller's working notebook for *Mikey and Nicky*, 1973, 5, Tom Miller Papers, Special Collections, Margaret Herrick Library, Academy of Motion Picture Arts and Sciences, Beverly Hills, CA.

6. Elaine May, "ACE [American Cinema Editors] Presents: *Mikey and Nicky* with Elaine May," interview by Phillip Schopper and Jeffrey Wolf, Metrograph Theater, New York, December 7, 2024.

7. For a discussion of variations on the gangster film formula, see Thomas Schatz, *Hollywood Genres: Formulas, Filmmaking, and the Studio System* (McGraw-Hill, 1981), 99–104.

8. Phillip Schopper, email to author, January 3, 2025.

9. Schopper, email to author.

10. Quentin Tarantino and Roger Avary, hosts, *Video Archives*, podcast, episode 106, "*Coma, Mikey & Nicky, Piranha*," September 27, 2022, 2:29:41.

11. Bordwell, "Classical Hollywood Cinema," 30.

12. Jeremy Carr writes, "What she holds back in terms of exposition and development, she communicates in behavior." Jeremy Carr, "*Mikey and Nicky* (1976)—Elaine May and the Cassavetes Connection," in *ReFocus: The Films of Elaine May*, ed. Alexandra Heller-Nicholas and Dean Brandum (Edinburgh University Press, 2019), 121.

13. Respectively: Jaime Rebanal, "*Mikey and Nicky* Review: Elaine May Breaks Down Masculinity to Its Core," *Cinema from the Spectrum* (blog), March 20, 2019, https://cinemafromthespectrum.com/2019/03/19/mikey; Ruth Batchelor, "With Such Friends—Who Needs Enemies?," *Los Angeles Free Press*, January 7, 1977, 9; Amy Longsdorf, "'Mikey and Nicky' Was Elaine May's Followup to Her Acclaimed 'The Heartbreak Kid,'" *Morning Call* (Allentown, PA), January 15, 2019; Alexandra Heller-Nicholas, "Introduction: Who's Kidding?—Approaching Elaine May," in Heller-Nicholas and Brandum, *ReFocus*, 10.

14. Alison Willmore et al., "The 101 Greatest Endings in Movies History," Vulture [*New York* magazine], February 22, 2021, https://www.vulture.com/article/the-101-best-movie-endings-of-all-time-ranked.html.

15. Elaine May, "MIKEY AND NICKY—Script," circa 1973, 126, Special Collections, Margaret Herrick Library.

6. Style

1. Respectively: Judith Crist, "Out of the Mouths of Admen . . . ," *Saturday Review*, January 22, 1977, 50; Desmond Ryan, "'Mikey and Nicky' Returns, but It Shouldn't Have Bothered," *Philadelphia Inquirer*, May 20, 1977, C9; Frank Rich, "'Mikey and Nicky' a Painful Mess," *New York Post*, December 22, 1976, 318; Charles Champlin, "'Mikey, Nicky' Play Cat and Mouse," *Los Angeles Times*, December 25, 1976, D1; Molly Haskell, "A Long Day's Journey into Buddy-Buddy Land," *Village Voice*, January 3, 1977, 37.

2. David Bordwell, *Figures Traced in Light: On Cinematic Staging* (University of California Press, 2005), 32.

3. Julie Salamon, "Buddy Love," *Wall Street Journal*, May 16, 1985, 30.

4. Jim Hemphill, "Mikey & Nicky (1976)," *American Cinematographer* 86, no. 4 (2005): 17.

5. Jessica Kiang, "Retrospective: The Directorial Career of Elaine May," IndieWire, August 8, 2013, archived October 23, 2021, https://web.archive.org/web/20211023014647/http://www.indiewire.com/2013/08/retrospective-the-directorial-career-of-elaine-may-95011/.

6. Jeremy Carr, "*Mikey and Nicky* (1976)—Elaine May and the Cassavetes Connection," in *ReFocus: The Films of Elaine May*, ed. Alexandra Heller-Nicholas and Dean Brandum (Edinburgh University Press, 2019), 121.

7. Julian Schlossberg, interview, *Mikey and Nicky* (1976), special ed. Blu-ray (Criterion Collection, 2019).

8. Patrick McMahon, interview with author, January 11, 2025. McMahon says that May brought in Albertson, perhaps for the studio's sake, to put together an entire cut of the movie, although it lacked the ending.

9. To return to the brief discussion of artistic value that I initiated in the introduction: *Mikey and Nicky*'s technical defects, to quote philosopher Jonathan Gilmore, do not work against the artist's "essential aims, ends, and purposes" (what Gilmore terms "constitutive functions"). Gilmore argues that an artistic property may be regarded as a defect when it "counts against the satisfaction" of an artwork's constitutive functions. Jonathan Gilmore, "A Functional View of Artistic Evaluation," *Philosophical Studies* 155, no. 2 (2011): 290. Hollywood filmmakers normally strive for technical perfection, but May did not—for her it was not an essential aim, end, or purpose in itself—so, in Gilmore's reasoning, we should not regard *Mikey and Nicky*'s technical defects as artistic defects.

10. John Cassavetes, interview, in Tom Miller's working notebook for *Mikey and Nicky*, 1973, Tom Miller Papers, Special Collections, Margaret Herrick Library, Academy of Motion Picture Arts and Sciences, Beverly Hills, CA.

11. McMahon, interview with author.

12. Vaughn Hazell, interview with author, January 17, 2025.

13. Paul F. Berliner, *Thinking in Jazz: The Infinite Art of Improvisation* (University of Chicago Press, 1994), 210.

14. Quoted in Berliner, *Thinking in Jazz*, 211.

15. Quoted in Berliner, *Thinking in Jazz*, 211.

16. Alexander Mackendrick, *On Film-Making: An Introduction to the Craft of the Director*, ed. Paul Cronin (Faber and Faber, 2004), 222–223.

17. Carr, "*Mikey and Nicky* (1976)," 134.

18. J. Hoberman, "May Days," *Village Voice*, February 14, 2006.

19. Ryan, "'Mikey and Nicky' Returns," C9.

7. Performance

1. Tom Miller's working notebook for *Mikey and Nicky*, 1973, 24, Tom Miller Papers, Special Collections, Margaret Herrick Library, Academy of Motion Picture Arts and Sciences, Beverly Hills, CA.

2. Julian Schlossberg, conveying answers from Elaine May to author, September 10, 2024.

3. Tom Canford [Miller], "'On the Whole, I'd Rather Be in Philadelpha' (Elaine May's *Mikey and Nicky*)," in *A Fever of the Mad: A Movie Publicist Works with Francis Coppola, Elaine May, John Cassavetes, Peter Falk, and Richard Gere and Survives to Tell the Tale!*, ed. Jonathan May (Hollow Square Press, 2013), Kindle. "Tom Canford" is the pen name of publicist Tom Miller.

4. Quoted in Michael Rivlin, "Elaine May: Too Tough for Hollywood?," *Millimeter* 3, no. 10 (1975): 17.

5. Carol Matthau, *Among the Porcupines: A Memoir* (Random House, 1992), 243.

6. Canford, "On the Whole," Kindle.

7. Peter Falk, *Just One More Thing* (Da Capo Press, 2007), 228.

8. Canford, "On the Whole," Kindle.

9. Miller's working notebook for *Mikey and Nicky*, 27.

10. Dan Rottenberg, "Elaine May . . . or She May Not," *Chicago Tribune*, October 21, 1973, 57.

11. Quoted in Dick Lemon, "Movies: How to Succeed in Interviewing Elaine May (Try, Really Try)," *New York Times*, January 4, 1970, D13.

12. Toni Morrison, "Write, Erase, Do It Over," interview by Rebecca Sutton, *American Artscape*, no. 4 (2014), https://www.arts.gov/stories/magazine/2014/4/art-failure-importance-risk-and-experimentation/toni-morrison.

13. E. P., "Buying & Booking Guide: *Mikey & Nicky*," *Independent Film Journal* 79, no. 1 (1976): 30–31.

14. Charles Champlin, "'Mikey, Nicky' Play Cat and Mouse," *Los Angeles Times*, December 25, 1976, D1.

15. Ruth Batchelor, "With Such Friends—Who Needs Enemies?," *Los Angeles Free Press*, January 7, 1977, 9.

16. Desmond Ryan, "'Mikey and Nicky' Returns, but It Shouldn't Have Bothered," *Philadelphia Inquirer*, May 20, 1977, 9.

17. Jeremy Carr writes of Cassavetes: "One need look no further than the actor's Oscar-nominated turn in *The Dirty Dozen* (Robert Aldrich, 1967) or his appearance in *Rosemary's Baby* (Roman Polanski, 1968)—two fine performances, but neither quintessential achievements—to see that [Cassavetes] and May are riding a similar wavelength." Jeremy Carr, "*Mikey and Nicky* (1976)—Elaine May and the Cassavetes Connection," in *ReFocus: The Films of Elaine May*, ed. Alexandra Heller-Nicholas and Dean Brandum (Edinburgh University Press, 2019).

18. Elaine May, interview by Haden Guest, November 12, 2010, Harvard Film Archive, Harvard University, Cambridge, MA.

19. Quoted in Joyce Haber, "Peter Falk Takes Off the Trench Coat," Calendar, *Los Angeles Times*, January 19, 1975, O27.

20. May, interview by Guest.

21. Matthau, *Among the Porcupines*, 243.

22. Carr, "*Mikey and Nicky* (1976)," 124.

23. Quoted in Guy Flatley, "Falk on 'Mikey': This Is No Romp in the Park," *New York Times*, December 17, 1976, 62.

24. Quoted in Michael Ventura, "The Passionate Art of Peter Falk," *LA Weekly*, November 23, 1984, 33–34.

25. Quoted in Ventura, "The Passionate Art of Peter Falk," 34.

26. Viola Spolin, *Improvisation for the Theater: A Handbook of Teaching and Directing Techniques* (Northwestern University Press, 1963), 6.

27. John Cassavetes, interview, in Miller's working notebook for *Mikey and Nicky*, 24.

Conclusion

1. Rachel Abramowitz, *Is That a Gun in Your Pocket? Women's Experience of Power in Hollywood* (Random House, 2000), 62.

2. Sam Wasson, *Improv Nation: How We Made a Great American Art* (Harper Perennial, 2018), 199–200.

3. Vaughn Hazell, interview with author, January 17, 2025.

4. Desmond Ryan, "'Mikey and Nicky' Returns, but It Shouldn't Have Bothered," *Philadelphia Inquirer*, May 20, 1977, C9. Along similar lines, an anonymous reviewer of this manuscript made one suggestion for improvement: modify the term *masterpiece*. The reviewer explained, "stagehands appearing inadvertently in two separate shots in light of her multi-camera coverage of the entire production are not the stuff of masterpiece films." The reviewer furthermore noted that many acknowledged seventies masterpieces—*A Clockwork Orange* (1971), *Badlands* (1973), *Nashville* (1975), *Days of Heaven* (1978), for example—were produced "on budgets smaller than *M/N*'s and in much less time." The reviewer makes a valid point, but it relies on the assumption that a Hollywood masterpiece must come in on time and on budget and achieve the technical perfection expected from commercial productions.

5. "While the identification of a work as a member of a category offers a *prima facie* reason for evaluating it in light of criteria associated with that category, the ends of the work furnished by the artist's successfully realized intentions can trump the ends of the category to which the work belongs." Jonathan Gilmore, "A Functional View of Artistic Evaluation," *Philosophical Studies* 155, no. 2 (2011): 296.

6. Frank Sibley, *Approach to Aesthetics: Collected Papers on Philosophical Aesthetics*, ed. John Benson et al. (Clarendon Press, 2006), 12.

BIBLIOGRAPHY

Abramowitz, Rachel. *Is That a Gun in Your Pocket? Women's Experience of Power in Hollywood*. Random House, 2000.

Alsop, Elizabeth. *Elaine May*. University of Illinois Press, 2025.

Arzner, Dorothy. Interview by Karyn Kay and Gerald Peary. In *Women and the Cinema: A Critical Anthology*, edited by Karyn Kay and Gerald Peary. Dutton, 1977.

Balio, Tino. "The Art Film Market in the New Hollywood." In *Hollywood and Europe: Economics, Culture, National Identity, 1945–95*, edited by Geoffrey Nowell-Smith and Steven Ricci. British Film Institute, 1998.

Bart, Peter. *Infamous Players: A Tale of Movies, the Mob (and Sex)*. Grand Central, 2012.

Basinger, Jeanine. "Giving Credit—Pioneering Women." Directors Guild of America. Winter 2011. https://www.dga.org/craft/dgaq/issues/1004-winter-2011/features-giving-credit.

Batchelor, Ruth. "With Such Friends—Who Needs Enemies?" *Los Angeles Free Press*, January 7, 1977.

Beaupre, Lee. "Elaine May's 'Mikey' to Paramount; Palomar in Scratch When Budget Rises." *Variety*, March 21, 1973, 3.

Beck, Marilyn. "Presley to Encore Satellite Show." *Atlanta Constitution*, July 29, 1974.

Bennett, Bruce. "Hope and Crosby They Were Not—Charles Grodin Recalls Making 'Ishtar.'" *Wall Street Journal*, May 16, 2011. Eastern Edition.

Benson, Sheila. "Elaine May Film Reborn and Praised." *Los Angeles Times*, November 14, 1984.

Berliner, Paul F. *Thinking in Jazz: The Infinite Art of Improvisation*. University of Chicago Press, 1994.

Berliner, Todd. *Hollywood Aesthetic: Pleasure in American Cinema*. Oxford University Press, 2017.

Berliner, Todd. *Hollywood Incoherent: Narration in Seventies Cinema*. University of Texas Press, 2010.

Biskind, Peter. "Inside *Ishtar*." *American Film*, May 1, 1987, 20–27, 66.

Blank, Edward. "'Exorcist II: Heretic' Amuses, 'Mikey and Nicky' Half and Half." *Pittsburgh (PA) Press*, June 17, 1977.

Blowen, Michael. "'Mikey and Nicky' Still Looking for the Right Formula." *Boston Globe*, October 4, 1985.

Blum, David. "The Road to *Ishtar*." *New York*, March 16, 1987, 34–43.

Booth, Stephen. *"King Lear," "Macbeth," Indefinition, and Tragedy*. Yale University Press, 1983.

Bordwell, David. "Classical Hollywood Cinema: Narrational Principles and Procedures." In *Narrative, Apparatus, Ideology: A Film Theory Reader*, edited by Philip Rosen. Columbia University Press, 1986.

Bordwell, David. *Figures Traced in Light: On Cinematic Staging*. University of California Press, 2005.

Bordwell, David. "Historical Poetics of Cinema." In *The Cinematic Text*, edited by R. Barton Palmer. AMS Press, 1989.

Boyum, Joy Gould. "Talented Artists, Dismal Movies." *Wall Street Journal*, January 17, 1977.

Bradshaw, Peter. "*Mikey and Nicky* Review—a Neglected Gem of 70s Cinema." *Guardian*, June 15, 2018.

Brady, John. *The Craft of the Screenwriter*. Simon and Schuster, 1982.

Brakhage, Stan. *Essential Brakhage: Selected Writings on Film-Making*. Edited by Bruce R. McPherson. Documentext, 2001.

Bramesco, Charles. "*Ishtar* at 30: Is It Really the Worst Movie Ever Made?" *Guardian*, May 15, 2017.

Brenner, Marie. "The Coast of Living." *Texas Monthly*, March 1, 1977, 116–120.

Brody, Richard. "A Man's World: Elaine May's Feminist Angle on the Gangster Film." *New Yorker*, May 1, 2015, 10.

Burton, Richard. *The Richard Burton Diaries*. Edited by Chris Williams. Yale University Press, 2012.

Butler, Alison. *Women's Cinema: The Contested Screen*. 2002. Wallflower Press, 2019.

Canby, Vincent. "Film View; It's That Time of Year When Unusual Movies Blossom." *New York Times*, April 28, 1985.

Canby, Vincent. "'Heartbreak Kid': Elaine May's 2d Effort as Director Arrives." *New York Times*, December 18, 1972.

Canby, Vincent. "Love Turns 'New Leaf' at Music Hall." *New York Times*, March 12, 1971.

Canby, Vincent. "'Mikey and Nicky,' Film on Amity." *New York Times*, December 22, 1976.

Canford, Tom. "'On the Whole, I'd Rather Be in Philadelphia' (Elaine May's *Mikey and Nicky*)." In *A Fever of the Mad: A Movie Publicist Works with Francis Coppola, Elaine May, John Cassavetes, Peter Falk, and Richard Gere and Survives to Tell the Tale!*, edited by Jonathan May. Hollow Square Press, 2013. Kindle.

Carney, Ray. "Mikey and Nicky." In *Magill's Cinema Annual 1985: A Survey of 1984 Films*, edited by Frank N. Magill. Salem Press, 1985.

Carney, Ray. "Pulp Affliction: The Sorry State of Contemporary Film." *Baffler*, no. 8 (December 1995): 41–49.

Carr, Jeremy. "*Mikey and Nicky* (1976)—Elaine May and the Cassavetes Connection." In *ReFocus: The Films of Elaine May*, edited by Alexandra Heller-Nicholas and Dean Brandum. Edinburgh University Press, 2019.

Carroll, Kathleen. "Et Tu, Mikey?" *New York Daily News*, December 23, 1976.

Carroll, Noël. "Forget Taste." *Journal of Aesthetic Education* 56, no. 1 (2022): 1–27.

Casella, Donna R. "What Women Want: The Complex World of Dorothy Arzner and Her Cinematic Women." *Framework: The Journal of Cinema and Media* 50, no. 1/2 (2009): 235–270.

Cassavetes, John. *Cassavetes on Cassavetes*. Edited by Ray Carney. Farrar, Straus and Giroux, 2001.

Champlin, Charles. "'Mikey, Nicky' Play Cat and Mouse." *Los Angeles Times*, December 25, 1976.

Champlin, Charles. "Warren Beatty: Two Sides to a Hollywood Story." *Los Angeles Times*, January 28, 1979.

Christian Science Monitor. "Movie Guide." February 11, 1977, 18.

Cocks, Jay. "Hit Men." *Time*, January 31, 1977, 59.

Coleman, Janet. *The Compass: The Improvisational Theatre That Revolutionized American Comedy*. University of Chicago Press, 1991.

Cook, David A. *Lost Illusions: American Cinema in the Shadow of Watergate and Vietnam, 1970–1979*. Charles Scribner and Sons, 1999.

Cooper, Patrick. *"Aren't You Gonna Die Someday?": Elaine May's* Mikey and Nicky: *An Examination, Reflection, and Making of*. BearManor Media, 2019.

Courogen, Carrie. *Miss May Does Not Exist: The Life and Work of Elaine May, Hollywood's Hidden Genius*. St. Martin's Press, 2024.

Crist, Judith. "Out of the Mouths of Admen . . ." *Saturday Review*, January 22, 1977, 49–50.

Crist, Judith. *Take 22: Moviemakers on Moviemaking*. Viking, 1984.

Cue. "Salute of the Week: Elaine May." September 20, 1969.

Danto, Arthur C. *The Transfiguration of the Commonplace: A Philosophy of Art*. Harvard University Press, 1981.

Dargis, Manohla. "Film." *New York Times*, February 5, 2006. Late Edition.

Deren, Maya. *Essential Deren: Collected Writings on Film*. Edited by Bruce R. McPherson. Documentext, 2005.

Donati, William. *Ida Lupino: A Biography*. University Press of Kentucky, 1996.

Ebert, Roger. "The Movies: 'A New Leaf.'" *Chicago Sun-Times*, April 6, 1971.

Falk, Peter. *Just One More Thing*. Da Capo Press, 2007.

Fine, Marshall. *Accidental Genius: How John Cassavetes Invented the Independent Film*. Reprint ed. Miramax, 2006.

Flatley, Guy. "Falk on 'Mikey': This Is No Romp in the Park." *New York Times*, December 17, 1976.

Freeman, Mark. "Teenagers on Stage—The Comedy of Elaine May and Mike Nichols." In *ReFocus: The Films of Elaine May*, edited by Alexandra Heller-Nicholas and Dean Brandum. Edinburgh University Press, 2019.

Gates, Racquel. "Subverting Hollywood from the Inside Out: Melvin Van Peebles's *Watermelon Man*." *Film Quarterly* 68, no. 1 (2014): 9–21.

Gelb, Barbara. "Mike Nichols: The Special Risks and Rewards of the Director's Art." *New York Times*, May 27, 1984. Late Edition.

Gilbey, Ryan. "From Improv to *Ishtar*: The Many Lives of Comedy Genius Elaine May." *Guardian*, November 18, 2018.

Gilmore, Jonathan. "A Functional View of Artistic Evaluation." *Philosophical Studies* 155, no. 2 (2011): 289–305.

Gilmour, Clyde. "Elaine May's *Mikey and Nicky* in Deep Trouble." *Toronto Star*, May 3, 1977.

Glassgold, C. Adolph. "The Films: Amateur or Professional." *Arts* 15, no. 1 (1929): 56–59.

Gomery, Douglas. *Shared Pleasures: A History of Movie Presentation in the United States*. University of Wisconsin Press, 1992.

Grodin, Charles. Interview by Jenni Matz and Bill Dana. American Comedy Archives, Emerson College, Boston, February 23, 2005.

Haber, Joyce. "Peter Falk Takes Off the Trench Coat." *Los Angeles Times*, January 19, 1975.

Haskell, Molly. "A Long Day's Journey into Buddy-Buddy Land." *Village Voice*, January 3, 1977, 36–37.

Haskell, Molly. "Woman Directors." *American Film* 1, no. 8 (1976): 18–23.

Hausman, Michael, and Victor Kemper. "The Making of *Mikey and Nicky* (1976)." Posted August 28, 2020, by Hollowshape, YouTube, 14:26. https://www.youtube.com/watch?v=qIXnPfJfy_I.

Heller-Nicholas, Alexandra. "Introduction: Who's Kidding?—Approaching Elaine May." In *ReFocus: The Films of Elaine May*, edited by Alexandra Heller-Nicholas and Dean Brandum. Edinburgh University Press, 2019.

Hemphill, Jim. "Mikey & Nicky (1976)." *American Cinematographer* 86, no. 4 (2005): 16–17.

Hendrickson, Kim. "10 Things I Learned: *Mikey and Nicky*." Criterion Collection. January 31, 2019. https://www.criterion.com/current/posts/6160.

Hoberman, J. "May Days." *Village Voice*, February 14, 2006.

Hoberman, J. "A Reclusive Auteur's Brilliant Career, from the Jewish New Wave to a Legendary Bomb." *Village Voice*, February 22, 2006.

Jackson, Lynne, and Karen Jaehne. "Eavesdropping on Female Voices: A Who's Who of Contemporary Women Filmmakers." *Cinéaste* 16, no. 1 (1987): 38–43.

James, Caryn. "The Fireworks of Elaine May." *New York Times*, February 24, 2006.

James, David E. "Amateurs in the Industry Town: Stan Brakhage and Andy Warhol in Los Angeles." *Grey Room*, no. 12 (Summer 2003): 81–93.

Jones, Kent. "In the American Grain." *Film Comment*, March/April 2016.

Kashner, Sam. "Who's Afraid of Nichols & May?" *Vanity Fair*, January 2013, 94–106.

Kauffmann, Stanley. *Before My Eyes: Film Criticism and Comment*. Da Capo Press, 1982.

Kauffmann, Stanley. "Films Worth Seeing." *New Republic*, May 27, 1985, 24.

Kauffmann, Stanley. Review of *Mikey and Nicky*. *New Republic*, January 1 and 8, 1977, 20–21.

Kauffmann, Stanley. "Stanley Kauffmann on Films." *New Republic*, December 8, 1978, 18, 36.

Kehr, Dave. "Critic's Choice: New DVD's." *New York Times*, December 21, 2004.

Kiang, Jessica. "Retrospective: The Directorial Career of Elaine May." IndieWire. August 8, 2013. Archived October 23, 2021. https://web.archive.org/web/20211023014647/http://www.indiewire.com/2013/08/retrospective-the-directorial-career-of-elaine-may-95011/.

Kissel, Howard. Review of *Mikey and Nicky*. *Women's Wear Daily*, December 20, 1976, 5.

Klevan, Andrew. *Aesthetic Evaluation and Film*. Manchester University Press, 2018.

Kroll, Jack. "Elaine's Night Out." *Newsweek*, December 27, 1976, 56.

Kuhn, Annette, and Susannah Radstone, eds. *The Women's Companion to International Film*. University of California Press, 1994.

Lang, Brent. "As Elaine May Turns 89, It's Time to Give the Filmmaking Giant the Credit She Deserves." *Variety*, April 21, 2021.

Leigh, Mike. *Mike Leigh on Mike Leigh*. Updated ed. Edited by Amy Raphael. Faber and Faber, 2022.

Lemon, Dick. "Movies: How to Succeed in Interviewing Elaine May (Try, Really Try)." *New York Times*, January 4, 1970.

Levinson, Jerrold. *The Pleasures of Aesthetics: Philosophical Essays*. Cornell University Press, 1996.

Lewis, Grover. *Academy All the Way*. Straight Arrow Books, 1974.

Longsdorf, Amy. "'Mikey and Nicky' Was Elaine May's Followup to Her Acclaimed 'The Heartbreak Kid.'" *Morning Call* (Allentown, PA), January 15, 2019.

Mackendrick, Alexander. *On Film-Making: An Introduction to the Craft of the Director*. Edited by Paul Cronin. Faber and Faber, 2004.

Maltby, Richard. *Hollywood Cinema: An Introduction*. 2nd ed. Wiley-Blackwell, 2003.

Maltby, Richard. "'Nobody Knows Everything': Post-Classical Historiographies and the Consolidated Entertainment." In *Contemporary Hollywood Cinema*, edited by Stephen Neale and Murray Smith. Routledge, 1998.

Matthau, Carol. *Among the Porcupines: A Memoir*. Random House, 1992.

May, Elaine. "ACE [American Cinema Editors] Presents: *Mikey and Nicky* with Elaine May." Interview by Phillip Schopper and Jeffrey Wolf. Metrograph Theater, New York, December 7, 2024.

May, Elaine. Interview by Haden Guest. November 12, 2010. Harvard Film Archive, Harvard University, Cambridge, MA.

May, Elaine. "Mikey and Nicky Release Dialogue Script." 1976. Special Collections, Margaret Herrick Library, Academy of Motion Picture Arts and Sciences, Beverly Hills, CA.

May, Elaine. "MIKEY AND NICKY—Script." Circa 1973. Special Collections, Margaret Herrick Library, Academy of Motion Picture Arts and Sciences, Beverly Hills, CA.

May, Elaine, and Julian Schlossberg. "Elaine May Chats with Julian Schlossberg About Her Comedy, Acting, and Directing Careers." 2023. Posted June 4, 2024, by Turner Classic Movies, YouTube, 16:06. https://www.youtube.com/watch?v=p-4POuAW_iU.

Miller, Tom. Working notebook for *Mikey and Nicky*. 1973. Tom Miller Papers. Special Collections, Margaret Herrick Library, Academy of Motion Picture Arts and Sciences, Beverly Hills, CA.

Monaco, James. *American Film Now: The People, the Power, the Money, the Movies*. Oxford University Press, 1979.

Morgan, Kim. Review of *Mikey and Nicky*. *Sight and Sound* 25, no. 10 (2015): 27.

Morrison, Toni. "Write, Erase, Do It Over." Interview by Rebecca Sutton. *American Artscape*, no. 4 (2014). https://www.arts.gov/stories/magazine/2014/4/art-failure-importance-risk-and-experimentation/toni-morrison.

Murf. Review of *Mikey and Nicky*. *Variety*, December 22, 1976, 20.

Nachman, Gerald. *Seriously Funny: The Rebel Comedians of the 1950s and 1960s*. Pantheon Books, 2003.

Naremore, James. *On Kubrick*. Rev. ed. British Film Institute, 2023.

A New Leaf production records. Paramount Pictures Special Collection, file 180. Margaret Herrick Library, Academy of Motion Picture Arts and Sciences, Beverly Hills, CA.

New York Times. "The Week Ahead: Feb. 26–March 4; Film." February 26, 2006.

Nichols, Mike. "Elaine May in Conversation with Mike Nichols." In *Nichols and May: Interviews*, edited by Robert E. Kapsis. University Press of Mississippi, 2020.

Nichols, Mike, and Elaine May. "Teenagers." 1958. Posted October 29, 2020, by Omnibus with Alistair Cooke, YouTube, 7:56. https://www.youtube.com/watch?v=XpYxH1BciHQ.

Nichols, Mike, and Elaine May. "The Teenagers in a Car Sketch." 1959. Posted March 17, 2015, by Cantara Christopher, YouTube, 10:39. https://www.youtube.com/watch?v=LJtUtF2gxK4.

P., E. "Buying & Booking Guide: *Mikey & Nicky*." *Independent Film Journal* 79, no. 1 (1976): 30–31.

Pollack, Joe. "At the Movies." *St. Louis (MO) Post-Dispatch*, September 23, 1977.

Pollack, Sydney. Papers. Special Collections, Margaret Herrick Library, Academy of Motion Picture Arts and Sciences, Beverly Hills, CA.

Probst, Leonard. *Off Camera: Leveling About Themselves*. Stein and Day, 1975.

Quart, Barbara Koenig. *Women Directors: The Emergence of a New Cinema*. Praeger, 1988.

Raucher, Herman. Interview by Preston Fassel. Cinedump, September 13, 2016. https://www.cinedump.com/interviews/2016/9/13/hermanraucher.

Rebanal, Jaime. "*Mikey and Nicky* Review: Elaine May Breaks Down Masculinity to Its Core." *Cinema from the Spectrum* (blog), March 20, 2019. https://cinemafromthespectrum.com/2019/03/19/mikey.

Rich, Frank. "'Mikey and Nicky' a Painful Mess." *New York Post*, December 22, 1976.

Rickey, Carrie. "Elaine May: Laughing Matters." *Sight and Sound* 28, no. 10 (2018): 40–43.

Rivlin, Michael. "Elaine May: Too Tough for Hollywood?" *Millimeter* 3, no. 10 (1975): 16–18, 46.

Robertson, Carol. *The Little Book of Movie Law*. American Bar Association, 2013.

Rosen, Marjorie. *Popcorn Venus: Women, Movies, and the American Dream*. Avon, 1973.

Rosenbaum, Jonathan. "Moving." *Film Comment*, July/August 1977.

Rosenthal, Phil, and David Wild, hosts. *Naked Lunch* podcast. "Elaine May" episode. July 21, 2022, 1:22:05.

Rottenberg, Dan. "Elaine May . . . or She May Not." *Chicago Tribune*, October 21, 1973.

Ryan, Desmond. "'Mikey and Nicky' Returns, but It Shouldn't Have Bothered." *Philadelphia Inquirer*, May 20, 1977.

Ryan, Desmond. "'Mikey and Nicky' Seeks a Second Opinion." *Philadelphia Inquirer*, May 27, 1985.

Sachs, Lloyd. "In May's Screen Gem, Women's Albums, Genius Shines." *Chicago Sun-Times*, January 2, 2005.

Salamon, Julie. "Buddy Love." *Wall Street Journal*, May 16, 1985.

Savile, Anthony. *The Test of Time: An Essay in Philosophical Aesthetics*. Oxford University Press, 1982.

Schatz, Thomas. *Hollywood Genres: Formulas, Filmmaking, and the Studio System.* McGraw-Hill, 1981.

Schlossberg, Julian. Interview. *Mikey and Nicky* (1976). Special ed. Blu-ray. Criterion Collection, 2019.

Schlossberg, Julian, and Elaine May. *Try Not to Hold It Against Me.* Beaufort Books, 2023.

Scorsese, Martin. *Scorsese on Scorsese.* Rev. ed. Edited by Ian Christie and David Thompson. Faber, 2003.

Shalit, Gene. "What's Happening: Instant Interview with Peter Falk." *Ladies' Home Journal,* March 1977, 14, 17.

Shepherd, Cybill, with Aimee Lee Ball. *Cybill Disobedience: How I Survived Beauty Pageants, Elvis, Sex, Bruce Willis, Lies, Marriage, Motherhood, Hollywood, and the Irrepressible Urge to Say What I Think.* HarperCollins, 2000.

Shuman, Michael L. "Accidental Outlaw: Agency and Genre in *The Bigamist.*" In *Ida Lupino, Filmmaker,* edited by Phillip Sipiora. Bloomsbury Academic, 2021.

Sibley, Frank. *Approach to Aesthetics: Collected Papers on Philosophical Aesthetics.* Edited by John Benson, Betty Redfern, and Jeremy Roxbee Cox. Clarendon Press, 2006.

Simon, John. "May, Bogdanovich, and Streisand: Varieties of Death Wish." *New York,* January 10, 1977, 55–77.

Simon, Neil. "Dialogue on Film." Interview by James Powers. *American Film,* March 1, 1978, 33–48.

Smukler, Maya Montañez. "Hollywood Can't Wait: Elaine May and the Delusions of 1970s American Cinema." In *ReFocus: The Films of Elaine May,* edited by Alexandra Heller-Nicholas and Dean Brandum. Edinburgh University Press, 2019.

Spolin, Viola. *Improvisation for the Theater: A Handbook of Teaching and Directing Techniques.* Northwestern University Press, 1963.

Steinberg, Cobbett. *Reel Facts: The Movie Book of Records.* Vintage Books, 1982.

Stempel, Tom. *Framework: A History of Screenwriting in the American Film.* 3rd ed. Syracuse University Press, 2000.

Stephens, Chuck. "Chronicle of a Disappearance." *Film Comment,* March/April 2006.

Sterritt, David. "'Voyage' Proves 'a Rather Dull Cruise': Also, Connery in 'Next Man' and New Elaine May Study." *Christian Science Monitor,* December 31, 1976, 19.

Stevens, Brad. "Male Narrative/Female Narration: Elaine May's *Mikey and Nicky.*" *Cineaction,* no. 31 (1993): 74–83.

Stevens, Kyle. "Tossing Truths: Improvisation and the Performative Utterances of Nichols and May." *Critical Quarterly* 52, no. 3 (2010): 23–46.

Tarantino, Quentin, and Roger Avary, hosts. *Video Archives,* podcast. Episode 106, *"Coma, Mikey & Nicky, Piranha."* September 27, 2022. 2:29:41.

Thomas, Bob. "Goodby, Columbo." *St. Louis (MO) Post-Dispatch,* March 8, 1976.

Thompson, Kristin. *Breaking the Glass Armor: Neoformalist Film Analysis.* Princeton University Press, 1988.

Thompson, Thomas. "Whatever Happened to Elaine May?" *Life,* July 1967, 54–59.

Thomson, David. "The Decade When Movies Mattered." In *The Last Great Amer-*

ican Picture Show: New Hollywood Cinema in the 1970s, edited by Thomas Elsaesser, Alexander Horwath, and Noel King. Amsterdam University Press, 2004.

Time Out. Review of *Ishtar*. September 10, 2012. https://www.timeout.com/movies/ishtar.

Tobias, Andrew. "For Elaine May, a New Film—But Not a New Leaf." *New West,* December 6, 1976, 59–69.

Variety. "50 Top-Grossing Films." January 12, 1977, 41.

Variety. "50 Top-Grossing Films." May 15, 1985, 9.

Variety. "Big Rental Films of 1973." January 9, 1974, 19.

Variety. "Elaine May's 'Bumpy Ride' on 'Leaf'; Manduke Sticks on 'Mikey & Nicky.'" August 27, 1969, 6.

Variety. "Par Charges Criminal Conduct in 'Mikey' Suit vs. Elaine May." September 15, 1976, 5.

Variety. "Par, Elaine May Sue Each Other; Film Over-Budget and Incomplete." October 29, 1975, 5.

Ventura, Michael. "The Passionate Art of Peter Falk." *LA Weekly,* November 23, 1984.

Ventura, Michael. "Pick of the Week: *Mikey and Nicky*." *LA Weekly,* December 30, 1984.

Walker, Alexander, Sybil Taylor, and Ulrich Ruchti. *Stanley Kubrick, Director: A Visual Analysis*. Rev. and enlarged ed. Norton, 1999.

Warga, Wayne. "Falk—Many a Sinking Ship's Saving Grace." *Los Angeles Times,* December 16, 1968.

Wasson, Sam. *Improv Nation: How We Made a Great American Art*. Harper Perennial, 2018.

Weismann, Brad. "*Ishtar* (Elaine May, 1987)." *Senses of Cinema* (blog), July 2019. https://www.sensesofcinema.com/2019/cteq/ishtar.

Willmore, Alison, Angelica Jade Bastién, and Bilge Ebiri. "The 101 Greatest Endings in Movies History." Vulture. February 22, 2021. https://www.vulture.com/article/the-101-best-movie-endings-of-all-time-ranked.html.

Wilson, Jake. "Dangerous Business—Elaine May as Existential Improviser." In *ReFocus: The Films of Elaine May,* edited by Alexandra Heller-Nicholas and Dean Brandum. Edinburgh University Press, 2019.

Zimmermann, Patricia Rodden. *Reel Families: A Social History of Amateur Film*. Indiana University Press, 1995.

INDEX

Page locators in *italics* refer to illustrations; *M&N* refers to *Mikey and Nicky*.

www.ingramcontent.com/pod-product-compliance
Lightning Source LLC
LaVergne TN
LVHW100411091026
849392LV00011B/40
* 9 7 8 1 4 7 7 3 3 5 7 1 0 *